A Trade Policy
for Free Societies

A
TRADE POLICY
FOR
FREE SOCIETIES

The Case Against Protectionism

Robert W. McGee

QUORUM BOOKS
Westport, Connecticut • London

Library of Congress Cataloging-in-Publication Data

McGee, Robert W.
  A trade policy for free societies : the case against protectionism
/ Robert W. McGee.
      p.   cm.
  Includes bibliographical references and index.
  ISBN 0–89930–898–8 (alk. paper)
  1. Protectionism. 2. Dumping (International trade). 3. Free
trade. I. Title.
HF1713.M37   1994
382'.71—dc20   93–42760

British Library Cataloguing in Publication Data is available.

Library of Congress Catalog Card Number: 93–42760
ISBN: 0–89930–898–8

First published in 1994

Quorum Books, 88 Post Road West, Westport, CT 06881
An imprint of Greenwood Publishing Group, Inc.

Printed in the United States of America

The paper used in this book complies with the
Permanent Paper Standard issued by the National
Information Standards Organization (Z39.48–1984).
10 9 8 7 6 5 4 3 2 1

Copyright Acknowledgments

Some chapters of this book are revisions of articles that appeared in the following
journals: *Capital University Law Review*, Volume 19, Issue 2 (Spring 1990); *The
Journal of Law and Commerce*, Volume 11, Issue 2 (Spring 1992), all rights reserved;
Northwestern Journal of International Law & Business (1993); *The George
Washington Journal of International Law and Economics*, Volume 26, No. 3 (1993).

Contents

Preface

Protectionist ideas and advocates have been around for thousands of years, at least since the time of Plato and Aristotle, and although protectionist ideas have been successfully refuted at least since the time of Adam Smith (1776), the protectionist mentality refuses to die. Each generation, a new group of protectionists is spawned and must be restrained from looting consumers.

Protectionism can take many forms, but the basic result of any protectionist policy is to protect producers at the expense of consumers. Protectionists often argue that domestic industry must be protected because cheap foreign imports are destroying jobs. Yet studies have consistently shown that protectionist policies destroy two or three jobs for every job saved, resulting in a net employment loss. Protectionists argue for "fair" trade, just as medieval scholars argued for a "fair" price, but there is no such thing as objectively determined fair trade. The only two kinds of trade are free trade and restricted trade. Either consumers are able to buy what they want from whom they want or they are not. If trade is restricted because of some tariff, quota, or antidumping policy, it is the result of special interests (producers) going to the legislature to seek the heavy hand of government to protect them from foreign competitors. Producers are using the force of government to pick consumer pockets. Government officials, who are supposed to be the servants of the people, are being captured by special interests to work against the interests of the general public.

This book is divided into three sections. The first section is on the philosophy of protectionism and reviews more than a dozen of the most commonly given reasons that have been used to justify protectionism over the past few hundred years. The author points out that these arguments generally support the producer's position, often to the detriment of consumers and the general public. Each argument is analyzed empirically and logically. A whole chapter is devoted to debunking the myth that trade deficits are bad and trade surpluses are good. The general conclusion is that the case against protectionism and in favor of free trade is strong from both an economic and a liberal democratic perspective.

Part II takes a look at the cost of protectionism, with emphasis on the case in the United States. The auto, steel, textile, and agricultural industries are given special attention. Some nonmonetary costs often overlooked or ignored by many commentators are also discussed. These costs include the net deadweight employment loss, social harmony costs, reduced choice, and the violation of rights that is inherent whenever consenting adults cannot trade. The general conclusion is that protectionist policies destroy more jobs than they save and raise the price that consumers must pay, which reduces the general standard of living.

Part III examines antidumping policy in the United States from both a theoretical and a practical viewpoint. After a review of the economic and legal background of the antidumping laws and a look at how they are administered, the author proceeds to examine the many problems inherent in the present policies, such as the many computational problems, the harmful effects of antidumping policy, and the weakness of the predatory pricing argument. Specific examples of dumping in the auto, steel, textile, agricultural, and television industries are also examined. The section concludes with a discussion of the philosophy of antidumping policy and examines issues such as the ethics of using the law to batter the competition, the irrationality of antidumping as a policy, a rights approach to antidumping, and the relationship between antidumping laws and the legitimate functions of government.

The final chapter discusses the implications of U.S. protectionism for international trade in Europe. The author examines the options for trade policy in Europe, with emphasis on emerging market economies, from both the rights and the utilitarian perspectives. The author concludes that total and immediate free trade is the best policy. The argument that policymakers may find it necessary, for practical reasons, to adopt a gradualist approach that involves temporary protection is also examined. Of the two options examined — infant industry protection and unemployment payments — the unemployment payment approach is the more efficient, but neither "second-best" approach is as desirable as total and immediate free trade.

Protectionism is like a tax in that it extracts wealth from the general public. However, rather than having the wealth transferred from the general public to the government or to the poor, it is transferred to producers, who can charge higher prices for their products as a result of protectionist policies. In effect, protectionist policies are subsidies for inefficient producers. Protectionist policies are an abuse of government power. Rather than protecting the property and contract rights of the vast majority, such policies disparage these rights in favor of special interests. In a free society, the purpose of government is to protect the life, liberty, and property of its citizens and otherwise leave them alone to lead their lives as they see fit. Protectionist policies have no place in a free society.

Acknowledgments

I thank Murray Sabrin and Fernando Alvarez for making many useful comments on portions of this manuscript. I would like to thank Joseph Wu, Valencia Lynch, John Tortora, and Vivian Lugo for helping me gather data.

I

THE PHILOSOPHY OF
PROTECTIONISM

1

The Protectionist Mentality

> In every country it always is and must be the interest of the great
> body of the people to buy whatever they want of those who sell it
> cheapest. The proposition is so very manifest, that it seems ridicu-
> lous to take any pains to prove it; nor could it ever have been called
> in question, had not the interested sophistry of merchants and man-
> ufacturers confounded the common sense of mankind.[1]

Protectionism is not new. Proponents were found in ancient Greece.[2]
Plato thought that trading with foreigners would allow undesirable
characters to enter the polis, along with gold and silver, all of which cor-
rupt the soul. Aristotle also thought exchanging products for money
had a corrupting influence and thought that the best state was one that
was self-sufficient, although both Plato and Aristotle recognized the
benefits of the division of labor (but not comparative advantage).

The theories supporting protectionism have been refuted for well
over 100 years — by Bastiat in France, Cobden and Bright in England
and John Prince Smith in Germany.[3] Adam Smith's refutation, *The
Wealth of Nations*, was published in 1776. Richard Cantillon's contri-
bution to the debate, *Essai Sur la Nature Du Commerce en Général*,
was written in the 1720s and 1730s and published in 1755.[4]

Protectionist sentiment remains strong. As Vilfredo Pareto pointed
out in 1927, the benefits of protectionism are concentrated while the
costs are diffused.

> Even if it were very clearly demonstrated that protection always entails the
> destruction of wealth, if that were taught to every citizen just as they learn
> the abc's, protection would lose so small a number of partisans and free trade
> would gain so few of them that the effect can be almost, or even completely,
> disregarded. The motives which lead men to act are quite different.
>
> In order to explain how those who champion protection make themselves
> heard so easily, it is necessary to add a consideration which applies to social
> movements generally. The intensity of the work of an individual is not

proportionate to the benefits which that work may bring him nor to the harm which it may enable him to avoid. If a certain measure A is the case of the loss of one franc to each of a thousand persons, and of a thousand franc gain to one individual, the latter will expend a great deal of energy, whereas the former will resist weakly; and it is likely that, in the end, the person who is attempting to secure the thousand francs via A will be successful.

A protectionist measure provides large benefits to a small number of people, and causes a very great number of consumers a slight loss. This circumstance makes it easier to put a protectionist measure into practice.[5]

With this clear-cut enormous benefit to some people, it is no wonder that protectionist ideas refuse to die — and even flourish — because the only thing preventing their enactment is a Congress that both understands basic economics and is honest enough to resist a well-financed lobby that wants them to enact something that will be to the detriment of their constituents. Robert Nozick explains what makes this abuse possible: "The illegitimate use of a state by economic interests for their own ends is based upon a preexisting illegitimate power of the state to enrich some persons at the expense of others."[6]

W. M. Curtiss puts it somewhat differently: "Through the years, some men have discovered how to satisfy their wants at the expense of others without being accused of theft: they ask their government to do the stealing for them."[7]

If it is immoral for Ford or General Motors executives to personally prevent a willing U.S. consumer from entering into a contract to buy a foreign automobile from a willing seller, is it any less immoral to ask government to do the job for them? The effect is the same whether the corporate executives physically restrain a consumer from walking into a Toyota or Hyundai dealership or whether they let the government intervene in their behalf by not allowing the automobile into the country in the first place. Also, are corporate executives who ask for government protection not acting immorally, because their action denies the right of consumers to exercise their right to property — to choose the product of their choice? Such action is a perversion of the law, because it allows some citizens to exploit the person, liberty, and property of others.[8] Bastiat tells how to determine when the law is being perverted: "See if the law takes from some persons what belongs to them, and gives it to other persons to whom it does not belong. See if the law benefits one citizen at the expense of another by doing what the citizen himself cannot do without committing a crime."[9]

According to this proviso, the welfare state is a perversion of the law, and protectionist measures such as tariffs and quotas are merely examples of one form of welfare — corporate subsidies.

Frank Chodorov provides one of the most succinct refutations of the protectionist mentality:

Let us test the claims of "protectionists" with an experiment in logic. If a people prosper by the amount of foreign goods they are not permitted to have, then a complete embargo, rather than a restriction, would do them the most good. Continuing that line of reasoning, would it not be better all around if each community were hermetically sealed off from its neighbor, like Philadelphia from New York? Better still, would not every household have more on its table if it were compelled to live on its own production? Silly as this reductio ad absurdum is, it is no sillier than the "protectionist" argument that a nation is enriched by the amount of foreign goods it keeps out of its market, or the "balance of trade" argument that a nation prospers by the excess of its exports over imports.[10]

WHAT IS AN IMPORT?

On the surface, it may seem simple to define an import, but a closer analysis reveals that defining what constitutes an import is not so cut and dried. For example, Sony makes televisions in San Diego. About half of U.S. Harley-Davidson motorcycles are made in Japan.[11] The Volvo 780 that is sold in the United States is the product of work done in several countries. The following are some of the countries involved:

France	Engine
Japan	Transmission
United States	Air conditioner
Germany	Electronic system
Singapore	Control valves
Canada	Exhaust system
Taiwan	Power antenna
South Korea	Electrical components
Sweden	Axles
Ireland	Tires
Italy	Design and assembly

How Swedish is this car, anyway? When you consider that some of the components that comprise the Volvo were made with machinery and equipment from other countries, the problem becomes even more difficult to determine. Part of the problem inherent in any attempt to restrict imports lies in the definition of an import. A whole body of literature has evolved around the concept of "domestic content" and domestic content legislation. In many ways, the definition is arbitrary, which causes problems that would not exist if trade were completely free.

Many arguments have been advanced in favor of regulating trade between consenting adults. The next few pages summarize and analyze these arguments.

THE SUBSIDY ARGUMENT

This argument will not stand up under close accounting analysis. Consumers who must pay higher prices for the goods they want or who are not able to get the products they want because of restrictive trade policies are obviously hurt by protectionism. They are not as well off as they would be in the absence of protectionism. Yet, advocates of protectionism continue to insist that forcing consumers to pay higher prices for farm products, for example, does not really harm them because the farmers will spend their extra income in the nonfarm sector. In other words, the extra money the farmers receive as the result of the subsidy all comes back to the consumer anyway, so there is no net loss.

This faulty thinking can be exposed by reference to the story of the beggar who asked the restaurant owner to give him $20.[12] The beggar points out that the restauranteur will be no worse off because the beggar promises to spend the entire $20 in the restaurant. What is seen is the sumptuous meal the beggar receives. The restauranteur also receives $20, so it appears that both have gained by the trade. What is less obvious is that the restauranteur, rather than having $20 and $20 worth of food now has only the $20 but not the food. Even though the beggar spent the entire proceeds of the subsidy in the restauranteur's restaurant, the restauranteur is poorer as a result.

Although this example may seen absurd, the same argument is being advanced by elected government officials and lobbyists who advocate subsidizing some industry. U.S. sugar farmers need a subsidy to survive, for example, but we will get it all back because their increased purchasing power will increase demand for goods and services throughout the economy.

The same argument is advanced by those who try to justify foreign aid on self-interest grounds. Give country X $100 million, so the argument goes. They promise to spend it all in the United States anyway, so we are getting it all back. Our exports increase and our trade imbalance decreases. What is seen is an extra $100 million in exports. What is more difficult to see is that the taxpayers are $100 million poorer in order to subsidize the purchases of some foreign country. In the case of aid to the Philippines, much of the aid found its way back to the United States in the form of prime Manhattan real estate, which is not an export at all, paid for by the U.S. taxpayer.

THE DUMPING ARGUMENT

"Dumping" can mean several things. It can mean that foreign producers are selling their products on domestic markets below cost. It also can mean that foreigners are selling their products in the United States for less than what they sell them for in their own country.[13] A corollary of this argument is that foreign governments are subsidizing these exports. In its extreme form, dumping has been likened to predatory pricing, whereby a foreign producer deliberately sells below domestic competitors with the intent of driving them out of business and gaining a monopoly for itself.

The popular view is that dumping is bad and those who dump should be penalized. Frédéric Bastiat pointed out the fallacy of this view in 1845, yet the view is still not only with us, but also widely believed to be true.[14] In Bastiat's example, foreigners flood the market with goods without asking for anything in return. Even if imports become infinite and exports shrink to zero, how can it be said that the economy, as a whole, is worse off?

Modern examples of dumping are only slightly less absurd. Rather than giving us free stereos and automobiles, the Japanese sell us their products at prices that are lower than what U.S. companies can afford to sell for. Such "dumping" saves U.S. consumers millions or even billions of dollars a year, thus raising their standards of living. The money we save on "dumped" goods can be spent on other goods and services that have a lower value on our subjective value scales. A few thousand United Auto Workers lose something because Americans choose to buy foreign motor vehicles, but 260 million Americans stand to benefit by being able to buy products of their choice rather than the products the United Auto Workers (and their friends in Congress) allow them to buy.

Actually, the domestic industry does not "lose" anything. It just does not gain, because U.S. consumers prefer to do business with someone else. U.S. producers would "lose" only if they did not receive something they were entitled to receive. Yet they have no right to sell their products to unwilling buyers, so it cannot be said that U.S. companies lose as a result of foreign competition.

The "below cost" argument does not hold up under analysis. Although it is sometimes necessary to sell a product below cost because the market says the product is not worth the cost of production, companies that make a practice of consistently selling below cost to gain market share usually go out of business. Some commentators respond to this argument by stating that foreign governments subsidize these exports, making it possible to sell below cost without going out of business.

Although some governments do indeed encourage exports, should the importing country complain? I, for one, would not complain if Japanese taxpayers want to pay for part of my Japanese automobile or stereo. The ones who should be complaining about such policies are the Japanese taxpayers.[15]

The predatory pricing argument also falls apart under analysis. For one thing, it is inefficient.[16] For another, predatory pricing is a myth.[17] In the few cases where it has been tried, it has been unsuccessful, at least from a consumer perspective, except in cases where government has stepped in to prevent competitors from entering the market.

Companies that try to drive their competitors out of the market by cutting prices must fail. First, they must sell below cost, which cannot go on indefinitely. As prices drop, demand increases, which means they must produce more to satisfy the increased demand, thus losing even more money. Second, even if a company does succeed in driving its competitors out of the market, it cannot keep them out. As soon as it starts to raise prices, competitors will start to reappear. If a company does engage in predatory pricing and manages to drive a competitor out of business, the bankrupt competitor will have its assets bought by another company, which will then be a low-cost producer, because it was able to acquire the bankrupt company's assets for perhaps ten cents on the dollar.

Even if a predator could drive all competitors into bankruptcy, it will not be able to charge a monopoly price. Once it raises prices, new competitors will come into the market. For example, assume General Motors was able to drive Ford and Chrysler out of business. First, it would still have to compete with Fiat, Volvo, Volkswagen, Toyota, Hyundai, Honda, and numerous other companies. Second, there are any number of other companies that could enter the market in the absence of barriers to entry. General Electric or IBM or hundreds of other companies could decide to pick up the pieces of a few bankrupt firms and compete against General Motors. All it takes is capital and know-how. Large companies have the capital, and they can purchase the know-how (perhaps by making better offers to a few top General Motors employees).

The only thing that can keep competitors out of the market is governmentally imposed barriers to entry. Congress can pass laws to prevent an IBM or General Electric from entering the automotive industry, it can use existing antitrust laws to do it, or it can prohibit foreign automobile manufacturers from competing with General Motors. In the absence of governmentally imposed entry barriers, competition occurs in the marketplace because entrepreneurs perceive profitable opportunities.

The United States and other countries have enacted legislation aimed at preventing dumping and penalizing those caught dumping. The number of antidumping and antisubsidy cases has increased dramatically since the late 1970s,[18] and one author asserts that "the dramatic rise of such unfair-trade cases is itself prima facie evidence of their use for harassment of successful foreign suppliers."[19] Patrick Messerlin examined more than 500 European Economic Community (EEC) antidumping cases brought between 1970 and 1985 and found that the General Agreement on Tariffs and Trade (GATT) rules were often used to harass and discriminate.[20]

In effect, antidumping laws are used to protect domestic producers, often (always?) at the expense of the consumer. Antidumping laws are based on a vague concept of "fairness," but the effect of enforcing such laws is to treat both producers and consumers unfairly.

THE JOB DESTRUCTION ARGUMENT

One of the most frequent arguments raised against unrestricted imports is that U.S. jobs will be lost. It is fairly easy to estimate the number of jobs lost in the U.S. automobile or steel industry by allowing imports into the country. One need only look at the number of such workers collecting unemployment insurance or look at the statistical compilations that have been made of automobile and steel industry employment totals, then discount that figure by some percentage based on the number of jobs that have been destroyed for other reasons, such as domestic competition, automation, and a decrease in domestic demand, and add back a percentage to represent the number of workers who were able to find other jobs. That is what is seen. However, what is not seen is the new jobs that are created as a result of free trade.

One source of jobs is the foreign auto and steel producers themselves. Foreign steel producers and motor vehicle manufacturers cannot spend U.S. dollars in their own countries. Those dollars must eventually return to the United States. They are deposited in the bank accounts of U.S. businesses that have sold goods to foreigners. The benefits of these sales permeate through the economy, expanding employment in many industries. For example, a Japanese automobile manufacturer investing in U.S. widgets increases employment in the U.S. widget industry. Widget industry workers spend their money on homes, autos, appliances, beer, food, and many other items, which expands employment in these areas as well. However, these benefits are impossible to trace back to their origin — the American who purchased a Japanese motor vehicle, who gave the Japanese auto company the money to spend on U.S. products. All that is seen is the jobs that are lost in the U.S. automobile industry. By allowing U.S. consumers to buy the car of their choice, 50,000 automobile industry jobs might be lost, but perhaps 70,000 jobs might be created in other industries. The exact number of jobs created is impossible to measure, but it is reasonable to conclude that it is better to let the free market create jobs than to protect auto industry jobs at an annual cost of $160,000 per job.[21]

Imports create jobs in other ways as well. The transportation, retail, wholesale, and service industries expand if imports are allowed into the country. Again, the exact number of jobs created in this manner is impossible to measure, but it is reasonable to assume that individuals must be hired to service all the imports that are entering the market.

There is also a cross-fertilization effect. If U.S. automobile companies can purchase foreign steel cheaper than U.S. steel, they may be able to sell their cars for less, thus making them more competitive with foreign automobile producers. U.S. consumers benefit by the import of foreign steel, as do U.S. automobile manufacturers.[22] If U.S. consumers do not have to spend as much on automobiles, they can spend more on other goods and services, such as home repairs, education, clothes, or any number of other things. All industries benefit by allowing foreign steel to "invade" our shores, with the possible exception of U.S. steel producers. However, even here, there may be some beneficiaries. U.S. steel producers that cannot compete will have an incentive to curtail steel production and channel their resources into areas where there is more demand. Some U.S. steelmakers have expanded into specialty steel and oil, for example, and their companies are now more healthy than before as a result.

Public officials and others view an excess of imports over exports as detrimental to the economy. Yet, although the U.S. current account deficit quadrupled between 1982 and 1987, more than 13 million jobs were created — more than were created in Europe and Japan combined in the past 10 years. Between 1982 and 1986, the United States created jobs 3 times as fast as Japan and 20 times as fast as West Germany.[23] Between 1983 and 1987, the U.S. unemployment rate declined by 28%, while Japan's rate increased by 17% and the common market's rate increased by over 20% at a time when both Japan and the common market showed a trade surplus with the United States.

Not only do imports create jobs, but also, placing restrictions on imports destroys jobs. One study found that imposing "voluntary" export restraints in the steel industry actually destroyed more jobs than it saved.[24] Although some jobs in the steel industry were saved, more jobs were lost in the industries that use steel products, which had to pay higher steel prices as the result of the "voluntary" restraints. As a result of the 1984 steel voluntary export restraints, the steel industry gained 16,900 jobs while steel-using companies lost 52,400 jobs, for a net loss of more than 35,000 jobs. One author goes even further and states that U.S. steel import policies destroy 50 jobs in other parts of the economy for each job saved in the steel industry.[25]

THE DEINDUSTRIALIZATION ARGUMENT

Another argument in the popular press (and in some academic circles) is that the United States is deindustrializing. Bluestone and Harrison[26] have been among the most frequently cited modern advocates of this notion, which Bhagwati[27] refers to as the "manufacturing matters muddle." Nicholas Kaldor[28] was one of the first modern commentators to spread the doctrine, although the doctrine is actually as old as mercantilism itself.[29] Yet, a simple analysis of the facts proves this charge to be untrue. Manufacturing employment, although fluctuating somewhat, has remained about the same over the past few decades. The decline is only in relative, not absolute, terms, because the service sector has been expanding. Furthermore, industrial production is increasing because of increased productivity.[30] Thomas DiLorenzo[31] attempted to measure the extent of industrial decline but found that there was none. In fact, between 1982 and 1986, the United States gained 406,000 manufacturing jobs, at a time when the trade deficit was increasing.[32] Yet arguments continue to be heard that the United States is deindustrializing,[33] and some even assert that the United States of the future will be devoid of manufacturing.[34]

THE HAMBURGER FLIPPER ARGUMENT

The hamburger flipper argument is a variation of the deindustrialization argument. Walter Mondale used it in his presidential campaign to argue that unless the United States adopts protectionist measures, the only jobs we will be able to get are flipping hamburgers at McDonalds or sweeping up around Japanese computers.[35]

As individuals lose their jobs because of a plant closure, they get new jobs to replace the jobs they lost. The Congressional Budget Office estimated that of the 8 million workers who were unemployed in January 1983, for example, only 20% lost jobs in a declining industry and most of the job losses were caused by the recession rather than by a structural change. Only 240,000 of the 1.6 million unemployed workers in declining industries had been unemployed for 26 weeks or more and only 60,000 — representing 0.05% — had been on the job for 10 years or more. So, although some workers are displaced, the number displaced is small, and those who are displaced are displaced only temporarily in most cases.[36]

Do workers who lose their jobs have to settle for lower wages when they eventually find another job? Yes and no. Obviously, a steel worker who is paid 20% to 50% more than he would be worth in a free market will find it difficult to match the previous, inflated income.[37] The steel company he worked for was able to pay an above-market wage and pass the cost on to consumers because the industry was protected from foreign competition. When the protection was removed, the steel company could no longer stay in business and continue to pay the inflated wage. However, this kind of unemployment represents only about 20% of total unemployment. Actually, there is a shift away from lower paying jobs into higher paying jobs.[38] Furthermore, many of the workers earning low incomes are individuals who recently entered the job market, such as students and housewives, as well as retirees who just want to work part-time. Many of these workers are not the primary earners in their families, and their earnings are regarded as supplements to family income rather than the main source of family income.[39]

THE LOW WAGE ARGUMENT

Protectionists often cite the fact that workers in foreign countries earn lower wages than domestic employees and claim that lower wages give foreign producers an unfair advantage. Although foreign workers often are paid less than their U.S. counterparts, U.S. labor productivity is often higher, which offsets this wage differential. Capital-intensive industries can afford to pay higher wages because wage costs form a smaller percentage of total costs than in labor-intensive industries.

Even if foreigners can undersell U.S. companies in some labor-intensive industries, consumers benefit because they can buy what they want for less money, which means they will have more to spend on other goods and services. Jobs will expand in other industries because of this increase in consumer spending in these other areas. It may be easy to see that industry A lost 5,000 jobs because of cheap foreign imports. What is less easy to see is the 4,000 or 7,000 or 10,000 jobs that have been created in other industries because consumers have more to spend on the goods and services these other industries produce.

A corollary of this low wage argument is that, in the absence of protectionism, Americans will also have to work for low wages or be forced into unemployment. However, although lifting protection may result in some downward pressure on nominal wage rates, lack of protection will also exert downward pressure on prices as competition increases, so Americans will be able to purchase the same amount of goods for less money. Overall, consumers will be better off under free trade because the price of goods will decline, quality will increase, and they will no longer have to pay the cost of enforcing restrictive trade legislation.

THE FULL EMPLOYMENT ARGUMENT

The full employment argument is a spin-off of the hamburger flipper and low wage arguments. Those who advocate it see full employment rather than consumption as the goal. However, employment is merely the means used to achieve the end. All production is ultimately for consumption.[40] A nation's standard of living depends on the amount of goods and services that are available for consumption, not on the number of people who are employed. If employment were the key to prosperity, China would be the richest nation on earth.

Creating full employment is easy. All one has to do is draft a few million men into the army or outlaw farm machinery. These actions will not raise the standard of living but will actually lower it. If full employment were the goal, then our modern technological society is headed in the wrong direction. Rather than working 14 or 16 hours a day, six days a week, as our ancestors did, we now work 7 or 8 hours a day, five days a week. Our children go to school until age 18 or 22, rather than work in dingy factories or mines. Women have the option of working or not, whereas before they had the option of working in a factory or on a spinning loom at home.[41]

THE FAIRNESS ARGUMENT

One of the most popular recent arguments in favor of protectionism is that trade should be "fair" rather than free. It is unfair that other countries protect their domestic producers or dump their products on the U.S. market at low prices. What advocates of this position fail to see is that fairness is a process, not an outcome. Because of this failure to see the nature of the fairness concept, they fall into any number of other fallacious arguments. They would argue that it is unfair that some individuals or countries are rich while others are poor. They would argue that it is unfair that women earn less than men, even though some women choose to become bookkeepers rather than accountants, nurses rather than doctors, and so forth or choose to stay at home raising a family rather than climb the corporate ladder during their most productive years. Would it also be logical to argue that it is unfair that blacks comprise only 12% of the population yet comprise 75% of all professional basketball players — and earn more than whites, on average, to boot?[42] The remedy to this "unfair" state of affairs would be to establish quotas for white and oriental basketball players, a solution that would be ridiculous as well as unfair to the blacks who would lose their jobs to less qualified members of other races. Yet those who see fairness as an outcome rather than a process must logically advocate positions that would lead to absurd (and unfair!) results such as this.

Fairness should be seen as a process. A transaction is fair if consenting adults are free to enter into it without being coerced. It is fair that consumers are able to buy foreign products without having to pay a higher price due to some government intervention such as a tariff or import quota. It is unfair if some special interest group such as the steel lobby or the United Auto Workers uses the force of government to increase the price that consumers must pay for the goods and services of their choice. We cannot determine fairness by looking at the way things are; we must look at how things got that way.[43] If the current arrangement is the result of coercion, such as tariffs or quotas, it is unfair. If it is the result of consumer choice, it is fair.

It is unfair that foreign governments erect trade barriers that prevent U.S. products from entering their countries. It is unfair to U.S. producers and to the consumers in the foreign country. Such coercive acts by government prevent consenting adults from entering into contracts or, at least, raise the cost of entering into voluntary agreements. It does not follow that the U.S. government should retaliate by erecting trade barriers of its own to punish foreign producers for their governments' unfair acts. Erecting trade barriers of our own is unfair to U.S. consumers, who must pay higher prices for foreign goods or who might have to settle for a product that would be their second or third choice, if they had to buy American. It is also unfair to foreign producers, who would prefer to sell their products to U.S. consumers at lower prices.

Two wrongs do not make a right. Although that conclusion might seem obvious, it is a fact that many individuals in positions of authority fail to see this simple point. If they did, they would not advocate retaliating against foreign manufacturers whose governments act unfairly regarding international trade.

A corollary of the fair trade argument is that we should reduce our trade barriers only for countries that reduce their trade barriers for us. Using this line of logic, we might also argue that the U.S. government should continue to make U.S. consumers pay an extra 10% or 20% or 50% for a Japanese radio or automobile — by keeping our high tariff — until Japan drops its tariff barriers against U.S. beef or fish or textiles. Our government will, thereby, reduce the standard of living of the millions of Americans who buy Japanese products until Japan's government lowers its tariffs for U.S. textile and food companies.

Millions of U.S. consumers suffer needlessly as a result of this irrational trade policy. The intelligent thing to do would be to unilaterally abolish our trade barriers, regardless of what other nations choose to do. That way, our standard of living will increase immediately, and we will not have to wait for years of delicate negotiations that may produce a less desirable result. A beneficial side effect of such a policy might be that consumers in other nations would see the results of our action and put pressure on their government officials to adopt the same policy. However, even if other nations do not reciprocate, U.S. consumers will still benefit because the prices consumers will be paying for foreign products will have been reduced.

Walter Block and Michael Walker point out another fallacy in the fair trade argument.[44] It is usually someone in a modern, industrialized country (first-world) who argues for fair trade. It is unfair to expect a company in a first-world country to compete with a company in a third-world country that has the advantage of lower wage rates. Yet it is fair for one first-world country to trade with another first-world country. For example, it is acceptable for Americans to buy Canadian shirts but not shirts made in Asia. The logical conclusion is that first-world countries should compete with first-world countries and third-world countries should compete with third-world countries. Yet if such a policy were followed to any great extent, the economies of the first-world countries would stagnate because they would have to pay more for many products, and third-world countries would also suffer because many of their major markets would be closed to them.

THE LEVEL PLAYING FIELD ARGUMENT

The level playing field argument is a variation of the fair trade and dumping arguments. Like the advocates of fair trade, those who advocate a level playing field fall victim to the fallacy that trade should be viewed as an outcome rather than a process. The level playing field argument starts with the premise that no country should have an "unfair" competitive advantage over another. However, as was pointed out above, fairness is a matter of voluntary exchange. Exchange is fair if it is voluntary and unfair if coercion (such as tariffs or quotas) is involved.

Advocates of the level playing field argument often point out that foreign governments subsidize their producers' exports. U.S. lumber producers are at a disadvantage over Canadian lumber producers because the Canadian government subsidizes the Canadian lumber industry. Of course, the U.S. government does the same thing for certain producers of agricultural products, but that is somehow different. The U.S. government (taxpayer) subsidizes wheat production to the point where the United States is driving Australian wheat farmers out of business by dumping U.S. wheat on the Australian market.

The way to analyze this subsidization policy is to look at who wins and who loses. U.S. wheat farmers win because they are able to sell their wheat to Australians, which they would not be able to do in the absence of a subsidy. U.S. taxpayers lose because they are the ones who pay the subsidy. In effect, U.S. taxpayers are picking up part of the tab for the average Australian's grocery bill. Australian wheat farmers lose because U.S. wheat farmers can undersell them. Australian consumers gain because they can buy wheat products at lower prices than would be possible without the U.S. taxpayer subsidy.

Overall, the U.S. economy loses and the Australian economy gains as a result of the wheat subsidy. The vast majority of Australians benefit because they can buy wheat products at a lower cost, which means they now have more money to spend on other goods and services. The resources that Australian farmers formerly used to produce wheat — land, labor, capital, and entrepreneurial time and effort — can now be used to produce something else that they were not able to produce before. The only Australians who lose are the wheat farmers, who must shift resources into the production of something else. From a utilitarian perspective, Australia benefits because the majority benefit and only a minority are less well-off. From a property rights perspective, Australia is also better-off because no one's property rights are infringed upon.

The result is just the opposite for the United States. A few wheat farmers benefit at the expense of the majority, who must subsidize their wheat sales. U.S. taxpayers have their standard of living reduced because they must use part of their income to subsidize wheat farmers (and Australian wheat eaters) rather than to purchase goods and services. The property rights of the vast majority (taxpayers) are infringed, while a small minority (wheat farmers) receive tax dollars that they are not entitled to receive. In effect, wheat farmers are receiving "stolen goods," inasmuch as taxpayers are forced to part with a portion of their income to subsidize the wheat farmers.

Those who argue for a level playing field are actually arguing against the best interests of the vast majority of the population, at least in cases where they want foreign governments to stop subsidizing the products that domestic consumers buy. Australians who argue for a level playing field in wheat are arguing against the best interests of the vast majority of Australians. The ones who should argue for a level playing field are the U.S. taxpayers, who must otherwise subsidize a tiny minority of wheat farmers (who control the powerful farm lobby).

One of the most illogical cases of this level playing field mentality is the case where an American advocates quotas or tariffs on the importation of Japanese video cassette recorders (VCRs). None of the VCRs sold in the United States are made in the United States. No U.S. company makes VCRs. The Japanese (and perhaps a few other foreign producers) are the only producers. Not a single U.S. job is lost as a result of the free importation of VCRs. The fact that U.S. companies do not manufacture VCRs means that their productive resources are available to produce other products that they can sell on domestic and foreign markets. Those who advocate restrictions on the importation of VCRs are, in effect, saying that U.S. consumers should pay higher prices for something with no corresponding benefit. If the higher price they are forced to pay is the result of a tariff, the U.S. government is, in effect, taxing consumers for buying a VCR. If the higher price is the result of the U.S. government forcing the Japanese manufacturer to raise the price of the VCR, the U.S. consumer is subsidizing the Japanese manufacturer with the assistance of the U.S. government. In either case, the U.S. government is working against the interests of its own citizens.

The level playing field argument is philosophically flawed for another reason as well. Protectionists see trade as a win-lose proposition, like a sporting event. If one party wins, another must lose. However, trade is a win-win proposition. If two parties enter into a trade agreement, it is because they both gain by the exchange. Otherwise, there would be no trade.

This fallacious view of trade is not new. Frédéric Bastiat exploded this myth more than a century ago. Bastiat used the example of a horse race to highlight the protectionist argument of his day.

We believe that our protective tariffs should simply represent the difference between the net cost of a commodity that we produce and the net cost of a similar commodity produced in a foreign country. . . . A protective tariff computed on this basis merely assures free competition; . . . free competition exists only where there is equality in the costs and conditions of production. In the case of a horse race, the weight that each of the horses is to carry is ascertained, and conditions are equalized; otherwise, the horses would no longer be competitors. In the case of commerce, if one of the sellers can bring his goods to market more cheaply than the others, he ceases to be a competitor and becomes a monopolist. . . . If you abolish this protection, which represents the difference in net costs, the foreigner will invade your market and acquire a monopoly.

Each person ought to wish, for his own sake as well as for the sake of his fellow citizens, that the production of the country be protected against foreign competition, *whenever a foreigner can furnish goods at a lower price.*[45]

In his response to this argument, Bastiat points out that the protectionists who take this position are taking the position of the producers, whereas those who advocate free trade take the position of the poor consumers, who must pay the price of protectionist measures. If the goal is to find out which horse is the fastest runner, then it makes sense to equalize the weight each horse must carry. However, if the goal is to get an important and urgent piece of news to a particular destination, it makes no sense to weigh down the horse that has the best chance of arriving first. If the goal is to satisfy the consumer at the lowest price, it does not make sense to increase the cost that consumers must pay by placing a tariff on cheaper foreign goods.

Inequality in the conditions of production between a foreign and a domestic industry does not mean that the higher cost industry will have to shut down completely. Low cost domestic producers will still be able to compete with foreign competitors, and high cost producers will have an incentive to enter another line of business where their resources can be used more productively.

THE STRONG DOLLAR ARGUMENT

Another popular argument that has been advanced is that a strong dollar is a source of our trade problems. Aside from the fact that this argument starts with a faulty premise — that trade deficits are always bad — it also assumes that there can be such a thing as a dollar that is too strong. Although it is true that imported goods cost less when the dollar is high relative to foreign currencies, there is no way to determine the correct price of the dollar. As long as exchange rates are flexible, consumers determine the relative strength of various currencies. It is nonsense to talk in terms of what the dollar should be valued at, because this value fluctuates constantly, along with the relative value of every other product and service.

A variation on this theme is the belief that the dollar should be measured in terms of some historical value, although it is never explained why this should be so. One popular benchmark is the 1980 dollar.[46] Yet when comparisons between 1980 prices of other commodities are made, the use of such benchmarks is seen to be ridiculous. Using 1980 as a benchmark, it appears that gasoline in 1989 is undervalued and hamburgers are overvalued. If a different benchmark is chosen — for example, 1960 — then it appears that gasoline is overvalued, because gasoline costs more today (and in 1980) than in did in 1960. Furthermore, because the dollar's value in 1980 was at a low point after going through a decade of inflation, comparing the relative value of the dollar today, using 1980 as a base, with the value of other currencies or commodities will produce distortions.

Because there is no such thing as a dollar that is too strong or too weak, it follows that attempts to restore the dollar to its correct value are absurd. Yet that is exactly what some individuals are advocating. Shifts in exchange rates are caused by changes in consumer preferences, in the absence of governmental tampering with exchange rates or the money supply. Furthermore, the market is a self-adjusting mechanism. If dollars rise too high to be sustained, imports will increase and dollars will flow into the international currency markets, thus reducing their relative value. There is no need to correct the market because the market corrects itself.

Exchange rates fluctuate based on the relative quantities of the various currencies that are in the international marketplace. Placing restrictions on imports causes fewer dollars to find their way into the international currency market, making the dollar relatively stronger. However, making the dollar artificially stronger by restricting imports tends to make imports even more attractive, which is the exact opposite of the policymaker's intention.

THE INFANT INDUSTRY ARGUMENT

Economists (including Adam Smith) advocating protectionism have cited the infant industry argument as the prime reason for shielding some domestic industries from foreign competition. It is one of the most basic and pervasive arguments, as well. Alexander Hamilton advocated it in his 1791 Report on Manufactures.[47] However, even this argument is based on faulty reasoning. According to the infant industry argument, government should protect a new industry from foreign competition so that it can, in time, grow strong enough to hold its own. Protection and various forms of subsidy are intended to be temporary, just until the new industry can get on its feet. The problem is that once an industry is protected or subsidized, it is difficult or nearly impossible to take away the protection. Interests become vested. In many cases, infant industries become midgets and never reach full height.[48] Furthermore, even when protection can help an infant industry, it does so by diverting resources from other industries, weakening them, and if the infant industry argument is used on many infant industries, the result will be no protection for any of them, because of the fallacy of composition.[49] In some cases, the infant industry approach does not work even when it is applied to only one industry.[50]

There is really no need to protect any industry, whether infant or mature. If foreigners can produce something better or cheaper than the domestic industry, it is to our advantage to buy foreign products and use our scarce resources to produce other products that we can do better than the competition. David Ricardo's law of comparative advantage comes into play here. Because we cannot produce everything, we should concentrate on what we can do well and buy everything else from foreigners.[51]

THE BREATHING ROOM ARGUMENT

Another popular argument in favor of protectionism is that U.S. industry only needs temporary protection. These industries, it is asserted, must have some breathing room so they can cut costs and improve productivity and then be able to compete with foreign producers. The steel, automobile, and textile industries are especially noted for using this argument, which is a variation on the "infant industry" theme. Murray Rothbard[52] calls it the senile industry argument.

The breathing room (senile industry) argument has not worked in practice. The U.S. auto industry is an example.[53] In 1981, the United States entered into a voluntary restraint agreement with Japan. Yet today, U.S. auto companies are still unable to compete with the Japanese, and there is pressure to continue the voluntary restraints and even tighten auto import restrictions. Temporary measures have a tendency to become permanent, to the detriment of consumers.

The steel industry is another example of where this breathing room strategy has failed. The U.S. steel industry has been cushioned from foreign producers since 1969 through quota agreements and restrictions. If the breathing room argument held water, steel industry production would be expected to increase and unit costs to fall. Yet just the opposite has been the case. Labor productivity has declined, and cost-cutting techniques have not been implemented. Investment in the steel industry actually declined after import restrictions were imposed, while foreign investment rose steadily.[54]

There is strong evidence to suggest that voluntary export restraints (VER) actually destroy more jobs than they save. For example, in Reagan's 1984 VER, aimed at reducing steel imports from 26% to 22% of domestic sales, employment in the steel industry increased by 17,000. However, employment in steel user industries declined by 52,000 because of the higher prices they had to pay for steel.[55]

The breathing room argument is also theoretically unsound. Competition provides incentives to improve quality and reduce costs. Taking away this incentive by insulating an industry from foreign competition retards these improvements. In effect, government restrictions on foreign imports give U.S. producers a monopoly. When there is monopoly, there is far less incentive to innovate, cut costs, and improve quality because consumers have fewer choices in the marketplace.

THE TAX BURDEN ARGUMENT

The tax burden argument states that foreign producers have a lower tax burden than do domestic producers, which gives them a built-in structural advantage. If foreign producers actually had a lower tax burden, the solution is simple — reduce domestic corporate tax rates to make U.S. industry more competitive. Yet this solution is seldom offered. An analysis of the tax burdens in various industrialized countries, however, reveals that the premise is incorrect. As a result of the various tax reform measures passed in the early 1980s, the United States has one of the lowest corporate tax burdens of any industrialized country. A Library of Congress study found that Japanese manufacturers pay an effective rate of 50.5%, compared with 27.7% for U.S. manufacturers.[56] The total tax burden of a Japanese automobile sold in the United States is actually slightly higher than the tax burden on a U.S. automobile sold in the United States. Furthermore, Japan does not impose a tariff on automobile imports, whereas the United States does.

THE VOLUNTARY RESTRAINT ARGUMENT

A voluntary restraint agreement is an agreement between the United States and some other country to limit imports of a certain product. For example, Japan has agreed not to export more than a certain number of automobiles to the United States. A number of countries have agreed not to do the same for steel.

One major problem with "voluntary" restraints is that they are not voluntary. These agreements are not between companies but between governments. The Japanese government prevents its automobile manufacturers from sending automobiles to the United States even though there are willing customers waiting to buy their products. The U.S. government uses threats and intimidation to get foreign governments to agree to these "voluntary" restrictions, because the absence of an agreement could lead to even less desirable trade terms.[57] U.S. consumers are hurt as a result, because some of them must settle on a choice that is lower down on their subjective value scale. The fact that it is called "voluntary" does not change the fact that consumers are hurt.

Robert Crandall[58] estimates that the VER on automobiles with Japan increased the price of a Japanese automobile by $2,500 in 1984 and allowed domestic manufacturers to charge $1,000 more than they would have been able to obtain in the absence of the quota. He estimated that this VER cost U.S. consumers about $16 billion in 1984 and 1985.

Another problem with so-called voluntary agreements is that they do not do what they are supposed to do. For example, Japan and the United States entered into an orderly marketing agreement in 1977 that limited the number of color televisions that Japan could send to the United States. As a result, the number of Japanese color televisions exported to the United States dropped from 2.50 million units to 1.56 million. However, domestic producers did not benefit from this decline, because the reduced number of Japanese imports was offset by increased imports from South Korea, Taiwan, and Canada. Furthermore, the restrictions were circumvented by starting production in the United States and then shipping the parts abroad, where the bulk of the manufacturing and assembly took place. The nearly completed units were shipped back to the United States for final assembly. This roundabout process undoubtedly increased costs, which would not have been necessary in the absence of the trade restriction.[59]

Voluntary restraints in the steel industry provide a further example. In 1968, the United States entered into a voluntary restraint agreement with Japanese and European exporters. They agreed to reduce the import tonnage by 22%, which they did. However, rather than maintain the previous product mix, the exporters shifted their exports from low-value basic steel to higher-value specialty steel products, so that even though the tonnage total was reduced, the market value of the steel they exported remained at about the same level as before.[60]

THE DEBTOR-NATION ARGUMENT

Those of the protectionist mentality point out that the United States is a debtor nation, meaning that Americans owe foreigners more than foreigners owe Americans. They think that being a debtor nation is harmful. Would they rather have it the other way? If so, then they must think that it would be better for Americans to invest overseas than at home. Do they also think that Americans should send their money overseas to buy foreign goods rather than buy American-made products?

This debtor-nation argument has a number of other weaknesses as well. Although borrowing to finance the federal deficit is irresponsible because it siphons off money that could be used for private investment and causes the nation's debt burden to increase, borrowing by business to finance growth is good business. If a company can borrow at 12% and invest the proceeds to earn 16%, then it is good business to borrow from anyone who wants to lend the money. If interest rates rise to 80%, it still makes good sense to borrow if the proceeds can be plowed into something that yields more than 80%. The fact that a business owes money does not mean that the business is unhealthy. In fact, it often means just the opposite. Sick businesses cannot find anyone to lend them money. The federal government, however, can borrow money because of its taxing power and ability to print money to repay both principal and interest.

Lending to business makes the economy healthy. Businesses expand production, create jobs, and flood the market with products that consumers (foreign and domestic) want to buy. Foreign investment helps make the U.S. economy stronger, so why should anyone be against it? Both parties benefit, the lender and the borrower. Other parties also benefit, such as the workers who must be employed to fill the newly created jobs and the consumers who now have more product choices. No one loses.

Historically, the U.S. economy has been healthiest when it was a debtor nation. The United States was a debtor nation during the rapid expansion of the nineteenth century. It was also a debtor nation during the economic expansion of the 1980s. It was a creditor nation during the depression of the 1930s, when no one wanted to lend U.S. business any money.[61] The whole debtor nation argument is based on faulty logic. On the one hand, protectionists complain that too much money is leaving the country because Americans are buying foreign goods. Then, when it comes back in the form of investment, they complain again because foreigners are pouring their money into the national economy (and creating jobs for Americans in the process).

THE RETALIATION ARGUMENT

Those who pay lip service to free trade argue that the United States should use trade as a weapon. We should threaten to erect trade barriers against nations that have erected trade barriers against the United States.[62] Those who advocate such policies are under the false impression that only the exporting country benefits by trade. Trade is mutually beneficial, and curtailing it for any reason hurts both sides. Restricting foreign imports is the same as restricting consumer purchases. There is no way to restrict one without restricting the other. Erecting trade barriers restricts consumer choice and causes prices to rise, because there is less competition.

If the U.S. government erects trade barriers, it can expect other countries to do likewise as a retaliatory measure. The effect of such restrictive policies is to reduce trade even more, hurting consumers. U.S. companies that export are also harmed by such policies, along with the employees of the exporters, who risk losing their jobs because of the government's restrictive trade practices.

Erecting trade barriers also cuts the foreign demand for U.S. products. If less dollars flow overseas, less dollars can flow back into the country. Foreign countries cannot spend dollars they do not have.

There is much empirical evidence to support the view that trade wars reduce exports. The Smoot-Hawley Tariff of 1930, for example, resulted in a dramatic decline in U.S. imports. In return, foreign countries retaliated by erecting high trade barriers of their own.[63] This act and its aftermath deepened and lengthened the depression.

THE NATIONAL DEFENSE ARGUMENT

Defense is more important than opulence.[64]

Another argument for protectionism is that we must protect Industry A or Industry B for reasons of national defense. The oil industry is often cited as an example.[65] The argument states that if the United States does not protect its oil industry by imposing quotas or import fees on foreign oil or by subsidizing the domestic industry, we will be overrun with foreign oil; our domestic oil industry will be devastated and unable to supply us with the needed oil if foreign supplies should be cut off in time of war.

Actually, the oil import restrictions the United States placed on oil during the 1960s drained domestic reserves and increased U.S. vulnerability in the 1970s.[66] Furthermore, a shortage of oil would make us think twice before getting involved in a foreign war, and lack of oil would be the least of our worries in the event of a nuclear war. If we really needed to fight a conventional war, there is enough oil in the ground to meet our needs, although it may take a few months to get the oil pumping. However, even this problem could be avoided by keeping a few months' worth of oil in reserve.[67] Conventional wars seldom start without warning, and if it appears that war might be on the horizon, the U.S. oil industry could make the necessary preparations. There is no need to protect the oil industry by placing trade restrictions on the importation or exportation of oil. Actually, refusing to protect the oil industry (or any other industry) against foreign competition will force it to become more efficient, which enhances national defense.

Another problem with the defense argument is that once one exception is made for one industry, there is no logical stopping point. Every industry in need of protection will assert national defense as a valid reason for government intervention. At one time in our history, a trade association for the U.S. glove industry stated that national defense required that Congress place a high tariff on the importation of gloves. U.S. soldiers needed gloves, and a future war effort would be imperiled if they could not get them because the foreign source was cut off. Section 104 of the 1952 Defense Production Act restricts peanut imports in the interests of national defense.[68] The cheese, fruit, watch manufacturing, railroad, airline, truck, and telephone industries have also used the defense argument when asking for protection.[69] Where does it all end?

A corollary of the idea that we should trade with our friends is that we should not trade with our enemies, but this second idea often does not hold water and harms us more than it harms our enemies. For example, the United States could decide not to sell wheat to the former Soviet Union, but that does not mean that the Soviets will not be able to obtain wheat. They can very easily get it from Canada or some other country. Also, if U.S. wheat sales are diverted to some other country, there is no guarantee that the wheat will not turn up in the Soviet Union eventually. The only predictable part of this restraint is that U.S. farmers will lose a sale to someone else.[70] Economic sanctions generally do not work.[71] At most, they will raise the price of the restricted goods for the country intended to be punished, and the countries that participate in the sanctions will lose sales without being able to show any corresponding benefit. In fact, sanctions often increase animosity between countries that are not currently on friendly terms.

A variation on the defense theme is the self-sufficiency theme. This argument calls for a country to be economically self-sufficient, because of nationalistic reasons, to encourage domestic employment, or because trading with others corrupts the soul. This latter reason was argued by Plato and Aristotle as sufficient reason for limiting trade with outsiders.[72] Durant[73] discusses Plato's thinking on this point. Schumacher[74] is a modern exponent of it. The problem with this position is that self-sufficiency greatly reduces the division of labor, which results in a reduced standard of living.[75] If every community has to make everything for itself, it cannot specialize in the things it does best and trade for everything else. It means that Canadian residents will not be able to eat bananas or pineapples and Honolulu residents will not be able to eat potato chips. This logic would have us believe that it is somehow bad to sell pineapples to Canadians but good to sell them to residents of Maine or New Hampshire, which is absurd. Free trade enhances harmony and peaceful cooperation, whereas self-sufficiency and trade restrictions lead to animosity between nations and actually increase the chance of war.

Rather than free trade being a threat to national defense, there is substantial evidence to suggest that lack of free trade is a threat to peace. Many wars were caused, at least in part, because of trade restrictions and the adoption of mercantilist trade policies. World Wars I and II are perfect examples. World War I was preceded by tariff and trade wars. The depression of the 1930s, which, along with the Treaty of Versailles, prepared the way for World War II, was aggravated by the erection of trade barriers such as the Smoot-Hawley Tariff that practically cut off the flow of imports into the United States.[76] Roosevelt's trade embargo of Japan, which hindered its invasion of Manchuria and crippled its domestic economy, practically forced it to bomb Pearl Harbor.[77]

One of the main causes of the American Revolution was England's mercantilist policies. The various Navigation Acts required cargo to be carried on English ships manned by English seamen. The Staple Act required goods that were imported to the colonies from Europe to first go through British ports. The Hat Act, the Woolens Act, and numerous other acts of Parliament prevented the colonies from exporting manufactured goods, making them dependent on British trade. High tariffs were placed on goods that did not come from Britain or a British colony, which increased their price to the point where British goods looked cheap by comparison.[78] Gold was not permitted to flow from England to the colonies, but a flow in the opposite direction was encouraged, under the mistaken mercantilist belief that wealth was measured by the amount of gold in the treasury rather than by the amount of goods and services the economy produced.[79]

Many other wars were caused, at least in part, by trade restrictions, which are often used as economic weapons — a substitute for military action. For example, the 1651 Navigation Act caused the First Anglo-Dutch War of 1652–54.[80] The second and third Anglo-Dutch wars were also caused by restrictive trade policies. Other wars in this era caused by nationalistic economic policies included King William's War, the French and Indian War (Seven Years' War), and the various other wars and skirmishes between England and France that did not end until the Congress of Vienna in 1815, various wars with Spain, including the War of Spanish Succession (Queen Anne's War) and the War of Jenkin's Ear, and the War of Austrian Succession.[81] All these wars had to be paid for, and the king and Parliament found it easier to finance them by borrowing than by taxing. The seeds of the American Revolution were sown in the 1760s, when England attempted to get the American colonists to help pay these war debts by taxing them. All these wars could have been prevented if England and the other European economic powers of the time had adopted free trade policies rather than mercantilism.

NOTES

1. Adam Smith, *An Inquiry into the Nature and Causes of the Wealth of Nations* (1776/1937), p. 461.

2. Plato, *Laws*, IV, 705a; Aristotle, *The Politics*, I, VII, chap. 4.

3. For Bastiat's views on free trade, see *Sophismes Économiques*, which is in Volume I of *Oeuvres Complètes de Frédéric Bastiat*, fourth edition (Guillaumin et Cie, 1878). Many of Bastiat's works have been translated into English. For example, see his *Economic Sophisms; Selected Essays on Political Economy* (Irvington-on-Hudson, N.Y.: Foundation for Economic Education, 1964); *Economic Harmonies* (Irvington-on-Hudson, N.Y.: Foundation for Economic Education, 1964). For information about John Prince Smith, see Ralph Raico, "John Prince Smith and the German Free-Trade Movement," in *Man, Economy and Liberty: Essays in Honor of Murray N. Rothbard*, eds. Walter Block and Llewellyn Rockwell, Jr. (Auburn, Ala.: Ludwig von Mises Institute, 1988), pp. 341–51; J. Becker, *Das Deutsche Manchestertum* (1907); W. O.

Henderson, "Prince Smith and Free Trade in Germany," *Economic History Review* 2 (1950): 295. Richard Cobden and John Bright have had literally hundreds of books and articles written about their work, many of which are in English. Literature on these two English economists is sometimes listed under "Anti-Corn Law League" or "The Manchester School" as well as under Cobden and Bright. Also see Francis W. Hirst (ed.), *Free Trade and Other Fundamental Doctrines of the Manchester School* (London and New York: Harper Brothers, 1903; New York: Augustus M. Kelley, 1968).

4.   Richard Cantillon, *Essai Sur la Nature Du Commerce en Général* [Essay on the Nature of Commerce in General] (1755; 1931). There is some speculation that Cantillon got some of his ideas, such as the monetary approach to the balance of payments, from David Hume, but there are doubts as to the validity of this allegation, because early drafts of *Essai* were in circulation long before Hume's essays *Of Money and of the Balance of Trade* first appeared in 1752. See Antoin E. Murphy, "Richard Cantillon — Banker and Economist," *Journal of Libertarian Studies* 7 (1985): 203. In fact, there is some speculation that Hume read Cantillon before he wrote his own essays on the subject. See F. A. Hayek, *Prices and Production* (London: Routledge & Sons, 1931/2 and 1935/9). For more on Hume's balance of payments and trade theories, see D. K. Fausten, "The Humean Origin of the Contemporary Monetary Approach to the Balance of Payments," *Quarterly Journal of Economics* 93 (1979): 655; H. G. Grubel, "Ricardo and Thornton on the Transfer Mechanism", *Quarterly Journal of Economics* 75 (1961): 292; Robert W. McGee, "The Economic Thought of David Hume," *Hume Studies* 15 (1989): 184; F. Petrella, "Adam Smith's Rejection of Hume's Price-Specie-Flow Mechanism: A Minor Mystery Resolved," *Southern Economic Journal* 34 (1968): 365; C. E. Staley, "Hume and Viner on the International Adjustment Mechanism," *History of Political Economy* 8 (1976): 252; M. I. Duke, "David Hume and Monetary Adjustment," *History of Political Economy* 11 (1979): 572.

5.   Vilfredo Pareto, *Manual of Political Economy* (1927), pp. 377, 379.

6.   Robert Nozick, *Anarchy, State, and Utopia* (New York: Basic Books, 1974), p. 272.

7.   W. M. Curtiss, *The Tariff Idea* (Irvington-on-Hudson, N.Y.: Foundation for Economic Education, 1953), p. 19.

8.   Frédéric Bastiat elaborates on this theme in *The Law* (Irvington-on-Hudson, N.Y.: Foundation for Economic Education, 1968). Dean Russell discusses the same phenomenon in *Government and Legal Plunder: Bastiat Brought Up to Date* (Irvington-on-Hudson, N.Y.: Foundation for Economic Education, 1985).

9.   Bastiat, *The Law*, p. 21.

10.   Frank Chodorov, "The Humanity of Trade," in *Free Trade: The Necessary Foundation for World Peace*, ed. J. K. Taylor (Irvington-on-Hudson, N.Y.: Foundation for Economic Education, 1986), p. 7.

11.   Bjorn Ahlstrom, "Protecting Whom from What?" *The Freeman* 39 (1989): 153.

12.   Ludwig von Mises, *Human Action*, third revised edition (Chicago, Ill.: Henry Regnery Company, 1966), p. 317.

13.   This second definition is the General Agreement on Tariffs and Trade (GATT), Article VII definition, but charging different prices in different markets is simply rational profit-maximizing behavior, as any student of price discrimination theory knows.

14.   The example, in the original French, may be found in *Oeuvres Complètes de Frédéric Bastiat*, Volume I, 4th ed., p. 57. The English translation is in Bastiat's *Economic Sophisms*, p. 55.

(London: Trade Policy Research Centre, 1975), p. xxxiii, as cited in Melvyn. B. Krauss, *The New Protectionism: The Welfare State and International Trade* (New York: New York University Press, 1978), p. 86.

16.   D. T. Armentano, *Antitrust Policy: The Case for Repeal* (Washington, D.C.: Cato Institute, 1986), p. 43.

17.   R. Koller, Jr., "The Myth of Predatory Pricing: An Empirical Study," *Antitrust Law & Economics Review* 4 (1971): 105; John McGee, "Predatory Price Cutting: The Standard Oil (N.J.) Case," *Journal of Law & Economics* 1 (1958): 137.

18.   J. Finger and J. Nogues, "International Control of Subsidies and Countervailing Duties," *World Bank Economic Review* 9 (1987): 707.

19.   Jagdish N. Bhagwati, *Protectionism* (Cambridge, Mass.: MIT Press, 1988), p. 48.

20.   P. Messerlin, *The Long Term Evolution of the EC Anti-Dumping Law: Some Lessons for the New AD Laws in LDCs* (Washington, D.C.: World Bank, 1987), p. 21, as cited by Bhagwati, *Protectionism*, p. 51.

21.   Robert Crandall, "Import Quotas and the Automobile Industry: The Costs of Protectionism," *Brookings Review* 2 (1984): 16.

22.   Restrictions on imported steel cost U.S. auto companies $300 per auto, according to one estimate. A Federal Trade Commission study found that limiting foreign steel producers to 18% of the U.S. market would cost consumers $8.5 billion in direct price increases and decreased economic efficiency. See Wayne Gable, *Myths About International Trade* (Washington, D.C.: Citizens for a Sound Economy, n.d.), p. 4; Walter Williams, *All It Takes Is Guts: A Minority View* (Washington, D.C.: Regnery Gateway, 1987), p. 78.

23.   A. Shapiro, "Why the Trade Deficit Does Not Matter," *Journal of Applied Corporation Finance* 2 (1989): 87–95.

24.   Arthur T. Denzau, *How Import Restraints Reduce Employment*, Publication No. 80 (St. Louis, Mo.: Washington University, Center for the Study of American Business, 1987).

25.   J. Michael Finger, "The Political Economy of Trade Policy," *Cato Journal* 3 (Winter 1983/84): 743.

26.   Barry Bluestone and Bennett Harrison, *The Deindustrialization of America* (New York: Basic Books, 1982).

27.   Bhagwati, *Protectionism*, p. 110.

28.   Nicholas Kaldor, *The Causes of the Slow Economic Growth of the United Kingdom* (Oxford: Oxford University Press, 1966).

29.   M. Folsom and S. Lubar (eds.), *The Philosophy of Manufactures: Early Debates Over Industrialization in the United States* (New York: Kelley, 1980).

30.   For more on this point, see Richard B. McKenzie, *Competing Visions: The Political Conflict Over America's Economic Future* (Washington, D.C.: Cato Institute, 1985), p. 38; Charles L. Schultze, "Industrial Policy: A Dissent," in *Plant Closings: Public or Private Choices?* ed. Richard B. McKenzie (Washington, D.C.: Cato Institute, 1984), p. 155; and William H. Branson, "The Myth of Deindustrialization," in *Plant Closings: Public or Private Choices?* ed. McKenzie, (1984), p. 177.

31.   Thomas DiLorenzo, *The Myth of America's Declining Manufacturing Sector*, Heritage Foundation Backgrounder (Washington, D.C.: Heritage Foundation, 1984).

32.   A. Shapiro, "Why the Trade Deficit Does Not Matter."

33.   T. White, "The Danger from Japan," *New York Times Magazine*, July 28, 1985, p. 23, as cited in Bhagwati, *Protectionism*, p. 64.

34.   S. Chaikin, "Trade, Investment, and Deindustrialization," *Foreign Affairs* 60 (1988): 836–48.

35.   Bhagwati, *Protectionism*, p. 64; *The New York Times*, October 13, 1982, p. A3; M. Schram, "'Big Fritz': Tough Talk and a Flag," *Washington Post*, October 7,

1982, p. 1; McKenzie, *Competing Visions: The Political Conflict over America's Economic Future*, p. 65.

36.   Richard B. McKenzie, *National Industrial Policy* (Dallas, Tex.: The Fisher Institute, 1984), p. 67.

37.   The rate of compensation in motor vehicles to that in all manufactures was about 165% in 1982. The ratio in iron and steel was 189%. Even if wages in these industries were cut to make them competitive with wages in Japan, the ratio would still be considerably above average, so it cannot be said that the tariff is needed to protect downtrodden labor. See M. Kreinin, "Wage Competitiveness in the U.S. Auto and Steel Industries," *Contemporary Policy Issues* 4 (January 1984): 39; Edward Tower, "Some Empirical Results on Trade and National Prosperity," *Cato Journal* 3 (Winter 1983/84): 639–40. However, the problem with the auto and steel industries is due to more than just excessive wages. Outmoded facilities and union work rules also play major roles. One study found that the group of nonfarm labor that would benefit most by unilateral tariff reductions would be unskilled labor. See J. Hartigan and E. Teller, "Trade Policy and the American Income Distribution," *Review of Economics & Statistics* 72 (May 1982): 261.

38.   N. Rosenthal, "The Shrinking Middle Class: Myth or Reality?" *Monthly Labor Review* (March 1985): 4; Richard B. McKenzie, *The American Job Machine* (New York: Universe Books, 1988), p. 102.

39.   McKenzie, *The American Job Machine*, pp. 108–12.

40.   The idea that all production is ultimately for consumption is Say's Law, which John Maynard Keynes attacked in his *General Theory of Employment, Interest and Money* (New York: Harcourt Brace, 1936). However, Keynes attacked a straw man, as has been pointed out by Mises, Hutt, and Sowell, among others. See Keynes, *The General Theory of Employment, Interest and Money*, p. 25; Ludwig von Mises, "Lord Keynes and Say's Law," *Freeman* 1 (October 30, 1950): 83, reprinted in Henry Hazlitt (ed.), *The Critics of Keynesian Economics* (New York: D. Van Nostrand, 1960); W. H. Hutt, *Keynesianism — Retrospect and Prospect* (Chicago, Ill.: Henry Regnery Company, 1963); W. H. Hutt, *A Rehabilitation of Say's Law* (Athens: Ohio University Press, 1975); W. H. Hutt, *The Keynesian Episode: A Reassessment* (Indianapolis, Ind.: Liberty Press, 1979); and Thomas Sowell, *Say's Law* (Princeton, N.J.: Princeton University Press, 1972), pp. 201–18.

41.   For more on this point, see Richard B. McKenzie, *The American Job Machine* (New York: Universe Books, 1988).

42.   Williams, *All It Takes Is Guts: A Minority View*, p. 80.

43.   Ibid., p. 81.

44.   Walter Block and Michael Walker, *Lexicon of Economic Thought* (Vancouver: Fraser Institute, 1989), pp. 131–32.

45.   Bastiat, *Economic Sophisms*, p. 28; *Sophismes Économiques*, pp. 27–28.

46.   Gable, *Myths About International Trade*, p. 7.

47.   Hamilton's report is reproduced in A. H. Cole (ed.), *Industrial and Commercial Correspondence of Alexander Hamilton* (New York: Kelley, 1968).

48.   Charles P. Kindleberger, "International Trade and National Prosperity," *Cato Journal* 3 (Winter 1983/84): 631; W. M. Corden, *Trade Policy and Economic Welfare* (New York: Oxford University Press, 1974).

49.   Kindleberger, "International Trade and National Prosperity," p. 630; Larry E. Westphal, *Empirical Justification for Infant Industry Protection*, World Bank Working Paper No. 445, Washington, D.C., March 1981; Tower, "Some Empirical Results on Trade and National Prosperity," p. 642.

50.   Anne O. Krueger and Baran Tuncer, "An Empirical Test of the Infant Industry Argument," *American Economic Review* 75 (1982): 1142; Lila J. Truett and

Dale B. Truett, *Economics* (St. Louis, Mo.: Times Mirror/Mosby College Publishing, 1987), p. 726.

51. However, comparative advantage is not the key here. Some economists have argued that because of modern technology or other reasons, the law of comparative advantage no longer applies. Although that view is questionable, the key is that it is better to buy cheap than to buy expensive, regardless of whether the law of comparative advantage still applies or not.

52. Murray N. Rothbard, "Protectionism and the Destruction of Prosperity," in *The Free Market Reader*, ed. Llewellyn H. Rockwell, Jr. (Burlingame, Calif.: The Ludwig von Mises Institute, 1988), pp. 148–59.

53. Gable, *Myths About International Trade*, p. 14.

54. Ibid.

55. Denzau, *How Import Restraints Reduce Employment*, pp. 5–6; McKenzie, *The American Job Machine*, pp. 148–49.

56. Gable, *Myths About International Trade*, p. 17.

57. Many voluntary restraint agreements are the result of an unfair trade practice petition. See J. Finger and J. Nogues, "International Control of Subsidies and Countervailing Duties"; J. Finger, H. Hall, and D. Nelson, "The Political Economy of Administered Protection," *American Economic Review* 72 (1982):452; Bhagwati, *Protectionism*, p. 53. "Orderly marketing agreements" and "adjustment assistance programs," although different in form, also have a negative effect on employment and free trade. See Leland B. Yeager and David G. Tuerck, "Realism and Free-Trade Policy," *Cato Journal* 3 (Winter 1983/84): 645–48; James Dorn, "Trade Adjustment Assistance: A Case of Government Failure," *Cato Journal* 2 (1982): 865.

58. R. Crandall, "Detroit Rode Quotas to Prosperity," *Wall Street Journal*, January 29, 1986, p. 30.

59. Victor A. Canto, "U.S. Trade Policy: History and Evidence," *Cato Journal* 3 (Winter 1983/84): 679–93; Victor A. Canto and Arthur Laffer, "The Effectiveness of Orderly Marketing Agreements: The Color TV Case," *Business Economics* 18 (January 1983): 38.

60. Canto, "U.S. Trade Policy: History and Evidence"; V. Canto, R. Eastin, and A. Laffer, "Failure of Protectionism: A Study of the Steel Industry," *Columbia Journal of World Business* 17 (1982): 43.

61. Gable, *Myths About International Trade*, p. 23.

62. "Talking Loudly and Carrying a Crowbar," *The Economist*, April 29, 1989, pp. 23–24; "The Myth of Managed Trade," *The Economist*, May 6, 1989, pp. 11–12; "Trade: Mote and Beam," *The Economist*, May 6, 1989, pp. 22–23; A. Dowd, "What To Do About Trade Policy," *Fortune*, May 8, 1989, p. 106.

63. Benjamin M. Anderson, *Economics and the Public Welfare* (New York: D. Van Nostrand, 1949; Indianapolis, Ind.: Liberty Press, 1979), p. 225; Hans F. Sennholz, *Age of Inflation* (Belmont, Mass.: Western Islands, 1979), pp. 52, 128; Gable, *Myths About International Trade*, pp. 24–25; The Smoot-Hawley Tariff Act of 1930, Pub. L. No. 71-361, 46 Stat. 590.

64. Smith, *An Inquiry into the Nature and Causes of the Wealth of Nations*, p. 431.

65. Robert L. Bradley, Jr., *The Mirage of Oil Protection* (Lanham, Md.: University Press of America, 1989).

66. Thomas D. Willett and Mehrdad Jalalighajar, "U.S. Trade Policy and National Security," *Cato Journal* 3 (Winter 1983/84): 717–18, 721; J. Cox and A. Wright, "A Tariff Policy for Independence from Oil Embargoes," *National Tax Journal* 28 (March 1975): 29.

67. J. Plummer, "United States Oil Stockpiling Policy," *Journal of Contemporary Studies* 4 (1981): 5; G. Horwich and E. Mitchell (eds.), *Policies for*

Coping with Oil-Supply Disruptions (New York: Praeger, 1982).

68. Curtiss, *The Tariff Idea*, p. 65.

69. Robert B. Ekelund, Jr., and Robert D. Tollison, *Economics*, second edition (Glenview, Ill., and Boston, Mass.: Scott, Foresman and Company, 1988), p. 868.

70. Earl Ravenal, "The Economic Claims of National Security," *Cato Journal* 3 (Winter 1983/84): 729–30.

71. There is ample empirical evidence to support this claim. For example, see M. Doxey, *Economic Sanctions and International Enforcement* (Washington, D.C.: Institute for International Economics, 1980); K. Knorr, *The Power of Nations* (New York: Macmillan, 1975); Willett and Jalalighajar, "U.S. Trade Policy and National Security," pp. 723–26.

72. Plato, *Laws*; Aristotle, *The Politics*; Lewis H. Haney, *History of Economic Thought* (New York: Macmillan, 1949), pp. 56–59. Walter Olson points out the irony of this "dependency" argument. Americans are dependent on foreigners for things like towels and tape decks, and foreigners are dependent on us for things like food and raw materials. See Walter Olson, "Don't Slam the Door," *National Review* 35 (March 4, 1983): 248.

73. Will Durant, *The Story of Philosophy* (New York: Washington Square Press, 1952), pp. 19–20, 37–38.

74. E. Schumacher, *Small Is Beautiful* (Englewood Cliffs, N.J.: Prentice-Hall, 1973).

75. V. Canto, A. Laffer, and J. Turney, "Trade Policy and the U.S. Economy," *Financial Analyst Journal* (September/October 1982): 237.

76. Murray N. Rothbard, *America's Great Depression* (Los Angeles, Calif.: Nash Publishing, 1963).

77. Willett and Jalalighajar, "U.S. Trade Policy and National Security," p. 725; Y. Wu, *Economic Warfare* (New York: Macmillan, 1952), p. 267; James J. Martin, "Pearl Harbor: Antecedents, Background and Consequences," in *The Saga of Hog Island* (Colorado Springs, Colo.: Ralph Myles, Publisher, 1977), p. 114. Discussing the economic factors leading to war in general, or to World Wars I and II in particular, would take another chapter, if not a book. For the causes of World War I, see L. C. F. Turner, *Origins of the First World War* (New York: W.W. Norton, 1970); Sidney Bradshaw Fay, *The Origins of the World War* (New York: Macmillan, 1939); Harry Elmer Barnes, *In Quest of Truth and Justice* (Chicago, Ill.: National Historical Society, 1928; Colorado Springs, Colo.: Ralph Myles, Publisher, 1972). For the causes of World War II, see A. J. P. Taylor, *The Origins of the Second World War* (New York: Athenium, 1983); Henry Elmer Barnes, "A. J. P. Taylor and the Causes of World War II," *New Individualist Review* 2 (1962): 3; William Henry Chamberlin, *America's Second Crusade* (Chicago, Ill.: Henry Regnery Company, 1950/62). For an in-depth study of 967 wars occurring between 500 B.C. and 1925 A.D., see Pitirim A. Sorokin, *The Crisis of Our Age: The Social and Cultural Outlook* (New York: Dutton, 1941). For an analysis of the relationship between economic nationalism and war, see Ludwig von Mises, *Omnipotent Government* (New Rochelle, N.Y.: Arlington House, 1969); Ludwig von Mises, "The Economics of War," in *Free Trade: The Necessary Foundation for World Peace*, ed. J. K. Taylor (Irvington-on-Hudson, N.Y.: Foundation for Economic Education, 1986), pp. 77–83; David Osterfeld, "The Nature of Modern Warfare," in Taylor (ed.), *Free Trade: The Necessary Foundation for World Peace*, pp. 84–90; Hans F. Sennholz, "Welfare States at War," in Taylor (ed.), *Free Trade: The Necessary Foundation for World Peace*, pp. 91–96; S. Husbands, "Free Trade and Foreign Wars," in Taylor (ed.), *Free Trade: The Necessary Foundation for World Peace*, pp. 97–105.

78. Clarence B. Carson, "The Mercantile Impasse," in Clarence B. Carson, *The Rebirth of Liberty: The Founding of the American Republic, 1760-1800* (Greenville,

Ala.: American Textbook Committee, 1973/76), reprinted in Taylor (ed.), *Free Trade: The Necessary Foundation for World Peace*, pp. 41–51.

79. Adam Smith pointed out this fallacy in *The Wealth of Nations* in 1776, yet the fallacy persists. The modern version of this mercantilist fallacy is that Americans are spending too much on imports, causing dollars to flow overseas, or that the United States is becoming a debtor nation. There is no such thing as spending "too much" on imports or on anything else. As long as consumers are free to choose what to spend their money on, they are always spending precisely the right amount. Also, what difference does it make whether the United States is a debtor nation or a creditor nation, as long as the result came about by consenting adults freely choosing to enter into the transactions that led to the current status?

80. Carson, "The Mercantile Impasse"; C. Nettels, *The Roots of American Civilization* (Irvington-on-Hudson, N.Y.: Foundation for Economic Education, 1963), p. 281.

81. Carson, "The Mercantile Impasse."

2

The Trade Deficit Mentality

This paper analyzes trade deficits from a law and economics perspective. The author concludes that trade deficits are the result of faulty accounting and that economic policy should not be influenced by the presence or extent of a trade deficit, because the balance of trade figure is an irrelevant statistic.

Hardly a day goes by that the media do not mention some international trade problem such as the trade deficit. The general tenor of the story is usually that trade deficits are bad for the U.S. national economy, with the implied or express conclusion that something should be done to reduce them. The choice of terms used to describe trade — voluntary exchange — makes it sound like trading with foreigners results in disaster: we are being "invaded" with foreign goods; foreign goods are "flooding" the market; foreigners are "dumping" their products. Senator Donald Reigle has been quoted as saying, "The continuing Japanese attack on our basic industries is another Pearl Harbor. The time has come to close America's door to the flood of Japanese imported products."[1]

ARE TRADE DEFICITS BAD?

Nothing . . . can be more absurd than this whole doctrine of the balance of trade. . . . When two places trade with one another, this doctrine supposes that, if the balance be even, neither of them either loses or gains; but if it leans in any degree to one side, that one of them loses, and the other gains in proportion to its declension from the exact equilibrium. Both suppositions are false . . . that trade which, without force or constraint, is naturally carried on between any two places, is always advantageous . . . to both.[2]

The author decided to test this view — that trade deficits are bad — by constructing a series of examples using elementary accounting principles.

Case No. 1

Situation A: Assume that Joe Consumer needs an automobile and has $10,000 to spend. After shopping around for the best buy, he decides to purchase a Japanese model for $7,000. His second choice would have been to purchase a Chevrolet for $10,000. With the $3,000 he has left over, he decides to hire a local carpenter to make $3,000 worth of improvements on his home, something he has wanted to have done for several years.

Situation B: Assume the same facts as in Situation A, except that the federal government imposes a $5,000 tariff on the importation of Japanese motor vehicles, so Joe decides to buy the Chevrolet instead. Assume that the U.S. and Japanese manufacturers each have a 20% gross margin, as do the carpenter and the automobile dealers. Is the United States better off as a result of the tariff? Who benefits and who loses? The following is an analysis of the two options.

Situation A: Joe Consumer has an automobile (his first choice) and $3,000 worth of home improvements. The carpenter makes a sale, as does the Japanese auto manufacturer and the U.S. auto dealer who sells Joe the automobile.

U.S. Auto Dealer (who sells Japanese cars)
Sales	$7,000
Cost of goods sold (80% of $7,000)	5,600
Gross profit	$1,400

Japanese Auto Manufacturer
Sales	$5,600
Cost of goods sold (80% of $5,600)	4,480
Gross profit	$1,120

Carpenter
Sales	$3,000
Cost of goods sold (80% of $3,000)	2,400
Gross profit	$ 600

Situation B: Joe has an automobile (his second choice) and no home improvements. The carpenter does not make a sale. The U.S. motor vehicle manufacturer and the U.S. dealer make a sale.

U.S. Auto Dealer (who sells Chevrolets)

Sales	$10,000
Cost of goods sold (80% of $10,000)	8,000
Gross profit	$ 2,000

U.S. Auto Manufacturer

Sales	$8,000
Cost of goods sold (80% of $8,000)	6,400
Gross profit	$1,600

The next question to be answered: who is better off and who is worse off (and by how much) if Joe buys the Japanese automobile instead of the U.S. one? Is there a net loss to the U.S. economy if Joe buys Japanese?

Party to the transaction	Better off	Worse off
Joe Consumer	$3,000	
Chevrolet dealer — United States		$2,000
U.S. auto dealer — Japanese autos	1,400	
Auto manufacturer — in United States		1,600
Auto manufacturer — in Japan	1,120	
Carpenter	600	
Totals	$6,120	$3,600

Net gain ("betteroffness"): $6,120 – $3,600 = $2,520

These are only the "first round" effects. Extending this analysis to the economy's total structure of production would reveal further betteroffness throughout the U.S. economy. Some economists might argue that differing propensities might alter this result, but the propensity and multiplier effects theories have been refuted for more than a generation and need not be discussed here. [3]

Joe Consumer is better off because he pays only $7,000 for a motor vehicle rather than $10,000. Also, he gets his first rather than his second choice, a gain that is intangible and, thus, not measurable. He also gets $3,000 worth of home improvements. The carpenter benefits, too, as well as the Japanese manufacturer and dealer (who is a local American). The "losers" are the U.S. automobile manufacturer and the dealer who sells U.S. automobiles.

The ethnocentric, protectionist (patriotic?) view is that we should not be looking at the entire transaction, only at the U.S. side. Are Americans better off or worse off as a result of allowing Americans to buy the car of their choice? Below is the analysis from that perspective:

Party to the transaction	Better off	Worse off
Joe Consumer	$3,000	
Auto dealer — United States		$2,000
Auto dealer — Japanese (a local American)	1,400	
Auto manufacturer — United States		1,600
Carpenter	600	
Totals	$5,000	$3,600

Net gain (betteroffness): $5,000 − $3,600 = $1,400

Conclusion: Even if we exclude the Japanese manufacturer's gain, Americans are better off, in total, if consumers are allowed to buy the product of their choice, even if it happens to be made in Japan. If Joe Consumer decides to buy Japanese electronics products rather than hire the services of a U.S. carpenter, the result does not change. The U.S. carpenter loses $600, which reduces the net gain to $800 ($1,400 − $600), but Joe gains because he gets his first choice rather than some lower choice on the hierarchical scale of preferences and the U.S. electronics store owner benefits by the sale as well.

There is another, less obvious factor to consider as well. What happens to the dollars that flow into the accounts of the Japanese businesses that sell their products to Americans? A number of things can happen. The Japanese can use the dollars to purchase U.S. products (or services). They can lend the money to Americans. They can invest in U.S. business, which creates jobs for Americans. Whatever they do with the dollars, the dollars eventually flow back into the United States, benefitting some American somewhere. The amount and timing of the benefit are impossible to measure, but a benefit does exist. U.S. dollars cannot be used in Japan, so they must eventually find their way back to the United States. Yet this basic fact is ignored by the vast majority of commentators who profess concern over the U.S. trade deficit. It is not necessary to be able to measure the effects to know that there must be certain effects.[4]

If the United States is better off, in total, by allowing free trade, why do so many Americans want to restrict consumer choices?[5] As the above analysis shows, some groups gain and some lose as a result of free trade. The groups who lost in the first case were U.S. automobile manufacturers (and the United Auto Workers Union) and the dealer who sells U.S. cars.[6] However, their loss was more than offset by the gains made by Joe Consumer, the carpenter, and the U.S. dealer who sells Japanese cars. Free trade is not a zero-sum game. The gains exceed the losses. The problem is that the parties who lose by free trade also have powerful lobbies in Washington, whereas Joe Consumer does not. The Public Choice School of Economics has spent a generation analyzing this phenomenon.[7] The carpenter, who fails to make a sale if Joe buys a U.S. car, does not even know Joe and cannot possibly see that he is losing a sale. What is seen is a U.S. automaker losing business. What is not seen is the gain Joe makes by buying a Japanese car and the gain the carpenter stands to make if Joe is allowed to buy the car of his choice.

Walter Williams points out that advocating tariffs is really just a scam on the U.S. public.[8] Politicians can show how their trade policies benefit one political constituency, while the many other constituencies that are harmed by barriers erected to trade do not even know that they are being harmed. Williams suggests that a more honest approach would be for the affected unions and companies to come to Washington each year for a handout rather than try to hide their subsidy in the form of trade restrictions. At least that way, the amount of the subsidy could be measured directly rather than being hidden from the taxpayers (and consumers), who must ultimately pay the price of government intervention. Congressmen who favor subsidizing the steel industry, for example, could ask their colleagues to vote for Aid to Dependent Steel Companies. Of course, if they tried this approach, many of the subsidies that are hidden at present would disappear, because they could not survive the light of day. It is difficult to justify protecting the job of a steelworker who earns $23 an hour in wages and fringe benefits when the average consumer who must subsidize this job earns only $11 an hour.

Case No. 2

Situation A: A U.S. automobile manufacturer buys $8,000 of steel from a Japanese producer. Because the U.S. automobile manufacturer's factory needs repairs, it also spends $2,000 to make them.

Situation B: Because of import quotas, tariffs, or antidumping laws, the automobile manufacturer finds that it is cheaper to purchase its steel from a U.S. steelmaker for $10,000. Because it has to spend an extra $2,000 for steel, it is not able to make repairs to its plant facility.

Assume in both cases that each steel company has a 20% gross margin, as does the construction company that would make the repairs.

Japanese Steel Company

Sales	$8,000
Cost of goods sold (80% of $8,000)	6,400
Gross profit	$1,600

U.S. Steel Company

Sales	$10,000
Cost of goods sold (80% of $10,000)	8,000
Gross profit	$ 2,000

Construction Company

Sales	$2,000
Cost of goods sold (80% of $2,000)	1,600
Gross profit	$ 400

Who is better off and who is worse off (and by how much) if the U.S. automobile manufacturer buys the domestically produced steel instead of the Japanese? Is there a net loss to the U.S. economy if the automobile company buys Japanese steel?

Party to the transaction	*Better off*	*Worse off*
U.S. auto company	$2,000	
Japanese steel company	1,600	
U.S. steel company		$2,000
U.S. construction company	400	
Totals	$4,000	$2,000

Net gain (betteroffness): $4,000 − $2,000 = $2,000

Conclusion: On a worldwide basis, the companies that are parties (or potential parties) to the transaction are $2,000 better off, in total, when the U.S. auto company purchases Japanese steel. However, some individuals are concerned only with "what's good for America." As it turns out, "America" is also better off when a U.S. auto company is free to buy Japanese steel.

Party to the transaction	*Better off*	*Worse off*
U.S. auto company	$2,000	
U.S. steel company		$2,000
U.S. construction company	400	
Totals	$2,400	$2,000

Net gain (betteroffness) : $2,400 − $2,000 = $400

Again, there are other benefits that are less easy to see. The Japanese steel company has to do something with those dollars. It cannot keep them in Japan indefinitely. When they return to the United

States, some American benefits. The dollars may be used to buy U.S. products or to build factories that create jobs for Americans. Even if the dollars are merely invested in certificates of deposit in U.S. banks, more loanable funds become available to U.S. businesses or consumers, and some American benefits somewhere down the line. As Milton and Rose Friedman point out, the best thing that could happen would be for U.S. consumers to trade dollars for Japanese automobiles and have the transaction end there. The Japanese could burn or bury the dollars, and Americans would never have to give up any goods or services for those green pieces of paper because they would never return to the United States. However, trade does not work that way. The dollars eventually flow back to the United States.[9]

An additional point needs to be made. Although the above examples regarding Japanese and U.S. automobile and steel companies may be acceptable from an accounting standpoint, they are philosophically flawed. When a U.S. consumer decides to buy a Japanese rather than a U.S. vehicle, it cannot be said that the U.S. automobile manufacturer loses, because the U.S. producer has no legal or ethical right to the consumer's money. To say that a U.S. manufacturer loses every time a U.S. consumer decides to buy a Japanese product is comparable to asserting that I lose $40 million because Walt Disney Company decides to pay Michael D. Eisner to be its chairman rather than me.[10] I do not lose, I just do not gain. Similarly, U.S. companies do not lose if consumers choose to purchase foreign goods and services. Consumers have decided that they (U.S. companies) are not entitled to the sale.

Consumers gain if they are free to buy the goods and services of their choice at a price that is not raised artificially by coercive government trade policy. They lose something if they must settle for their second or third choice because government trade policy prevents them from making what would be their first choice in the absence of intervention.

AN ACCOUNTING ANALYSIS OF TRADE DEFICITS

Those who think that trade deficits are always bad and trade surpluses are always good need a lesson in basic accounting. Fortunately, Frédéric Bastiat provided such a lesson in the 1840s. Unfortunately, he provided it in French, and the 1964 English-language translation of his example has been all but ignored by economists (and journalists, who are partly responsible for spreading this economic fallacy).[11] Although his example related to France and the United States, I will use a similar example that pertains to the United States and Japan, because there is a good deal of Japan-bashing going on in today's press (and the halls of Congress).

Example 1: Let us say that a ship left Los Angeles for Tokyo, loaded with U.S. products, totalling $200,000. Upon arrival in Tokyo, a 10%

shipping charge and a 30% tariff were paid, bringing the total cost to $280,000. The cargo was sold at a $40,000 profit, a total price of $320,000. The proceeds were used to purchase Japanese electronic equipment. Another 10% had to be paid for transportation, insurance, and so forth; therefore, by the time the shipment arrived in Los Angeles, the total cost amounted to $352,000. This cargo was sold for $422,400, or a 20% profit, $70,400 above cost.

Two profits have been made — $40,000 and $70,400. Yet the books of the customhouse show that exports were $200,000 and imports were $352,000 — a $152,000 trade deficit![12]

Example 2: A few weeks later, the same U.S. exporter sent another ship to Japan with a cargo worth $200,000, but this ship sank shortly after leaving the harbor. The U.S. exporter has incurred a $200,000 loss. Yet the books of the customhouse show exports of $200,000 and imports of $0. Obviously, the United States has gained by this event to the extent of $200,000!

Such accounting is simple and straightforward — and wrong. The way trade deficits are measured, the obvious solution would be to load all our ships to the hilt, then sink them before they reach their destination. That way, we would have massive exports and no imports — a large trade surplus! The correct way to measure profits and losses is to focus on the difference between what has been sold and the cost of what has been sold. In the first example, the U.S. exporter made profits of $40,000 one way and $70,400 on the return trip. In the second example, he incurred a $200,000 loss. Yet those of the trade deficit mentality would have us believe that the United States lost on the first series of transactions and gained on the second.

A simplified, correct accounting presentation of the first example would be as follows, assuming the merchant started operations with nothing but $500,000 cash and $500,000 common stock:

	Cash	+	Inventory	=	Common Stock	+	Retained Earnings
Start	$500,000				$500,000		
Purchase U.S. products	−200,000		+200,000				
Totals	300,000		200,000		500,000		
Pay shipping & tariff	−80,000		+80,000				
Totals	220,000		280,000		500,000		
Sell U.S. goods	+320,000		−280,000				+40,000
Totals	540,000		0		500,000		40,000

	Cash +	Inventory =	Common Stock +	Retained Earnings
Purchase electronic equipment	−320,000	+320,000		
Totals	220,000	320,000	500,000	40,000
Pay shipping	−32,000	+32,000		
Totals	188,000	352,000	500,000	40,000
Sell electronic equipment	+422,400	−352,000		+70,400
Totals	$610,400	$ 0	$500,000	$110,400

Assets and retained earnings have both increased by $110,400. Obviously, the U.S. merchant has profited by the transactions, and if the U.S. merchant benefits, so does the United States.

PHILOSOPHICAL FLAWS AND INTERVENTIONISM

If trade deficits are so bad, the obvious solution would be to annex Japan and make it the fifty-first state. Our trade deficit with Japan would be eliminated immediately by this shuffling of papers. Yet if a trade deficit can be eliminated by a mere shuffling of papers, how bad can it be to begin with? New Jersey may have a trade deficit with Montana, but nobody complains. I have a trade deficit with my local grocery store because I buy more from it than it buys from me; yet saying that I am worse off by dealing with my local grocery store is absurd. So is the argument that trading with Japan makes us worse off.

Ironically, the trade deficit with Japan is at least partially caused by U.S. protectionist trade policies. Special interest groups such as the seamen's unions and domestic shipbuilders convinced Congress to pass legislation requiring Alaskan oil producers to use high-cost U.S. tankers to carry their cargo to uneconomic U.S. ports, cutting off Japanese consumers (who must import 99% of their oil) from our Alaskan oil fields. Had the Alaskan oil producers been allowed to trade directly with the Japanese using the ships of their choice, the amount of oil shipped to Japan would be more than enough to wipe out the entire merchandise trade deficit we have with Japan! However, because Alaskan oil producers had to use high-cost shipping and had to ship the oil to Western and Gulf ports, the Japanese found it less expensive to buy their oil from the Middle East and Africa rather than from Alaska, which would otherwise have been the lowest-cost producer.[13]

Domestic lumber producers are in a similar predicament. Japan would love to buy U.S. logs, but a law passed in 1968 makes it illegal to export logs cut on federal land (65% of all logs) unless they are first processed in a U.S. mill. Japan has 20,000 mills of its own, so it does not need its logs processed. Therefore, rather than buying U.S. logs, it buys from Canada and other countries.[14] Timber companies that own private plots of timber support the ban because they are not subject to it. Mills like the ban because they think the ban on unprocessed logs will increase their business. Environmentalists like the ban in the mistaken belief that limiting the cutting of logs will preserve natural resources.[15]

Those who are concerned with trade deficits take the narrow view that all trade is bilateral, when in fact it is multilateral. I buy more from the grocery store than it buys from me, but the grocery store buys more from wholesalers than the wholesalers buy from it. If I work for a wholesaler, I sell my labor to the wholesaler and buy nothing from it in return. The grocery store, the wholesaler, and I each run a trade deficit, yet we are all better off for it. Japan runs a trade surplus with the United States, yet it runs a trade deficit with western Europe.[16] The United States has a trade surplus with western Europe (or did until recently, anyway) and a deficit with Japan.[17] So what?

Those who are alarmed by a trade deficit are looking at only one side of the transaction. An elementary knowledge of double-entry bookkeeping would clear up the confusion immediately. Any merchandise trade deficit must be exactly offset by a surplus in capital flows or services. Otherwise, the transaction does not balance, which means the transaction is being recorded improperly.

Which brings us to another point. The accounting for trade accounts is faulty and violates generally accepted accounting principles. For example, in 1984, when U.S. merchandise exports were measured at $220 billion, the balance of payments statement was out of balance by an unexplained $30 billion.[18] The statement was made to balance by "plugging" it with a $30 billion account called "statistical discrepancy." This practice was not limited to the 1984 statement, however. It is common practice to force a balance. If a corporation used this technique for such a large imbalance, it would not be able to get its financial statements certified by any reputable accounting firm, and any firm that did certify the statements could be sued for malpractice. If the company were publicly traded, its stock would be taken off the stock exchange by the Securities and Exchange Commission. Yet government officials can get away with the practice because there are no generally accepted accounting principles for the federal government. The principles are whatever government officials say they are.

Jacques Rueff, the eminent French economist, went so far as to suggest that foreign trade statistics be abolished.

The duty of governments is to remain blind to trade statistics, never to worry about them, and never to take any steps with a view to altering them. . . . I would not hesitate to recommend the elimination of foreign trade statistics if the question were put to me, in view of all the harm that they have done in the past, that they are still doing and, I am very much afraid, will continue to do in the future.[19]

Other economists have also pointed out the problems inherent in foreign trade statistics.[20] The figures announced one day are subject to change the next, and in some cases, the figures first announced as a surplus can be revised to reveal a deficit later. For example, in 1951, 20 reports reveal 20 different balance of payment figures, ranging from a surplus of $5 billion to a deficit of $1 billion.[21] Not all changes are the result of new information. Some changes "represent changes of mind rather than changes of information."[22] Furthermore, the balance of payment figures reported by the International Monetary Fund are always different than those reported by the Department of Commerce because the groups classify certain items differently.[23]

Those who view trade as a zero-sum game also fall prey to another fallacy. All economic values are subjective. No trade can take place unless the parties to the trade value the objects in question differently. I would rather have a widget than $5 and the widget manufacturer would rather have my $5 than one of its widgets. A trade is possible under such circumstances if we each communicate our wishes and if no one prevents us from making the trade. We both gain because we give up something we value less for something we value more. If I choose to buy my widget from Widget Company A rather than Widget Company B, Company B does not lose, it just does not gain. If Company A is Japanese and Company B is American, the result does not change. I (an American) gain and so does the Japanese company. The U.S. company does not lose, it just does not gain. If I trade with a Japanese company, one American gains (me). If I trade with a U.S. company, two Americans gain. In either case, the United States benefits by the trade. If a law is passed that prevents me from trading with the Japanese company, the U.S. company gets a sale it would not otherwise get, but I lose something because I am not able to choose the widget I want; I must settle for a less desirable widget. If it costs more to buy a U.S. widget, my standard of living is reduced because I now have less money to spend on other goods and services. The sellers of the products I cannot now buy also lose, because they are unable to sell me their products or services. Even if the price of a U.S. widget is identical to that of the Japanese widget, I still lose if I am not able to purchase the widget of my choice because I must settle for a widget that is not my first choice.

The way gross national product (GNP) is measured contributes to this faulty logic — that trade surpluses are good and trade deficits are bad. GNP measures the value of goods and services produced in the economy for a given quarter or year. Increases in GNP (supposedly) indicate that the economy is growing, and declines indicate that the economy is doing poorly. Exports increase GNP, and imports decrease it. Thus, it can be concluded that exports are good and imports are bad, the same conclusion the mercantilists reached in the eighteenth century. Yet Americans benefit by both imports and exports, so this conclusion is faulty.[24] Furthermore, imports often exceed exports during periods of economic expansion.[25]

Another problem with the trade deficit mentality is that it totally ignores the effect of measuring bilateral trade between countries of different sizes.[26] For example, Japan has about half the population of the United States. Even if the Japanese buy the same amount of products from the United States per capita as the United States buys from Japan, there will be a trade deficit because the United States has twice the population of Japan. In order to have a zero trade deficit with Japan, Japan would have to buy twice as much from the United States per capita as the United States buys from Japan. Yet, both sides benefit by voluntary trade, so, even though there is a trade "deficit," there is no cause for concern.

Richard B. McKenzie suggests that a trade deficit can be a sign of health rather than sickness.[27] Jacques Rueff makes the same point: "notwithstanding the commonly accepted opinion, a trade deficit — which is the essential feature of the situation of all the countries that are both long-established and rich — is a sign of wealth, whereas an excess of exports over imports is nearly always the hallmark of real poverty."[28] McKenzie points out that the trade deficit is simply the excess of imports over exports. Real imports grew by more than 50% between 1981 and 1986 while real exports fell by more than 13%, thus increasing the trade deficit. However, part of the decline in exports is attributable to the fact that the U.S. economy was expanding during this period, and manufacturers sold their products to other Americans rather than to foreigners. Domestic demand grew more rapidly than foreign demand, which is a sign of a healthy economy. Thus, the healthy economy helped to produce the trade deficit.

CONCLUDING COMMENTS

Trade is not a zero-sum game where one party benefits and the other loses. Both parties benefit by trade. Otherwise, no trades would be made, because individuals do not enter into trade with the idea of making themselves worse off. Whether or not a country's exports exceed its imports is completely irrelevant as far as determining whether the economy benefits by trading with foreigners. Trade deficits "matter" only in the sense that those who are concerned with them might make incorrect policy decisions if they attempt to reduce imports, because such a move will also reduce exports.[29]

Those who worry about the U.S. trade deficit are looking at only one side of the coin. They see dollars leaving the country, but they do not see them returning to create jobs and economic growth. They see foreigners getting dollars in the mistaken belief that Americans should get those dollars, even though consumers have decided otherwise. What is more difficult to see is the harm that is caused when consumers are not free to choose the goods and services of their choice because of some governmentally constructed barrier, which either increases the cost they must pay to obtain their first choice or prevents them from getting their first choice. When government interferes with consumer choice, it benefits some special interest at the expense of the consumer. It commits an act that would be illegal if done by an individual. If an individual prevented a consumer from purchasing a foreign automobile unless the consumer paid a $2,500 bribe, that individual would be both acting unethically and breaking the law. Yet when the government slaps a tariff or quota on foreign automobiles, that act is viewed as being perfectly legitimate or even beneficial. The government is doing the job of the extortionist, in effect, because it is preventing consumers from making the purchases of their choice unless they are willing to pay something extra. Some special interest (in this case, the auto industry) benefits at the expense of consumers, who must pay more because the government (which is supposed to represent them and protect their property rights) has chosen to force them to subsidize the auto industry. Unless and until this form of interventionism is stopped and trade barriers are removed, government will continue to reduce our standard of living and force us to subsidize special interests.

NOTES

1.   Robert B. Ekelund, Jr., and Robert D. Tollison, *Economics*, second edition (Glenview, Ill.: Scott Foresman, 1988), p. 875. The quote was taken from "Uno's Surprise: Uncertainty about Auto Imports," *Time*, July 11, 1983, p. 19.

2.   Adam Smith, *An Inquiry into the Nature and Causes of the Wealth of Nations* (1776; reprinted, New York: Random House, 1937), book IV, chap. III, part 2.

3.   See Henry Hazlitt, *The Failure of the "New Economics": An Analysis of the Keynesian Fallacies* (Princeton, N.J.: D. Van Nostrand, 1959); Henry Hazlitt, *The Critics of Keynesian Economics* (Princeton, N.J.: D. Van Nostrand, 1960); W. H. Hutt, *Keynesianism — Retrospect and Prospect* (Chicago, Ill.: Henry Regnery, 1963); W. H. Hutt, *The Keynesian Episode: A Reassessment* (Indianapolis, Ind.: Liberty Press, 1979). For example, there is no way to measure or even predict propensities to consume or save for any particular group, so it is impossible to predict the unintended consequences of attempting to shift purchasing power away from or to one group over another. Furthermore, the theory of the multiplier looks at only part of the transaction while completely ignoring the other parts.

4.   Ludwig von Mises, *The Ultimate Foundation of Economic Science* (Kansas City: Sheed, Andrews and McMeel, 1978); Ludwig von Mises, *Epistemological Problems of Economics* (New York: New York University Press, 1981); Hans-Hermann Hoppe, *Praxeology and Economic Science* (Auburn, Ala.: The Ludwig von Mises Institute, 1988). Major portions of these works are devoted to the a priori approach to economic theory, which takes the position that it is possible to arrive at valid conclusions in the social sciences without examining empirical evidence by using logic.

5. About 300 protectionist pieces of legislation were introduced in Congress in 1985. See Wayne Gable, *Myths about International Trade* (Washington, D.C.: Citizens for a Sound Economy, n.d.), p. 1.

6. According to one estimate, auto import quotas add about 5% to the price of a car and the annual cost per job saved is about $160,000. See Robert W. Crandall, "Import Quotas and the Automobile Industry: The Costs of Protectionism," *The Brookings Review* 2 (1984): 8–16. Another author states that lack of a free market costs auto buyers an extra $2,000 per car, or $250,000 for each domestic job saved. See S. Wells, "The Myth of the Trade Deficit," in *The Free Market Reader*, ed. Llewellyn H. Rockwell, Jr. (Burlingame, Calif.: The Ludwig von Mises Institute, 1988), pp. 138–40. It would be cheaper just to give each job loser $20,000 or $40,000 and tell them to go find another job rather than subsidizing their present positions at such a high cost. However, even this solution, although better than a subsidy for inefficiency, would violate the property rights of anyone called upon to contribute the $20,000 or $40,000.

7. For an early treatise on this topic, see James M. Buchanan and Gordon Tullock , *The Calculus of Consent* (Ann Arbor: University of Michigan Press, 1962). For a more recent analysis, see James D. Gwartney and R. E. Wagner, *Public Choice and Constitutional Economics* (Greenwich, Conn.: JAI Press, 1988).

8. Walter Williams, *All It Takes Is Guts: A Minority View* (Washington, D.C.: Regnery Books, 1987), p. 66.

9. Milton Friedman and Rose Friedman, *Free To Choose* (New York: Harcourt Brace Jovanovich, 1979/80), p. 42.

10. "Is the Boss Getting Paid Too Much?" *Business Week*, May 1, 1989, pp. 46–93.

11. The example, in the original French, may be found in Frédéric Bastiat, *Oeuvres Complètes de Frédéric Bastiat* (Paris: Guillaumin et Cie, 1878), vol. I, pp. 52–57. The English translation is in Frédéric Bastiat, *Economic Sophisms* (Irvington-on-Hudson, N.Y.: Foundation for Economic Education, 1964), pp. 51–55. A similar example is given in Frédéric Bastiat, *Selected Essays on Political Economy* (Irvington-on-Hudson, N.Y.: Foundation for Economic Education, 1964), pp. 321–24. These examples were first given in 1845 and 1850, respectively.

12. The actual accounting is somewhat more distorted than this. Since the early 1980s, shipping costs have been included in the cost of imports but excluded from the cost of exports, giving a bias weighted toward imports. See Lawrence W. Reed, *Free Trade or Protectionism?* (cassette tape) (Englewood, Colo.: Independence Press, 1985).

13. Beth deHamel, James R. Ferry, William W. Hogan, and Joseph S. Nie, Jr., *The Export of Alaskan Crude Oil: An Analysis of the Economic and National Security Benefits* (Cambridge, Mass.: Putnam, Hayes and Bartlett, 1983); Steve H. Hanke, "U.S. - Japanese Trade: Myths and Realities," *Cato Journal* 3 (1983/84): 757; Hans F. Sennholz, "Protectionism and Unemployment," in *Free Trade: The Necessary Foundation for World Peace*, ed. Joan Kennedy Taylor (Irvington-on-Hudson, N.Y.: Foundation for Economic Education, 1986), pp. 63–72.

14. Hans F. Sennholz, "Protectionism and Unemployment," in *Free Trade: The Necessary Foundation for World Peace*, ed. Joan Kennedy Taylor (Irvington-on-Hudson, N.Y.: Foundation for Economic Education, 1986), pp. 63–72; Barney Dowdle and Steve H. Hanke, "Public Timber Policy and the Wood-Products Industry," in *Forest Lands, Public and Private*, eds. M. Bruce Johnson and Robert Deacon (Cambridge, Mass.: Ballinger Publishing, 1984); Steve H. Hanke, "U.S.-Japanese Trade: Myths and Realities," *Cato Journal* 3 (1983/84): 757; Erick Larson, "Logging Sales," *Wall Street Journal*, May 7, 1982.

15. Steve H. Hanke, "U.S.-Japanese Trade: Myths and Realities," *Cato Journal* 3 (1983/84): 757–68; Sherry H. Olson, *The Depletion Myth: A History of Railroad Use*

of Timber (Cambridge, Mass.: Harvard University Press, 1971).

16. Richard B. McKenzie, *Competing Visions: The Political Conflict over America's Economic Future* (Washington, D.C.: Cato Institute, 1985), p. 176.

17. Murray L. Weidenbaum, "The High Cost of Protectionism," *Cato Journal* 3 (1983/84): 777–79..

18. Lila J. Truett and Dale B. Truett, *Economics* (St. Louis, Mo.: Times Mirror/Mosby College Publishing, 1987), p. 692.

19. Jacques Rueff, "An All-Time Fallacy: The Trade Balance Argument," in *Balance of Payments: Proposals for Resolving the Critical World Economic Problem of Our Time* (New York: Macmillan, 1967), pp. 116–129. This chapter was extracted from a lecture given at the new Ecole de la Paix on February 27, 1933, entitled, "De quelques hérésies économiques qui ravagent le monde" (A Few Economic Heresies that Plague the World). The original text was published in the *Revue d'Economie Politique* (Librairie du Recueil Sirey), No. 2, 1933.

20. Fritz Machlup, "The Mysterious Numbers Game of Balance-of-Payments Statistics," in *International Payments, Debts, and Gold: Collected Essays* (New York: New York University Press, 1976), p. 140; Alan C. Shapiro, "Why the Trade Deficit Does Not Matter," *Journal of Applied Corporate Finance* (1989): 87.

21. Machlup, "The Mysterious Numbers Game of Balance-of-Payments Statistics," p. 145.

22. Ibid., p. 142.

23. Ibid., p. 143.

24. The mercantilist mentality leads to many interesting paradoxes. For example, at the start of the U.S. Civil War, the North attempted to blockade southern ports to prevent imports from coming into the country. At the same time, Congress was erecting high tariff barriers to protect northern industry from destructive foreign competition. If free trade destroys the domestic economy, would the North not have been better off calling off the blockade of southern ports and just let free trade destroy the southern economy? William L. Baker makes this point in "Native Pottery Only," in *Free Trade: The Necessary Foundation for World Peace*, ed. Joan Kennedy Taylor (Irvington-on-Hudson, N.Y.: Foundation for Economic Education, 1986), pp. 52–55.

25. Murray N. Rothbard suggests that GNP is a faulty statistic and that a better way to measure economic growth would be to deduct government spending from GNP and adjust for taxation, leaving us with a figure that represents actual growth rather than government bloat. See Murray N. Rothbard, *America's Great Depression* (Kansas City: Sheed and Ward, 1963), pp. 224–26, 296–304. For an exposition on Rothbard's proposal, see Robert Batemarco, "GNP, PPR, and the Standard of Living," *Review of Austrian Economics* 1 (1987): 181–86.

26. Wayne Gable, *Myths about International Trade* (Washington, D.C.: Citizens for a Sound Economy, n.d.), p. 11.

27. Richard B. McKenzie, *The American Job Machine* (New York: Universe Books, 1988), pp. 136–41.

28. Rueff, "An All-Time Fallacy: The Trade Balance Argument," p. 129.

29. Paul Heyne, "Do Trade Deficits Matter?" *Cato Journal* 3 (1983/84): 705.

3

Arguments for Free Trade

EFFICIENCY

The primary economic argument for free trade is one of efficiency. It is simply easier and cheaper to trade your textile products for bananas if you live in New Hampshire than to raise your own bananas. Ricardo's law of comparative advantage[1] and Adam Smith's division of labor examples[2] make it obvious that it is more economical to specialize in the things you do best and trade for everything else than to attempt to provide everything all by yourself. Not only would it be more expensive to try to provide everything all by yourself, it also would be impossible. Bananas do not grow in New Hampshire, so New Hampshire residents who want bananas must either trade for them or travel to a warmer climate. Yet protectionists would argue that a high tariff must be placed on bananas so that New Hampshire farmers, who can grow bananas only in hothouses, will be able to compete with Central American farmers, who can grow them much cheaper without hothouses.

No single individual even knows how to make a pencil, let alone more complex products, such as automobiles and airplanes.[3] The wood for a pencil might be grown in Northern California or Oregon. The saw that cut the tree down was made somewhere else from iron ore that was mined a thousand miles away, converted into steel in Gary, Indiana, Pittsburgh, Chicago, Japan, or Germany, and converted into a saw blade at some Black & Decker factory. The blade and other parts of the saw may have been assembled in Mexico and shipped to some warehouse in St. Louis on a railroad car that was made in Chicago or on a truck that was made in Detroit, out of parts that were imported from 10 or 20 foreign countries. Irish and Chinese immigrants helped lay the track that the railroad used, and designs for the train might have originated in Erie, Pennsylvania, Germany, or England. The loggers' food came from places as diverse as Hawaii (pineapples), Colombia (coffee), Texas (hamburgers), Washington (apples), Idaho and Maine (potatoes),

Kansas (wheat), Illinois (corn), and perhaps a few dozen other states and foreign countries. Once the lumber is cut, it is converted into small, pencil-length slats a few hundred miles away at a mill, processed, and converted into a finished product with lacquer that is imported from Delaware or the Far East, graphite that is mined in Ceylon, and an eraser that comes from chemicals originating in the Dutch East Indies and Italy.

Trade is essential to economic growth, and restricting trade inhibits growth, which results in a lower standard of living. Another, utilitarian argument for free trade is that the masses benefit by it.[4] It is only the special interest groups that stand to lose by free trade, and even the special interest groups may gain more than they lose, at least in the long run. For example, an automobile company may benefit in the short run by convincing Congress to limit foreign imports because it will be able to sell its automobiles for a higher price than would be possible in a free market. However, if the steel industry also convinces government that it needs protection, then auto companies will have to pay more for their steel, so they are harmed. If tire companies also get government protection from foreign competition, the automobile companies will have to pay more for tires. If Japanese or German companies are prevented from selling automobile parts to U.S. automobile manufacturers, the automobile manufacturers will have to buy domestic-made parts that probably cost more and may be of lower quality. Policies that restrict trade are essentially welfare programs for corporations that are paid for by consumers. It is a form of redistribution. It is a classic example of special interest groups using the force of government to obtain benefits at the expense of the majority. "'Protection' really means exploiting the consumer."[5]

Perhaps the strongest utilitarian argument against protectionism is the cost. Numerous studies have been made that determine the cost of specific protectionist policies in a number of industries. Trade protection cost consumers $80 billion in 1988.[6] Trade restrictions raise the cost of imported goods about 20% on average and boost prices of comparable U.S. goods by 10% to 14%.[7] Through 1985, Americans paid over $17 billion in higher prices for new cars, both foreign and domestic, because of quotas.[8] The annual cost of tariffs on vans and on two- and four-door sports/utility vehicles was $250 million.[9] The cost of Japan's voluntary quotas on their exports to the United States from 1981 to 1984 was $16.75 billion.[10] The additional cost of an imported Japanese car due to Japanese export quotas from 1984 to 1985 was $2,400 per car.[11] The additional cost of a U.S. car due to Japanese export quotas from 1984 to 1985 was between $750 and $1,000 per car.[12] The annual cost of Japanese voluntary export quotas on autos was $1.1 billion.[13] The annual cost of each protected auto job was $241,235.[14]

Protectionism is inefficient in other industries, too. In the steel industry, the annual cost of each protected job is $113,622.[15] The annual cost to steel-using manufacturers because of steel protection is $7 billion.[16]

Textile and apparel protection cost the poorest 20% of U.S. households an estimated 3.6% of their annual income in 1987.[17] Eliminating existing tariffs and quotas would cut domestically produced apparel prices by 18.9% and prices for imports by 34.6%.[18]

Although textile protection saved 46,000 jobs in the textile industry, it destroyed an estimated 52,440 jobs in retailing, transportation, and other areas that depend on imports.[19] The annual cost of apparel and textile protectionism, based on wholesale values, is $20.3 billion.[20] The annual cost to households of apparel and textile protectionism is $238.[21] The annual cost of each protected textile job is $52,204.[22] The annual cost of each protected apparel job is $46,052.[23] The annual cost of restraints on nonrubber footwear imports is $700 million.[24] The annual cost of each protected nonrubber footwear job is $55,000.[25] The annual cost of restraints on rubber footwear is $230 million.[26] The annual cost of each protected rubber footwear job is $30,000.[27]

The annual cost of tariffs on ceramic tiles is $116 million.[28] The annual cost of each protected ceramic tile job is $135,000.[29]

The annual cost of quotas on imported dairy products is $5.5 billion.[30] The annual cost of each protected dairy product job is $220,000.[31] The annual cost of sugar protection is $3 billion.[32] The annual cost of peanut protection is $170 million.[33] The annual cost of peanut protection per acre is $1,000.[34] The annual cost of meat protection is $1.8 billion.[35] The annual cost of each protected meat job is $160,000.[36]

The price system works as a signaling system. It alerts entrepreneurs that consumers want either more or less of a particular good or service. If U.S. automobile companies cannot sell their automobiles at the going market price, it is a signal from consumers that the companies are doing something wrong: either they are charging too much or their quality is not as high as that of their competitors. The price system lets companies know what consumers want to have produced. If this price system, this communication system, is not garbled by intervention such as a subsidy, tariff, or import quota, companies will get the information they need to make the most efficient use of their resources. If the message is garbled, companies will not get the message that consumers are trying to send. Also, with less competition, there is less incentive to reduce costs and improve quality. If it is easier to get protection from Congress than to cut costs and improve quality, there is less incentive to innovate and cut costs. Companies will take the easiest path, the path of least resistance. If old, rust-belt steel companies do not get the message that they should try another line of business, they will continue to make steel rather than something that consumers would prefer. In the absence of government protection, these steel companies would have gotten the message much earlier than they did, and they could have branched out into other, more productive lines of business rather than go into bankruptcy.

Krauss shows that a subsidy (although not advocated by the present author) is more efficient than a tariff because a subsidy distorts only production decisions, whereas a tariff distorts both production and consumption decisions.[37] The loss to the overall community is less with a subsidy than with a tariff, although there is an overall loss in both instances. Haberler ranks quotas as being more harmful than tariffs because tariffs, although harmful, do not interfere as seriously with the market economy and do not destroy the price mechanism of a market economy, whereas quotas do tend to have that effect.[38] However, there is no need to settle for second or third choice. Tariffs are less harmful than quotas, but both quotas and tariffs are more harmful than the free market, which allocates resources in the manner most consistent with consumer preferences. The logical choice would be to favor free markets over either tariffs or quotas.

Another reason for free trade is that it enhances international cooperation. Countries that trade with each other are less likely to go to war than are countries that erect trade barriers to prevent foreign goods from crossing their borders. If goods do not cross borders, armies will.[39] Trading with our neighbors is friendly and neighborly. Peaceful exchange between individuals enhances harmony. Erecting trade barriers, resorting to name calling and "Buy American" campaigns, and other forms of economic nationalism are unfriendly and promote ill-will and discord. Military conflicts often start as trade wars, then escalate.

"Buy American" campaigns also are costly to taxpayers. Several federal, state, and local laws mandate that preference be given to U.S.-made products even if they cost more than foreign goods.[40] Federal agencies must pay up to a 6% premium for domestically produced goods, and some defense purchases have premiums of up to 50%. New York state agencies must buy U.S. steel. New Jersey requires that all state automobiles be made in the United States. States have many other restrictions on the purchase of foreign-made products that cost taxpayers millions. Many other questionable practices are often resorted to in order to keep inexpensive foreign goods off the domestic market. For example, when Japanese ceramic tile was capturing an increasingly large share of the domestic market, the ceramic tile industry convinced many municipalities to change their building codes to exclude the Japanese tiles. However, they did not name Japan specifically. They changed the codes to require the tiles to be of a certain thickness, which just happened to be a different thickness than that of Japanese tile.[41]

Inhibiting the flow of imports into the country also makes it impossible to export. If foreign countries cannot receive U.S. dollars for their products, they will not be able to use U.S. dollars to purchase U.S. goods and services. Dollars that flow out of the country must eventually flow back into the country, because dollars will not buy anything in Japan, Germany, or France. Trade is multilateral, not bilateral. Stopping the flow in one direction also reduces the flow in other directions. A tax on imports is also a tax on exports. The relationship is symmetrical.[42]

Free trade results in a higher standard of living than does protectionism. If individuals can buy the goods and services of their choice at the market price, they are better off than if restrictive trade policies prevent the products and services they want to buy from crossing the border or if restrictive laws and regulations increase the price they must pay. Consumers cannot be made better off by limiting their choices or increasing the prices they must pay; yet, that is exactly what occurs when trade is not free.

DEMOCRATIC ASPECTS OF FREE TRADE

Ultimately, it is consumers who determine who works and who does not, what is produced and what is not.[43] Consumers vote with their dollars. If they vote for Japanese automobiles, their dollars will flow into the accounts of Japanese automobile manufacturers. Employment will shrink or expand based on these consumer voting patterns. Whereas 49% of the votes in a close political election are wasted, none of the consumers' votes are wasted, because each dollar vote has an effect on what is produced and by whom. However, unlike votes in a political election, not all consumers have an equal number of votes. Those individuals who have better served consumers in the past have been able to accumulate more dollars (consumer votes) than those who have served consumers less well in the past. By serving consumers, individuals are able to accumulate consumer votes (dollars), which they can then use to cast votes in the future to determine what is produced and by whom.

The Public Choice School approach to trade would focus on the disparities in the intensity of interest between different groups and how this disparity can result in a small but intense minority (special interest group) gaining dominance over a large majority (consumers). For example, a vast majority of consumers would rather buy a shirt for $20 than for $25, but very few of them would be willing to expend the time, effort, and money to go to Washington to lobby Congress so that the cost of shirts could be reduced. Yet the special interest groups that stand to benefit by stemming the flow of imported shirts into the country are willing to spend the time, effort, and cash to protect their interests and get what they want. They have a powerful and effective lobby in Washington that looks after their interests, with the result that shirts cost perhaps $5 more than they would in the absence of government protection. The majority will is thwarted by the minority because the minority is concentrated and powerful while the majority is dispersed and powerless. Public Choice economists would call this behavior "rent seeking" because the power-wielding minority uses the power of government to extract rent from the powerless majority (consumers).[44]

Consumers are penalized by higher prices whenever a special interest group has the ear of Congress, but a study by Destler and Odell shows that there is room for hope.[45] Although Congress tends to side with special interest groups at the expense of individual consumers, a number of special interest groups opposing protectionism have become more vocal in recent years and are making themselves heard. The Destler and Odell study is perhaps the first to systematically analyze the forces that oppose protectionism. They found that a vocal antiprotectionist interest group is sometimes able to reduce or even neutralize the power of a proprotectionist special interest by using the same tactics that the proprotectionist group uses — lobbying Congress. For example, steel companies and steel unions lobby Congress to place tariffs, quotas, or other trade restrictions on steel. Steel users, such as the automobile industry, lobby Congress not to impose restrictions on the importation of steel, because doing so will raise the price of steel and make their products less competitive in world markets. Textile mills, led by the American Textile Manufacturers Institute, lobbied for protection against foreign clothing imports, and retail stores, led by the Retail Industry Trade Action Coalition, lobbied against the mills because placing quotas or tariffs on clothes would hurt their business.[46] The automobile manufacturers and automobile unions lobbied in favor of import quotas and domestic content legislation for automobiles, and the American International Auto Dealers Association lobbied against the restrictions because the restrictions would hurt their business. The Jenkins Bill, which would have placed restrictions on the importation of textiles, was fought[47] by an antiprotectionist group that cited a study[48] that showed 58,000 apparel retailing jobs would be lost but only 36,000 apparel manufacturing jobs would be gained. So it appears that individual consumers are not totally at the mercy of the special interests as long as there is a competing special interest that stands to lose by the protectionist measure under consideration. It is ironic that individuals have to rely on any special interest for protection from Congress, inasmuch as Congress is supposed to be protecting the rights of individuals to use their property as they see fit and to enter into contracts to purchase the goods and services of their choice.

PROPERTY AND CONTRACT RIGHTS

Until now, the arguments in favor of free trade have been based for the most part on economic and utilitarian theory — the greatest good for the greatest number. Yet there are even stronger philosophical arguments that can be made based on natural rights theory. At its core, natural rights theory starts with the premise that an individual owns his own body and the fruits of his own labor.[49] From that premise is derived the axiom that individuals should be able to trade the fruits of their labor with anyone who is willing to trade, without outside interference. Anyone who places obstacles in their path violates their property rights. If consenting adults want to enter into a contract, no one else has a right to interfere, regardless of how stupid their choice of terms might be. If someone wants to buy a Japanese rather than a U.S. automobile, it is no one's business except the buyer and the present owner of the vehicle.

Placing a tariff on the automobile increases the price the buyer must pay, reducing his standard of living. If quotas prevent the automobile from even coming into the country, the consumer is forced to settle for a choice that is lower down his scale of subjective values, lowering his standard of living. By what right can anyone block transactions between a willing seller and a willing buyer? Furthermore, passing trade laws that allow General Motors to maintain a monopoly or oligopoly position at the expense of 260 million consumers is unethical. Representatives, who are supposed to represent the interests of everyone, have become the pawns of special interest groups — the automobile industry in Detroit, the farm lobby in the midwest, tobacco interests in the southeast, the lumber industry in the northwest, aircraft manufacturers in Long Island, and so forth.

There is only a certain amount of power to go around. Either individuals possess it or government bureaucrats possess it. To the extent that individuals can determine what they buy, they are free. To the extent that government has the power to dictate what goods flow into the country and what price is charged, individuals are not free. The moral basis for free trade is property rights. The right to own property includes the right to use, sell, trade, or give it away. Individuals own the fruits of their labor and have the right to exchange those fruits for the fruits of others' labor. Individuals who prevent consenting adults from voluntarily exchanging the fruits of their labor are acting immorally. The fact that trade restrictions are imposed to protect a few steel jobs or some other special interest group does not alter the immorality of the act. The fact that a majority may approve of the restriction does not alter the immorality of the act, either. Wrong does not become right if the majority approves. If majority approval were all that were needed to make something moral, then slavery and human sacrifice should be considered moral, because both were once approved by vast majorities.

CONCLUDING COMMENTS

Although the prospects for totally free trade seem remote, at least for the foreseeable future, there are a number of actions that can be taken by individuals and groups to increase the possibility of freer trade in the not too distant future.

1. Pressure the legislature to repeal all antidumping and countervailing duty laws as soon as possible. These laws are often used to bludgeon foreigners and are always against the best interests of consumers. The laws are applied arbitrarily and are used as a weapon by various special interest groups to protect their positions of power — positions they did not achieve by the dollar votes of consumers. Until these laws can be repealed, publicize the cost of these laws to the consumer in every way possible. Alert consumer groups, the media, and legislators as to how much each existing or proposed piece of legislation costs consumers.[50]

2. Make the legislature gun-shy about passing or advocating new antitrade legislation. Just as businesses often must conduct an environmental impact study before they can engage in many kinds of activity, the legislature must feel morally compelled to conduct a consumer impact study before it can consider trade (antitrade) legislation. Presently existing consumer groups can implement this idea immediately by badgering the protectionists in the legislature to conduct an independent study before introducing legislation, or the consumer groups can conduct their own study or publicize existing studies.[51]

3. Encourage the legislature or the chief executive to abolish any agency charged with enforcing antidumping or countervailing duty laws. Cut off their funding. Refuse to appoint replacements as employees quit, retire, or die. Even if the antidumping and countervailing duty laws cannot be abolished outright in the near future, the teeth can be removed from these laws by removing the ability to enforce them. Of course, such an approach might cause a temporary crisis between the legislature and the chief executive officer over the separation of powers, but the crisis would be resolved quickly and consumers would stand to benefit while the legislature and the chief executive are fighting it out.

4. Pressure the legislature to abolish all tariffs and quotas and voluntary import restrictions, because these policies are anticonsumer and exist only to protect vested interests. Until these restrictions can be repealed, their cost should be publicized.

5. Pressure the legislature to abolish all subsidies to all domestic industries. Stop supporting farm prices and steel, auto, and other manufacturers. Such support policies involve hidden costs, are anticonsumer, result in needless friction with our trading partners, and increase the possibility of retaliation.

6. Quit complaining that foreign governments subsidize exports. This practice is good for domestic consumers because it reduces the price they must pay for foreign products. If foreign taxpayers want to subsidize domestic consumer purchases, that is their business.[52]

7. Pass a constitutional amendment that prevents government at all levels from interfering in acts between consenting adults. Although repealing trade restrictions will allow individuals to buy the products of their choice,

laws that can be repealed can also be reenacted. Repealing restrictive trade legislation is only a temporary measure. A constitutional amendment would be more likely to permanently protect consumers, although there are no guarantees that some future Supreme Court would not make the amendment a dead letter, like it has already done with the contract clause.[53] Passage of such a constitutional amendment would have many other beneficial effects as well, but outlining even the major beneficial effects would take an article at the very least, or perhaps a book or two.

The ultimate cure for protectionism is education. The same protectionist arguments that mercantilists used in the eighteenth century are still alive and well in the halls of the legislature, in the media, and in the hearts and minds of many individuals. Unlike false theories in the natural sciences, which are quickly and permanently discarded when better theories are advanced, false theories in the social sciences can remain alive for hundreds (or thousands) of years, and each generation has to relearn the wisdom gained by previous generations. Free trade advocates must be ever vigilant and must refute protectionist arguments at every opportunity. Fortunately, one does not have to be a genius to do this. Having a working knowledge of the past 200 years of free trade literature should be sufficient, because the same arguments that have been advanced in favor of protectionism in the eighteenth century are still with us. All the protectionist arguments that are being advanced today were refuted 200 years ago, so there is no need to develop new arguments. Using the arguments of Smith, Cobden, Bright, Bastiat, and others will be sufficient. When a sufficiently large number of voting-age citizens have heard the arguments and had a chance to reflect upon them, it will be increasingly difficult for Congressional candidates to sell their protectionist programs, and the special interest groups that contribute to their campaigns will find they are not able to buy the number of votes they need to get their programs passed.

NOTES

1. David Ricardo, *Principles of Political Economy and Taxation* (1817).

2. Adam Smith, *The Wealth of Nations* (1776).

3. Leonard Read makes this point in "I Pencil," *Freeman* (December 1958), reprinted in Bettina Bien Greaves, ed., *Free Market Economics: A Basic Reader* (Irvington-on-Hudson, N.Y.: Foundation for Economic Education, 1975), pp. 40–42.

4. M. Krauss, *The New Protectionism: The Welfare State and International Trade* (New York: New York University Press, 1978), p. 6; Ludwig von Mises, *Human Action* (Chicago, Ill.: Henry Regnery, 1966), p. 750.

5. Milton and Rose Friedman, *Free To Choose* (New York: Harcourt Brace Jovanovich, 1979/80), p. 41.

6. P. Blustein, "Unfair Traders: Does the U.S. Have Room to Talk?" *Washington Post*, May 24, 1989, p. F1.

7. A. Murray, "As Free-Trade Bastion, U.S. Isn't Half as Pure as Many People Think," *Wall Street Journal*, November 1, 1985, p. 1.

8. Worldwide Information Resources, "New Competitive Realities Show Japanese Auto Quota Is Obsolete," (November 20, 1987), p. 4.

9. American International Auto Dealers' Association (AIADA), "Auto Import Group Calls Reclassification of Multi-Purpose Vehicles a 'Consumer Rip-Off,'" January 17, 1989; AIADA, "Import Dealers See Continuing Fight Over MPV Tariffs; Demand End of 25% Duty," February 16, 1989.

10. C. Collyns and S. Dunaway, "The Cost of Trade Restraints: The Case of Japanese Automobile Exports to the United States," *International Monetary Fund Staff Papers* (March 1987): 150–75.

11. Robert Crandall, "The Effects of U.S. Trade Protection for Autos and Steel," *Brookings Papers on Economic Activity* (July/August 1987): 271–88.

12. Ibid.

13. David Tarr and Morris E. Morkre, "Aggregate Costs to the United States of Tariffs and Quotas on Imports," Bureau of Economics Staff Report to the Federal Trade Commission (December 1984).

14. Ibid.

15. Ibid., p. 131.

16. R. Shapiro, "A Hidden Tax on All Our Houses," *U.S. News and World Report*, March 21, 1988, p. 52.

17. William R. Cline, "Reverse the Course on Textiles," *Washington Post*, August 7, 1987, p. A33.

18. William R. Cline, *The Future of World Trade in Textiles and Apparel* (Washington, D.C.: Institute for International Economics, 1987); E. Hudgins, *Robust U.S. Textile Industry Needs No More Protection* (Washington, D.C.: The Heritage Foundation, 1987).

19. L. Baughman, *Analysis of the Impact of the Textile and Apparel Trade Act of 1987* (International Business and Economics Research Corporation, 1987), p. 7.

20. William R. Cline, *The Future of World Trade in Textiles and Apparel* (Washington, D.C.: Institute for International Economics, 1987), p. 193.

21. Ibid.

22. Ibid., p. 191.

23. Ibid.

24. Gary Clyde Hufbauer, Diane T. Berliner, and Kimberly Ann Elliott, *Trade Protection in the United States: 31 Case Studies* (Washington, D.C.: Institute for International Economics, 1986), p. 15.

25. Ibid.

26. Ibid., p. 14.

27. Ibid.

28. Ibid., p. 96.

29. Ibid.

30. Shapiro, "A Hidden Tax on All Our Houses"; Hufbauer, Berliner, and Elliott, *Trade Protection in the United States*, p. 15.

31. Hufbauer, Berliner, and Elliott, *Trade Protection in the United States*, p. 15.

32. R. Ives and J. Hurley, *United States Sugar Policy: An Analysis* (Washington, D.C.: U.S. Department of Commerce, 1988), p. v.

33. A. Murray, "As Free-Trade Bastion, U.S. Isn't Half as Pure as Many People Think," *Wall Street Journal*, November 1, 1985, p. 1; Hufbauer, Berliner, and Elliott, *Trade Protection in the United States*, p. 15.

34. Hufbauer, Berliner, and Elliott, *Trade Protection in the United States*, p. 15.

35. Ibid.

36. Ibid.

37. Krauss, *The New Protectionism*, pp. 13, 32–34.

38. Ibid., pp. 13–14; Gottfried Haberler, *Quantitative Trade Controls, Their Causes and Nature* (Cambridge, Mass.: Harvard University Press, 1943), p. 20.

39. For an elaboration on this theme, see Frédéric Bastiat, *Economic Harmonies* (Irvington-on-Hudson, N.Y.: Foundation for Economic Education, 1964), pp. 478–86; Samuel H. Husbands, "Free Trade and Foreign Wars," in *Free Trade: The Necessary Foundation for World Peace*, ed. Joan Kennedy Taylor (Irvington-on-Hudson, N.Y.: Foundation for Economic Education, 1986), pp. 97–105.

40. Murray Weidenbaum, *Business, Government, and the Public* (Englewood Cliffs, N.J.: Prentice-Hall, 1981), pp. 253–55.

41. Murray Weidenbaum, "The High Cost of Protectionism," *Cato Journal* 3 (Winter 1983/84): 777–82.

42. Abba Lerner, "The Symmetry between Import and Export Taxes," *Economica* 3 (August 1936): 306; Victor Canto, "U.S. Trade Policy: History and Evidence," *Cato Journal* 3 (1983/84): 679–95. One recent study states that prudence requires the United States to cut its $154 billion 1987 trade deficit by at least $100 billion in the next few years. See William R. Cline, *American Trade Adjustment: The Global Impact* (Washington, D.C.: Institute for International Economics, 1989), p. 1. Such a goal will be extremely difficult to attain and is not desirable in any event. Because cutting imports also reduces exports, according to the Lerner thesis, we could cut imports by $100 billion and still have a $154 billion trade deficit because exports would also be cut by $100 billion. Besides, trade deficits are nothing to be concerned about. See Frédéric Bastiat, *Economic Sophisms* (Irvington-on-Hudson, N.Y.: Foundation for Economic Education, 1964), pp. 51–55; Paul Heyne, "Do Trade Deficits Matter?" *Cato Journal* 3 (1983/84): 705; Jacques Rueff, "An All-Time Fallacy: The Trade Balance Argument," in Jacques Rueff, *Balance of Payments: Proposals for Resolving the Critical World Economic Problem of Our Time* (New York: Macmillan, 1967), pp. 116–29, extracted from a lecture given at the new Ecole de la Paix on February 27, 1933, entitled "De quelques hérésies économiques qui ravagent le monde" (A Few Economic Heresies that Plague the World), published in the *Revue d'Economie Politique* (1933).

43. Mises, *Human Action*, p. 271.

44. B. Baysinger, R. Ekelund, and R. Tollison, "Mercantilism as a Rent Seeking Society," in *Towards a Theory of the Rent Seeking Society*, eds. James M. Buchanan, Robert Tollison, and Gordon Tullock (College Station, Tex.: Texas A&M University Press, 1980), pp. 235–68.

45. I. M. Destler and John S. Odell, *Anti-Protection: Changing Forces in United States Trade Politics* (Washington, D.C.: Institute for International Economics, 1987).

46. Ibid., p. 19.

47. Ibid., p. 56.

48. L. Baughman and T. Emrich, *Analysis of the Impact of the Textile and Apparel Trade Enforcement Act of 1985* (International Business and Economics Research Corporation, 1985).

49. John Locke, *Second Treatise on Government* (Buffalo, N.Y.: Prometheus Books, 1690/1986); Hans-Hermann Hoppe, *A Theory of Socialism and Capitalism: Economics, Politics, and Ethics* (Boston, Mass.: Kluwer Academic Publishers, 1989), chap. 2.

50. J. Michael Finger has some interesting ideas for informing the public about the cost of a particular restrictive trade practice. For example, an Argentine meat packer might run a TV ad in Japan showing an Argentine family enjoying roast beef, then show how much roast beef a Japanese family would have after the Japanese government got through imposing its restrictive trade practices. See J. Michael Finger, "Incorporating the Gains from Trade into Policy," *World Economy* 5 (December 1982):

367; J. Michael Finger, "The Political Economy of Trade Policy," *Cato Journal* 3 (Winter 1983/84): 743–49.

51.   I. M. Destler has suggested that a special Trade Barrier Assessment Agency be established to analyze the cost of specific protectionist measures. See I. Destler, *American Trade Politics: System Under Stress* (Washington, D.C.: Institute for International Economics, 1986), p. 220; Destler and Odell, *Anti-Protection*, p. 132. The problem with this approach is that it would increase the bureaucracy rather than reduce it. A better approach might be to abolish the U.S. International Trade Commission, which is charged with the task of determining how much special interest groups stand to gain by particular protectionist measures but does not compute how much other groups stand to lose. Such an approach makes its calculations biased in favor of the special interests and against consumers.

52.   Some libertarians would object to this view on ethical grounds, because their purchases are being subsidized with stolen property — taxes. From an ethical viewpoint, there may be a duty to try to reduce the amount of subsidization that goes on, or at least not to encourage it.

53.   For more on the death of the contract clause, see Henry Butler and Larry Ribstein, "State Anti-Takeover Statutes and the Contract Clause," *Cincinnati Law Review* 57 (1988): 611; Richard Epstein, "Toward a Revitalization of the Contract Clause," *Chicago Law Review* 51 (1984): 703; E. Mack, "In Defense of 'Unbridled' Freedom of Contract," *American Journal of Economics and Sociology* 40 (1981): 1; Robert W. McGee, "Mergers and Acquisitions: An Economic and Legal Analysis," *Creighton Law Review* 22 (1988/89): 665–93; M. Phillips, "The Life and Times of the Contract Clause," *American Business Law Journal* 20 (1982): 139; Bernard H. Siegan, *Economic Liberties and the Constitution* (Chicago, Ill.: University of Chicago Press, 1980).

II

THE COST OF PROTECTIONISM

4

Introduction to Protectionism

There is no doubt that protectionism costs, but it is less clear exactly how much it costs and who pays.[1] Also, although protectionism results in a deadweight loss — there are more losers than winners — some individuals and groups gain from protectionism, and it is those who stand to gain who have the ear of the legislature, at least for the most part.

Protectionism can take several forms. Protectionism in the form of quotas limits the number of units of the foreign product that can come into the country. Tariffs are another form of protectionism, which can be used to raise the price to consumers and, therefore, reduce the price competition on domestic producers that would otherwise result. One study estimates that trade restrictions raise the cost of imported goods by 20% on average and raise the price of comparable domestically produced goods by 10% to 14% because of the reduced price competition.[2] Curiously, slapping quotas on foreign producers gives them an incentive to upgrade the quality of the units they can send into the country and encourages them to build plants in the United States, thereby increasing competition with the very companies the government is trying to protect.[3]

A study of 203 International Trade Commission investigations in five industries between 1972 and 1982 concluded that protection is not an effective way to stimulate domestic output because the reactions of users tend to offset the actions of producers.[4] Other studies have reached similar conclusions.[5] This evidence makes it difficult to justify even the most plausible excuse for protectionism — the infant industry argument.

Baldwin and Green found that trade policy changes that enable industries to get import protection sooner and easier than before make it easier for foreign suppliers to avoid reducing exports to the protected market. Governments find it easier to quantitatively restrict imports from a few foreign suppliers rather than from all foreign suppliers.

However, restrictions lead to quality upgrades, a shifting of production to noncontrolled countries, and a rise in exports by suppliers that are not controlled, all of which tend to offset the purpose of the protection — to expand domestic output. When government defines an industry narrowly in order to show serious injury from imports, users and foreign suppliers shift to substitute items, which defeats the purpose of the protection.[6]

Another problem with protectionism is that temporary measures, designed to help an ailing industry strengthen itself to compete in international markets, tend to become permanent. Industries that are relieved of the pressures of competition sometimes choose to use their resources to convince the legislature to renew protection of their industry rather than investing in cost reduction, because the profits from protectionism might be higher and more sure than the profits from competition.[7]

Granting subsidies is also a form of protectionism, in the broad sense, because it reduces a domestic producer's risk and/or increases profits. Regulations also can reduce competition and protect domestic producers from foreign competition if the regulation has the effect of raising barriers to market entry. According to one estimate, regulation costs Americans between $400 and $500 billion annually — about $4,000–$5,000 per household — in addition to the costs that appear in the government budget.[8] However, not all regulations can be classified as protectionist, although many of them do have a protectionist effect. Sometimes two or more of these forms of protectionism may be used in conjunction with each other, which makes it difficult to calculate the exact cost and benefit of each policy. One study estimated that the annual cost of protection in industries with trade volumes exceeding $100 million in the mid-1980s was $65 billion.[9] William Niskanen also estimates that trade protection cost U.S. consumers about $65 billion in 1986, which represents almost a 100% increase since 1980.[10] Another study estimated that trade protectionism cost consumers $80 billion in 1988.[11] However, these studies understate the true cost of protectionism, because they exclude the effect that the filing of antidumping petitions have on prices. The mere filing of an antidumping petition, or the threat of filing, induces firms to raise their prices, which costs consumers. Also, there is tremendous incentive — and no downside risk — to file such a petition: it is a tool (weapon) that a company can use to force a competitor to raise its prices without any cost to the firm that files, because the federal government pays the cost of prosecution.[12]

Another factor that is often overlooked is the disparate impact that protectionism has on subgroups. Trade restrictions on automobiles, clothing, and sugar cost consumers $14 billion in 1984, which amounted to a 23% income tax surcharge for families that had less than $10,000 in income but amounted to only 3% for families with incomes over $60,000.[13] Protection in the textile industry alone has been estimated to cost poor families almost 9% of their disposable income.[14] Another study found that textile quotas cost the poorest fifth of the U.S. population 3.6% of their incomes, compared with 0.3% for the top fifth.[15] Protectionist trade policies also tend to harm developing countries more than developed countries. One study found the average tariff on manufactured products coming into the United States from developed countries to be 2.9%, whereas the rate for products coming from developing countries averaged 7.6%.[16]

"Costs" of protectionism include not only direct costs, such as higher prices, but also many indirect costs. Protectionism destroys more jobs than it creates, so there is the employment cost.[17] Quality may also decline if higher quality products become less available or totally unavailable as a result of protectionism. There are losses of individual rights, because consumers and producers — buyers and sellers — are less free to enter into contracts. There is a cost involved in administering the various protectionist schemes, which must be paid by taxpayers and consumers. Also, because protectionism raises prices, reduces quality, and incurs administrative costs, it reduces the general standard of living.

NOTES

1. One treatment of this question is by Tracey Horton and Hal Colebatch, *Who Pays for Protection* (Australian Institute for Public Policy, 1988).

2. Alan Murray, "As Free-Trade Bastion, U.S. Isn't Half as Pure as Many People Think," *Wall Street Journal*, November 1, 1985, p. 1.

3. Jose A. Gomez-Ibanez, Robert A. Leone, and Stephen A. O'Connell, "Restraining Auto Imports: Does Anyone Win?" *Journal of Policy Analysis and Management* 2 (1983): 196–219.

4. Robert E. Baldwin and Richard K. Green, "The Effects of Protection on Domestic Output," in *Trade Policy Issues and Empirical Analysis*, ed. Robert E. Baldwin (Chicago, Ill.: University of Chicago Press, 1988), pp. 205–26.

5. A Congressional Budget Office study concluded that "protection has not substantially improved the ability of domestic firms to compete with foreign producers." Congressional Budget Office, *Has Trade Protection Revitalized Domestic Industries?* (Washington, D.C.: U.S. Government Printing Office, 1986), p. 96, quoted in Daniel Oliver, *Protectionism's Adverse Economic Impact*, written testimony before the U.S. International Trade Commission, Investigation No. 332-325, October 14, 1992, p. 4.

6. Baldwin and Green, "The Effects of Protection on Domestic Output," pp. 223–24.

7. Aaron Tornell, "On the Ineffectiveness of Made-to-Measure Protectionist Programs," in *International Trade and Trade Policy*, eds. Elhanan Helpman and Assaf Razin (Cambridge, Mass.: MIT Press, 1991), p. 76.

8. Thomas D. Hopkins, *Cost of Regulation* (Rochester, N.Y.: Rochester Institute of Technology, 1991), p. 1.

9. Gary Clyde Hufbauer, Diane T. Berliner, and Kimberly Ann Elliott, *Trade Protection in the United States: 31 Case Studies* (Washington, D. C.: Institute for International Economics, 1986), pp. 14–15.

10. William A. Niskanen, "U.S. Trade Policy," *Regulation* 1 (1988): 34–42.

11.   Paul Blustein, "Unfair Traders: Does the U.S. Have Room to Talk?" *Washington Post*, May 24, 1989, p. F1.

12.   A large percentage of the antidumping petitions that are filed are later withdrawn or voluntarily terminated. Only about a third of the petitions filed result in having dumping duties levied. One study has shown that the cases that are withdrawn have at least as much effect on trade as do those cases that eventually result in duties. Thomas J. Prusa, "Why Are So Many Antidumping Petitions Withdrawn?" *Journal of International Economics* 33 (1992): 1–20.

13.   Susan Hickok, "The Consumer Cost of U.S. Trade Restraints," *Federal Reserve Bank of New York Quarterly Review* (Summer 1985): 1–12.

14.   James Bovard, "High Cost of Textile Protection," *Journal of Commerce*, December 10, 1991, p. A12; also cited in Oliver, *Protectionism's Adverse Economic Impact*, p. 7.

15.   Peter Passell, "The Victim Has a Blue Collar, But Free Trade Has an Alibi," *New York Times*, August 16, 1992, p. E4, cited by Oliver, *Protectionism's Adverse Economic Impact*, p. 7. For a detailed breakdown of how textile protectionism affects different income groups, see William R. Cline, *The Future of World Trade in Textiles and Apparel* (Washington, D.C.: Institute for International Economics, 1990), pp. 201–6.

16.   J. Michael Finger and Patrick A. Messerlin, *The Effects of Industrial Countries' Policies on Developing Countries* (Washington, D.C.: The World Bank, 1989), p.7, cited in Oliver, Protectionism's Adverse Economic Impact, p. 8.

17.   We will discuss this point below.

5

Monetary Costs

This chapter summarizes the cost of protectionism in various major industries.

AUTOS

According to a Brookings Institution study, voluntary export restrictions on autos cost consumers about $14 billion in 1984, and auto manufacturers gained $9 billion in profits, for a deadweight loss of $5 billion.[1] Because the quantity of foreign autos coming into the United States was crimped, unit prices rose — by nearly one-third, according to one estimate.[2] Also, because foreign auto prices were higher than would be the case in a free market, domestic auto manufacturers were able to raise their prices because of reduced price competition from imports.[3] Other sources report the mid-1980s figure at $17 billion,[4] which includes the increased cost of new foreign and domestic cars as a result of quotas.[5] More recent studies have estimated the U.S. deadweight loss attributable to quotas to be between $200 million and $1.2 billion.[6] Quota rents — the amount by which foreign sellers can raise prices because of the quota — have been estimated to be between $2.2 billion and $7.9 billion a year.[7]

The foreign deadweight loss of U.S. auto quotas has been estimated to be somewhere between 0 and $3 billion.[8] It is reasonable to expect that some foreign deadweight loss will occur, because the quantity they can sell will be reduced by quotas, even though they may be able to charge a higher unit price for the units they are able to sell. However, these deadweight losses may be on the conservative side, because they do not take other inefficiency factors into account. For example, when a company chooses what to export, it might tend to choose to produce the product it can make most efficiently, but when some quota causes a manufacturer to upgrade, as is the case with auto and steel products, to name a few, the company will have to shift its production from what it can do most efficiently to something else which, by definition, it must do less efficiently.[9] These efficiency losses are difficult to estimate, but they probably do exist.

Various other studies have also calculated the cost of protection in the U.S. auto industry from different perspectives. The annual cost of tariffs on vans and two- and four-door sports/utility vehicles has been estimated to be $250 million.[10] Japan's voluntary quotas on exports to the United States were estimated to cost consumers $16.75 billion annually a few years ago.[11] Another study estimated the annual cost of Japanese export quotas to be $1.1 billion.[12]

On a cost per auto basis, one study estimated that import quotas added $2,400 to the price of a Japanese car, on average.[13] A different study found the figure to be between $750 and $1,000.[14] One study determined that the annual cost of quotas was $241,235 per auto job saved.[15] Another study put the estimate at between $181,000 and $188,000, depending on the year.[16] A study of the effect that the VER program had just on Japanese cars for 1983 estimated the cost per job saved to be at least $1,444,267.[17] However, even if the annual cost of saving one job in the auto industry is only $100,000, it would still pay, in terms of overall welfare, to remove the blockages to free trade and pay each displaced auto worker $40,000 or $50,000 a year for awhile,[18] until he can find another job. One study of import restraints in the auto industry concludes that "The effects of quantitative import restrictions on the behavior of firms in a market as imperfectly competitive as the car market seem likely to be of sufficient magnitude to make such restrictions an expensive and inefficient form of policy intervention."[19]

STEEL

A study of the pre-1985 restraint agreement with the European Community estimated that the induced increase in the price of imported steel was 30%.[20] This study also estimated that the induced increase in the price of domestic steel resulting from this agreement was 12%.[21] Various studies[22] have estimated the cost of restraints to U.S. consumers to be $1.1 billion,[23] $2.0 billion,[24] or from $4.3 billion to $5.9 billion.[25]

Studies have estimated that the U.S. deadweight loss due to import protection is between $100 million and $300 million a year.[26] Quota rents from steel industry protection have been estimated to be somewhere between $700 million and $2 billion a year.[27] The annual foreign deadweight loss has been estimated to be $100 million.[28]

Another cost, although more difficult to trace, is the cost that protection in one industry has on other industries. For example, if the steel industry receives protection, steel-using industries have to pay more for their steel. A government study of the effect of voluntary restraint agreements on steel-consuming industries estimated that the agreements caused sales in these industries to decline by as much as $1.9 billion in 1985, $5 billion in 1986, $4.8 billion in 1987, and $0.6 billion in 1988.[29] Also, the foreign companies that are willing to sell steel for lower prices are forced to raise their prices as a condition of doing business in the United States. U.S. trade policies sometimes actually increase the profits of foreign companies because the reduced quantity they can sell is more than offset by the higher price they can charge. Korean steel companies would actually make less profit if the United States removed its trade restrictions, which puts the U.S. Congress in the curious position of helping foreign companies that are competing with domestic producers.[30]

Another phenomenon that occurs is that the market mix shifts when a tariff or quota places restraints on one product or another. For example, when quotas were placed on the importation of basic steel, foreign producers increased their shipments of specialty steel.[31] Also, users of specialty steel had to keep larger than usual inventories of specialty steel at the start of each quota period, because foreign suppliers surged to fill their country quota.[32] Thus, quotas increased their holding costs, because they were not able to manage their inventories at optimum levels. There can be interindustry shifts, as well. For example, if government restricts steel imports, causing the price of steel to rise, domestic consumers will have a tendency to buy foreign-made autos, machinery, and equipment that are made with lower-cost foreign steel, taking business away from domestic producers of these items.[33]

TEXTILES[34]

One study conducted a few years ago estimated the induced increase in the price of textiles to be 21%.[35] A more recent study estimated the price increase to be 28%.[36] For apparel, various studies have estimated the cost increase attributable to protectionism to be 39%,[37] 50%,[38] 46% to 76%,[39] and 53%.[40] The induced increase in the price of domestic goods has been estimated to be between 3%[41] and 17%[42] for textiles and 19%,[43] 31%,[44] or 46%[45] for apparel. Figures differ among the studies because of differing methodologies, assumptions, sample populations, and years, but the findings are consistent in their conclusions that protectionism results in higher prices.

Various studies have placed the cost of restraints to U.S. consumers at between $8.5 billion to $12.0 billion[46] and $18 billion[47] for apparel and between $2.8 billion[48] and $9 billion for textiles.[49] The annual welfare cost of restraints to the United States has been estimated to be $650 million for textiles[50] and $6 billion for apparel.[51] A more recent study estimated that the annual welfare gains to be reaped by removing quantitative restrictions on textiles and apparel would be $11.92 billion.[52] The same study estimated foreign capture rents to be more than $6 billion. A study of trade in 14 key textile and apparel categories involving 3 developed and 34 developing countries estimated the annual global gains to be had by eliminating quotas and tariffs on developed country textile and apparel imports to be about $23 billion, about $12.3 billion of which would accrue to the United States.[53] The distortionary effect of the Multi-Fiber Arrangement, which has been in place since 1974, is estimated to be between $4 billion and $6 billion a year.[54] Protectionism costs between $50,000[55] and $134,686[56] a year for each textile job saved and between $39,000[57] and $81,973[58] for each apparel job.

Textile protection also results in deadweight losses to foreign producers, because quotas prevent them from selling the quantity that would be possible to sell in a free market. One study estimates that developing countries suffer $8 billion in losses because of the quotas and tariffs that the industrialized countries place on textiles.[59] About half of this loss is attributable to trade policy in the United States.[60]

AGRICULTURAL PRODUCTS

The various farm commodity programs had an annual deadweight loss of about $6 billion in 1987, according to one estimate.[61] However, there were gainers and losers. Producers gained $16.6 billion, while consumers lost $4.8 billion and taxpayers lost $17.7 billion. About $4.1 billion of the $4.8 billion consumer loss represents income redistribution as the result of regulation. Another study estimated that the subsidies to farm programs and peripheral programs such as the food stamp program had an annual net deadweight loss of $31 billion as of the mid-1980s. These programs cost consumers and taxpayers $6.9 billion and $32.1 billion, respectively, and resulted in producer gains of $8.0 billion.[62]

Dairy

Milk marketing order programs in the United States redistribute about $500 million a year from consumers to producers. However, the deadweight loss is smaller than that because there are some producer gains that partially offset the cost. Exact estimates are difficult because of the cross effect of import quotas and price supports, which are estimated to produce $1.3 billion in annual producer gains while costing consumers and taxpayers $1.2 billion and $800 million a year, respectively.[63]

One study of the dairy industry estimated the annual U.S. deadweight loss caused by protectionism to be $1.4 billion.[64] Another study estimated that the quota rents in the dairy industry cost $250 million a year.[65] A study from the mid-1980s found that there is a small amount of foreign deadweight loss from U.S. dairy industry protectionism.[66]

Peanuts

One study concluded that peanut marketing quotas result in the transfer of $140 million a year from U.S. consumers to producers.[67] Another study put the cost of restraints to U.S. consumers at $200 million, which amounts to $1,000 per acre.[68] The price of both domestic and imported peanuts is 28% higher than would be the case without quotas.[69]

Sugar

This "infant industry" has been protected by the U.S. government since 1816, which, one would think, would be a sufficient amount of time for the industry to become competitive. Instead, protection has allowed the sugar industry to charge up to four times the world sugar price for domestically produced sugar.[70] Restrictions on the importation of sugar in 1987 cost U.S. consumers between $2.1 billion and $3 billion.[71] The benefit to domestic sugar producers was $1.7 billion.[72] However, because the sugar restrictions stimulated corn sweeteners, there was an additional annual cost to consumers of $1 billion, for a deadweight loss of $1.4 billion.[73] The price of sugar became so high that both Coke and Pepsi decided to switch to high fructose corn syrup, which caused U.S. sugar consumption to drop by more than 500,000 tons a year, an amount that is equal to the entire quotas of 25 of the 42 countries that are allowed to sell sugar in the United States.[74]

Another study estimated that protectionism causes the price of both domestic and imported sugar to increase by 30%.[75] The cost of constraints to U.S. consumers has also been estimated to be $660 million (1978),[76] $1 billion (1981 quotas),[77] $1.7 billion (1980 tariffs),[78] $2.4 billion (FY1983),[79] $1.88 billion (FY1983),[80] $735 million (1983),[81] $1 billion (1984),[82] $3 billion (1984),[83] and $3 billion plus (1988).[84] The quota rents that foreigners reap from sugar protectionism has been estimated to be between $410 million[85] and $1.3 billion.[86]

Trade barriers in the sugar industry cause other economic distortions as well. For example, some sugar farmers in the Caribbean and other third world countries switched to growing marijuana because U.S. trade barriers prevented them from selling sugar in the United States.[87] So, it might be valid to add a portion of the costs of policing U.S. borders to keep out marijuana to the more direct costs of subsidizing the domestic sugar industry in the United States. Also, domestic sugar refineries are hurt because they are not able to buy cheaper foreign raw sugar. Those refineries that can survive in this environment by being more efficient than their competitors are able to increase their market share by buying up the refineries that go bankrupt because of U.S. sugar policy, making the refinery end of the business more monopolistic and less competitive. Between 1980 and mid-1989, 10 of the 22 U.S. sugar cane refineries went out of business.[88]

Tobacco

One study estimated that tobacco marketing quotas result in $600 million in annual producer gains and $600 million in consumer losses — $400 million for U.S. consumers and $200 million for foreign consumers.[89]

The point of citing all these statistics is not to show that different economists arrive at different numbers[90]or that the numbers change from one year to the next but to illustrate that there is clear and convincing evidence to show that protectionism costs, and costs plenty, in monetary terms. However, protectionism involves more than just monetary costs.

NOTES

1.   Clifford Winston and Associates, *Blind Intersection? Policy and the Automobile Industry* (Washington, D.C.: Brookings Institution, 1987), pp. 65–66. This study is summarized in Thomas D. Hopkins, *Cost of Regulation* (Rochester, N.Y.: Rochester Institute of Technology, 1991), pp. B8–9.

2.   Elias Dinopoulos and Mordechai E. Kreinin, "Effects of the U.S.-Japan Auto VER on European Prices and on U.S. Welfare," *Review of Economics & Statistics* 70 (1988): 484–91. These authors also found that the U.S. welfare loss to Europe exceeded its loss to Japan.

3.   Dinopoulos and Kreinin found that the European auto manufacturers that sold cars in the United States raised their prices at the same time that the United States slapped import quotas on Japanese cars.

4.   "New Competitive Realities Show Japanese Auto Quota Is Obsolete," *Worldwide Information Resources*, November 20, 1987, p. 4.

5.   One factor that these studies often do not consider is the effect that upgrading has on consumer welfare. For example, when Japan got hit with quotas, it increased the size, horsepower, and luxury equipment of the autos it sent to the United States. These changes added $1,500 to the cost of the average Japanese car, but some studies ignored this factor when estimating the cost of quotas. Robert C. Feenstra, "Quality Change under Trade Restraints in Japanese Autos," *Quarterly Journal of Economics* 103 (February 1988): 131–46; Robert C. Feenstra, "How Costly Is Protectionism?" *Journal of Economic Perspectives* 6 (Summer 1992):159–78. It has been estimated that the upgrading from basic steel to specialty steel as a result of quotas caused as much of a consumer loss as did the conventional deadweight loss. Randi Boorstein and Robert C. Feenstra, "Quality Upgrading and Its Welfare Cost in U.S. Steel Imports, 1969–74," in *International Trade and Trade Policy*, eds. Elhanan Helpman and Assaf Razin (Cambridge, Mass.: MIT Press, 1991), pp. 167–86.

6.   Jaime de Melo and David Tarr, "Welfare Costs of U.S. Quotas in Textiles, Steel and Autos," *Review of Economics and Statistics* 72 (August 1990): 489–97; also reported in Feenstra, "How Costly Is Protectionism?" p. 163.

7.   de Melo and Tarr, "Welfare Costs of U.S. Quotas in Textiles, Steel and Autos"; C. Fred Bergsten, Kimberly Ann Elliott, Jeffrey J. Schott, and Wendy E.

Takacs, *Auction Quotas and United States Trade Policy* (Washington, D.C.: Institute for International Economics, 1987), p. 42.

8. Feenstra, "Quality Change under Trade Restraints in Japanese Autos."

9. Carlos A. Rodriguez makes this point in "The Quality of Imports and the Differential Welfare Effects of Tariffs, Quotas, and Quality Controls as Protective Devices," *Canadian Journal of Economics* 12 (August 1979): 439–49. Feenstra, "How Costly Is Protectionism?" p. 168, also mentions it.

10. AIADA, "Auto Import Groups Call Reclassification of Multi-Purpose Vehicles a 'Consumer Rip-Off,'" January 17, 1989; AIADA, "Import Dealers See Continuing Fight over MPV Tariffs: Demand End of 25% Duty," February 16, 1989.

11. Charles Collyns and Steven Dunaway, *The Cost of Trade Restraints: The Case of Japanese Automobile Exports to the United States*, International Monetary Fund Staff Papers, March 1987, pp. 150–75. This study covered the period 1981–84.

12. David Tarr and Morris Morkre, *Aggregate Costs to the United States of Tariffs and Quotas on Imports*, Bureau of Economics Staff Report to the Federal Trade Commission, December 1984. This study was also cited in Gary Clyde Hufbauer, Diane T. Berliner, and Kimberly Ann Elliott, *Trade Protection in the United States: 31 Case Studies* (Washington, D.C.: Institute for International Economics, 1986), pp. 256–58.

13. Robert Crandall, "The Effects of U.S. Trade Protection for Autos and Steel," *Brookings Papers on Economic Activity* 1 (July/August 1987): 271–88. This study covered the period 1984–85. Reducing the supply of Japanese autos that could enter the United States allowed them to raise their prices. It should be mentioned that the United States is not the only country that tries to protect its auto industry. South Korea is even more protectionist. A U.S. car with a base price of $16,000 costs South Korean consumers about $43,000 by the time its government gets done adding on tariffs and taxes. Pete du Pont, "Tigers by the Tail," *American Spectator* (September 1992): 41–42.

14. Crandall, *The Effects of U.S. Trade Protection for Autos and Steel*. Because the price of Japanese autos was artificially raised because of a crimp in the supply, domestic auto makers could raise their prices because of reduced price competition.

15. Tarr and Morkre, *Aggregate Costs to the United States of Tariffs and Quotas on Imports*; computed by dividing the total cost of protection by the estimated number of jobs saved by protection. Other studies have computed different costs per job saved, depending on the year in question and the specific piece of legislation being considered. Crandall estimated the 1983 cost to be $160,000 per job saved. Robert W. Crandall, "Import Quotas and the Automobile Industry: The Costs of Protectionism," *Brookings Review* 2 (Summer 1984): 8–16. Hufbauer, Berliner, and Elliott, *Trade Protection in the United States*, p. 258, estimated the 1984 cost to be $105,000.

16. Dinopoulos and Kreinin, "Effects of the U.S.-Japan Auto VER on European Prices and on U.S. Welfare," p. 490. They arrived at their figures by dividing the average labor productivity (output/labor) ratio into the VER-induced additional auto output.

17. Michael F. Bryan and Owen F. Humpage, "Voluntary Export Restraints: The Cost of Building Walls," *Economic Review*, Federal Reserve Bank of Cleveland (Summer 1984), pp. 17–37. This estimate is conservative, for several reasons. Although it estimated that the VER program transferred about $2 billion from consumers to producers and dealers and generated $166.4 million in efficiency losses, it did not consider secondary price effects, such as the price rise for substitute cars. Also, the number of jobs saved by the policy was estimated to be 1,500 at most. If the number of jobs saved had been only 1,000, then the cost per job saved would have been $2,166,400, without taking secondary effects into account.

18.   Average annual compensation in the auto industry for the years in question was about $35,000.

19.   Alasdair Smith and Anthony J. Venables, "Counting the Cost of Voluntary Export Restraints in the European Car Market," in *International Trade and Trade Policy*, eds. Elhanan Helpman and Assaf Razin (Cambridge, Mass.: MIT Press, 1991), p. 213.

20.   Hufbauer, Berliner, and Elliott, *Trade Protection in the United States*, pp. 178–79. This figure represents a 5% tariff and a 25% scarcity premium that resulted from the pre-1985 restraint agreement with the European Community and the informal understanding with Japan.

21.   Ibid. This estimate was based on the price rise associated with the crimp in supply that resulted from restraint agreements.

22.   Ibid., p. 179, summarizes these studies.

23.   Tarr and Morkre, *Aggregate Costs to the United States of Tariffs and Quotas on Imports*, p. 25. The figures are for 1983.

24.   Susan Hickok, "The Consumer Cost of U.S. Trade Restraints," *Quarterly Review* 10 (Summer 1985): 8. The figures are for 1984.

25.   Hufbauer, Berliner, and Elliott, *Trade Protection in the United States*, p. 179. The figures are for 1983 and are based on a U.S. Congressional Budget Office study that reflected the projected additional cost of the 15% quota under the proposed Fair Trade in Steel Act.

26.   de Melo and Tarr, "Welfare Costs of U.S. Quotas in Textiles, Steel and Autos"; Hufbauer, Berliner, and Elliott, *Trade Protection in the United States*. These studies were also cited by Feenstra, "How Costly Is Protectionism?" p. 163.

27.   de Melo and Tarr, "Welfare Costs of U.S. Quotas in Textiles, Steel and Autos"; Bergsten et al., *Auction Quotas and United States Trade Policy*, p. 42.

28.   Randi Boorstein, "The Effect of Trade Restrictions on the Quality and Composition of Imported Products: An Empirical Analysis of the Steel Industry," Ph.D. dissertation, Columbia University, 1987; cited by Feenstra, "How Costly Is Protectionism?" p. 163.

29.   *The Effects of the Steel Voluntary Restraint Agreements on U.S. Steel-Consuming Industries*, Report to the Subcommittee on Trade of the House Committee on Ways and Means on Investigation No. 332-270 under Section 332 of the Tariff Act of 1930, U.S. International Trade Commission Publication 2182, May 1989, p. viii. Another estimate of steel-user costs for 1988 is $800 million. Janet Novack, "Does Big Steel Really Need Protection?" *Forbes*, March 16, 1992, p. 37.

30.   David Tarr, "Effects of Restraining Steel Exports from the Republic of Korea to the United States and the European Economic Community," *World Bank Economic Review* 1 (1987): 379–418; J. Michael Finger, "Trade Policies in the United States," in *National Trade Policies*, ed. Dominick Salvatore (New York and Westport, Conn.: Greenwood Press, 1992), p. 79.

31.   Quality upgrading is a common phenomenon when a tariff or quota is placed on certain items. For a study on quality upgrading as applied to the steel industry, see Boorstein and Feenstra, "Quality Upgrading and Its Welfare Cost in U.S. Steel Imports, 1969–74."

32.   Robert E. Baldwin and Richard K. Green, "The Effects of Protection on Domestic Output," in *Trade Policy Issues and Empirical Analysis*, ed. Robert E. Baldwin (Chicago, Ill.: University of Chicago Press, 1988), p. 212.

33.   Crandall, "The Effects of U.S. Trade Protection for Autos and Steel."

34.   Some of these studies are summarized in Hufbauer, Berliner, and Elliott, *Trade Protection in the United States*, pp. 146–48.

35.   Ibid., p. 146.

36. William R. Cline, *The Future of World Trade in Textiles and Apparel* (Washington, D.C.: Institute for International Economics, 1990).

37. Hufbauer, Berliner, and Elliott, *Trade Protection in the United States*, p. 146.

38. Carl Hamilton, *An Assessment of Voluntary Restraints on Hong Kong Exports to Europe and the U.S.A.* (Stockholm: Institute for International Economic Studies, University of Stockholm, 1985), p. 8; Carl Hamilton, "An Assessment of Voluntary Restraints on Hong Kong Exports to Europe and the U.S.A." *Economica* 53 (1986): 339–50.

39. Hickok, "The Consumer Cost of U.S. Trade Restraints," p. 6.

40. Cline, *The Future of World Trade in Textiles and Apparel*, p. 15.

41. Ibid., p. 191.

42. Hufbauer, Berliner, and Elliott, *Trade Protection in the United States*, p. 146.

43. Cline, *The Future of World Trade in Textiles and Apparel*, p. 191.

44. Hufbauer, Berliner, and Elliott, *Trade Protection in the United States*, p. 146.

45. Carl Hamilton, *Voluntary Export Restraints on Asia: Tariff Equivalents, Rents and Trade Barrier Formation.* (Stockholm: Institute for International Economic Studies, University of Stockholm, 1984), p. 8.

46. Hickok, "The Consumer Cost of U.S. Trade Restraint," pp. 18–19.

47. Hufbauer, Berliner, and Elliott, *Trade Protection in the United States*, p. 148. Cline, *The Future of World Trade in Textiles and Apparel*, p. 191, also estimated the cost to be about $18 billion at wholesale, which could understate the true (retail) cost by as much as 100%.

48. Cline, *The Future of World Trade in Textiles and Apparel*, p. 191 (at wholesale).

49. Hufbauer, Berliner, and Elliott, *Trade Protection in the United States*, p. 148.

50. Ibid., p. 149.

51. Ibid.

52. de Melo and Tarr, "Welfare Costs of U.S. Quotas in Textiles, Steel and Autos," p. 493.

53. Irene Trela and John Whalley, "Global Effects of Developed Country Trade Restrictions on Textiles and Apparel," *Economic Journal* 100 (1990): 1190–205. This paper is a revised and shortened version of *Do Developing Countries Lose from the MFA?* National Bureau of Economic Research Working Paper No. 2618, June 1988. This paper is discussed in Feenstra, "How Costly Is Protectionism?" p. 167.

54. Feenstra, "How Costly Is Protectionism?" p. 164.

55. Hufbauer, Berliner, and Elliott, *Trade Protection in the United States*, p. 149.

56. Cline, *The Future of World Trade in Textiles and Apparel*, p. 191.

57. Hufbauer, Berliner, and Elliott, *Trade Protection in the United States*, p. 149.

58. Cline, *The Future of World Trade in Textiles and Apparel*, p. 191.

59. Trela and Whalley, "Global Effects of Developed Country Trade Restrictions on Textiles and Apparel."

60. Ibid.

61. Bruce L. Gardner, "The United States," in *Agricultural Protectionism in the Industrialized World*, ed. Fred H. Sanderson (Washington, D.C.: Resources for the Future, 1990), p. 52.

62. Clifton B. Luttrell, *The High Cost of Farm Welfare* (Washington, D.C.: Cato Institute, 1989), pp. 121–22.

74   TRADE POLICY FOR FREE SOCIETIES

63.   Gardner, "The United States," pp. 49–50.
64.   Hufbauer, Berliner, and Elliott, *Trade Protection in the United States.* Feenstra, "How Costly Is Protectionism?" p. 163, also cites this figure. Ibid., p. 164, mentions that most of this deadweight loss is due to restrictions on cheese imports.
65.   Bergsten et al., *Auction Quotas and United States Trade Policy,* p. 42.
66.   James E. Anderson, "The Relative Inefficiency of Quotas," *American Economic Review* 75 (March 1985): 178–90. He estimated the loss to be $20 million.
67.   Gardner, "The United States," pp. 49–50.
68.   Hufbauer, Berliner, and Elliott, *Trade Protection in the United States,* p. 319.
69.   Ibid., p. 318.
70.   James Bovard, *The Fair Trade Fraud* (New York: St. Martin's Press, 1991), p. 71. The farm program Congress passed in 1985 guaranteed U.S. sugar beet and sugar cane farmers about 21.5 cents a pound for their product when the world market price was about 4 cents a pound. Janet Novack, "Three Yards and a Cloud of (Sugar) Dust," *Forbes,* September 4, 1989, p. 39.
71.   Bruce L. Gardner estimated the cost to be $2.1 billion. A Commerce Department study estimated the cost to be $3 billion. U.S. Department of Commerce, *United States Sugar Policy — An Analysis* (Washington, D.C.: Government Printing Office, 1988), p. v. This latter study was cited by Bovard, *The Fair Trade Fraud,* p. 72.
72.   Since 1980, the U.S. sugar program has cost taxpayers and consumers more than $2 million for each domestic sugar producer. Bovard, *The Fair Trade Fraud,* p. 71.
73.   Gardner, "The United States," p. 47.
74.   Bovard, *The Fair Trade Fraud,* pp. 72–73.
75.   Hufbauer, Berliner, and Elliott, *Trade Protection in the United States,* p. 294.
76.   Robert W. Crandall, "Federal Government Initiatives to Reduce the Price Level," *Brookings Papers on Economic Activity* (1978): 2.
77.   Consumers for World Trade, *How Much Do Consumers Pay for U.S. Trade Barriers?* (Washington, D.C.: Consumers for World Trade, 1984).
78.   Michael C. Munger, *The Costs of Protectionism: Estimates of the Hidden Tax of Trade Restraint* (Washington University, Center for the Study of American Business, 1983), pp. 10, 14.
79.   U.S. Department of Agriculture, *Sugar: Background for 1985 Legislation* (Washington, D.C.: U.S. Department of Agriculture, 1984), p. 38.
80.   Rachel Dardis and Carol Young, "The Welfare Loss from the New Sugar Program," *Journal of Consumer Affairs* 19 (1985): 127.
81.   Tarr and Morkre, *Aggregate Costs to the United States of Tariffs and Quotas on Imports,* p. 76. Hufbauer, Berliner, and Elliott, *Trade Protection in the United States,* p. 297, point out that this is a conservative estimate because it is based on a long-run analysis in which the world sugar price is assumed to be 15 cents per pound, when, in fact, the 1983 world price was 9.4 cents per pound.
82.   Hickok, "The Consumer Cost of U.S. Trade Restraints," p. 7.
83.   Estimated cost of import quotas and price supports to consumers, cited by Paul Mirsky, *Journal of Commerce* 21 (May 1985): 15A.
84.   U.S. Department of Commerce, *United States Sugar Policy — An Analysis* (Washington, D.C.: Government Printing Office, 1988), p. v, cited in Bovard , *The Fair Trade Fraud,* p. 72.
85.   Bergsten et al., *Auction Quotas and United States Trade Policy,* p. 42.
86.   Gwo-Jiun M. Leu, Andrew Schmitz, and Ronald D. Knutson, "Gains and Losses of Sugar Program Policy Options," *American Journal of Agricultural*

Economics 69 (August 1987): 591–602. These authors also estimated the annual foreign deadweight loss to be $200 million.

87.   Paul Magnusson, "U.S. Shoots Itself in Foot in Tariff Skirmish," *Detroit Free Press*, May 24, 1987, p. F7, cited in Daniel Oliver, *Protectionism's Adverse Economic Impact*, written testimony before the U.S. International Trade Commission, Investigation No. 332-325, October 14, 1992, p. 8; Bovard, *The Fair Trade Fraud*, p. 74, also mentions this point.

88.   Novack, "Three Yards and a Cloud of (Sugar) Dust," pp. 39–40.

89.   Gardner, "The United States," p. 50.

90.   The authors of these studies used a number of different techniques, methodologies, assumptions, data, and demand and supply elasticities to arrive at their conclusions.

6

Nonmonetary Costs

EMPLOYMENT COSTS

Protectionist policies can save jobs. In fact, one of the main reasons advocates of protectionism support protection is because jobs will be lost in the absence of protection. That is what is seen. What is *not* seen is the jobs that will be destroyed or the jobs that will never be created as the result of some protectionist policy. If auto imports are restricted, the people who depend on auto imports for their livelihood, such as importers, foreign car dealers and their employees, and so forth, may be thrown into the unemployment lines. However, the effects on these groups are often ignored when computing the number of jobs to be saved by a particular protectionist policy.

One of the problems with protectionism is that protectionists look at only one side of the coin — the jobs that will be saved by adopting a particular protectionist policy. It is more difficult to see the jobs that will be destroyed or the jobs that will never be created by adopting the policy. Adopting the correct policy is also complicated by the fact that the special interest groups — for example, the auto companies and auto unions — have much to gain or lose and so are willing to expend more time, energy, and resources to get their policies adopted than will the average consumer, who may not even be aware that a particular policy might cost a few hundred or a few thousand dollars. The special interest groups are organized, whereas consumers are not. Thus, the special interests have a built-in advantage. The special interests can organize to get government to pass protectionist policies that will benefit them at the expense of the general public. Public Choice economists call this behavior rent-seeking, which they define as seeking special privileges from government or getting others to pay for your benefits.[1]

It makes sense to expect that if consumers have to spend an extra $2,000 for an automobile, they will have $2,000 less to spend for other things. If they have to pay more for autos, the industries that would otherwise receive their $2,000 will receive less. If Jane has to spend $14,000 for a car instead of $12,000, she will not be able to spend $2,000 on a vacation, and the airline, hotel, and restaurants that would otherwise get a portion of the $2,000 will be poorer as a result of the policy protecting the automobile industry from foreign competition. Jane will be $2,000 poorer, too, because instead of having a car and a vacation, she has just a car.

It is impossible to predict which nonauto industries will be injured by the protectionist policy, and it is unlikely that the average workers in the airline, hotel, or restaurant business will even be aware that they are being hurt by the auto interests. However, it is reasonable to expect that they are being hurt, because the loss to these and other industries is substantial when one multiplies the $2,000 welfare loss by the number of autos that are sold. Billions of dollars that would otherwise be available to these other industries become unavailable. As a result, these other industries will not expand as rapidly — and, thus, will not create as many jobs — and may even have to fire some employees because of reduced demand for their products and services.

Do the employment gains exceed the employment losses? Will a protectionist policy save more jobs than it destroys? In the absence of intervention, it is reasonable to expect that resources will gravitate to their most productive uses. The price system is known for doing exactly that. An intervention in the market process, such as the adoption of a protectionist policy, distorts this flow into less productive areas, so it is reasonable to expect that there will be some deadweight loss. The studies that have been done confirm this expectation. For example, one study[2] found that a particular protectionist policy would save 36,000 apparel manufacturing jobs but cause 58,000 apparel retailing jobs to be lost, for a loss/gain ratio of more than 1.6 to 1, and that figure is conservative, because it does not measure the job losses that would occur in other industries as a result of the protectionist policy. Other studies found that imposing "voluntary" export restraints in the steel industry actually destroyed more jobs than it saved. One study found that 16,900 jobs in the steel industry were saved as a result of the 1984 voluntary restraints on steel imports, but 52,400 jobs were destroyed in the industries that use steel, for a loss/gain ratio of 3.1 to 1.[3] Another study[4] estimated that 27,072 jobs would be saved and 40,927 jobs would be lost, for a ratio of slightly more than 1.5 to 1. Another study[5] estimated that a 15% import quota in the steel industry would save 26,000 jobs in the steel industry but destroy 93,000 jobs in steel-importing industries, for a loss/gain ratio of 3.6 to 1. A study that estimated the effects that voluntary restraint agreements have had on 75 steel-using industries concluded that the agreements destroyed 170,825 more jobs than were saved,[6] and the job gains occurred in industries that had lower value added per worker. The industries that gained jobs had an average added value of $32,400 per worker; the industries that lost jobs averaged $61,825 in added value, nearly twice as much.[7] Therefore, protectionism in the steel industry is destroying relatively high quality jobs and replacing them with relatively low quality jobs, which is just the opposite of what the protectionists would have us believe. Rather than blaming free trade for turning Americans into a country of broom pushers and hamburger flippers,[8] it is protectionist policies that are causing high paying jobs to be replaced with low paying jobs.

The Cline study[9] estimated that the various protectionist policies[10] in the United States preserve 214,200 direct jobs in the apparel industry and 20,700 jobs in the textile industry, at an annual cost of $17.6 billion for apparel and $2.8 billion for textiles.[11] That means that it costs about $82,000 to save one job in the apparel industry for one year and $135,000 to save a textile job. That amounts to $238 per household per year, or 0.72% of household disposable income.[12]

The statistics in the sugar industry are especially shocking. Since 1980, sugar quotas have destroyed more jobs than the total number of sugar farmers in the United States.[13] According to a Commerce Department estimate, high sugar prices have destroyed nearly 9,000 jobs in the food manufacturing industry since 1981. One company, Brach Candy Company, announced plans to close its candy factory in Chicago and move 3,000 jobs to Canada because of the high cost of U.S. sugar. Also, ten sugar refineries had to close in recent years — destroying 7,000 refinery jobs — because of cutbacks in sugar imports. However, the United States has just 11,000 sugar farmers,[14] who received an average of more than $2 million each in price supports and subsidies since 1980.[15]

In the next few paragraphs, I will attempt to estimate the cost of protectionist trade policies in terms of the net number of jobs lost. These estimates are based on an expansion and extrapolation of the studies reported by Hufbauer, Berliner, and Elliott, who looked at 31 cases of protectionism in industries having at least $100 million in annual trade volume.[16] In cases where they conducted more than one study of the same industry, I will use the statistics from their most recent study.

Employment losses are conservative for several reasons. For one, only industries with volume of at least $100 million are included; smaller industries are excluded. Also, in cases where the cost per job saved was expressed by Hufbauer, Berliner, and Elliott in terms such as "over one million," as was the case for benzenoid chemicals, my computations were based on the figure at the low end of the spectrum ($1 million). Finally, in computing the number of jobs lost in each category, I used the more conservative 1.6 to 1 ratio from the Baughman and Emrich study rather than the much larger 3.1 to 1 ratio cited in the Denzau paper.

Table 6.1 estimates the jobs saved by protectionism. Statistics for the total cost to consumers and cost per job saved were taken from Hufbauer, Berliner, and Elliott. Jobs saved was computed by dividing cost to consumers by cost per job saved.

Table 6.2 estimates the jobs lost by protectionism and the deadweight loss. The "jobs saved" and "cost per job saved" columns are taken from Table 6.1. The column showing the ratio of jobs lost to jobs saved was taken from the Baughman and Emrich study. "Jobs lost" is computed by multiplying "jobs saved" by the ratio of jobs lost to jobs saved. "Deadweight loss" is computed by subtracting jobs saved from jobs lost.

One point comes to mind immediately when looking at Table 6.1. When looking at the "Cost per Job Saved" column, it becomes obvious immediately that the cost of saving jobs in some industries is

Table 6.1
Jobs Saved by Protectionism

Industry	Cost to Consumers (millions of dollars)	Cost per Job Saved (dollars)	Jobs Saved
Benzenoid Chemicals	2,650	1,000,000+	2,650
Glassware	200	200,000	1,000
Rubber Footwear	230	30,000	7,667
Ceramic Articles	95	47,500	2,000
Ceramic Tiles	116	135,000	859
Orange Juice	525	240,000	2,187
Canned Tuna	91	76,000	1,197
Textiles and Apparel	27,000	42,000	642,857
Carbon Steel	6,800	750,000	9,067
Ball Bearings	45	90,000	500
Specialty Steel	520	1,000,000	520
Nonrubber Footwear	700	55,000	12,727
Color Televisions	420	420,000	1,000
CB Radios	55	93,000	591
Bolts, Nuts, Large Screws	110	550,000	200
Prepared Mushrooms	35	117,000	299
Automobiles	5,800	105,000	55,238
Motorcycles	104	150,000	693
Maritime Industries	3,000	270,000	11,111
Sugar	930	60,000	15,500
Dairy Products	5,500	220,000	25,000
Meat	1,800	160,000	11,250
Fish	560	21,000	26,667
Petroleum	6,900	160,000	43,125
Lead and Zinc	67	30,000	2,233

*Computed by dividing cost to consumers by cost per job saved.

Source: Data from Gary Clyde Hufbauer, Diane T. Berliner, and Kimberly Ann Elliott, *Trade Protection in the United States: 31 Case Studies* (Washington, D.C.: Institute for International Economics, 1986); compiled by the author.

Table 6.2
Jobs Lost by Protectionism

Industry	Jobs Saved[a]	Cost per Job Saved[a]	Ratio of Jobs Lost to Jobs Saved[b]	Jobs Lost[c]	Deadweight Loss[d]
Book Manufacturing	5,000	$100,000	1.6 to 1	8,000	3,000
Benzenoid Chemicals	2,650	1,000,000+		4,240	1,590
Glassware	1,000	200,000		1,600	600
Rubber Footwear	7,667	30,000		12,267	4,600
Ceramic Articles	2,000	47,500		3,200	1,200
Ceramic Tiles	859	135,000		1,374	515
Orange Juice	2,187	240,000		3,499	1,312
Canned Tuna	1,197	76,000		1,915	718
Textiles and Apparel	642,857	42,000		1,028,571	385,714
Carbon Steel	9,067	750,000		14,507	5,440
Ball Bearings	500	90,000		800	300
Specialty Steel	520	1,000,000		832	312
Nonrubber Footwear	12,727	55,000		20,363	7,636
Color Televisions	1,000	420,000		1,600	600
CB Radios	591	93,000		946	355
Bolts, Nuts, Large Screws	200	550,000		320	120
Prepared Mushrooms	299	117,000		478	179
Automobiles	55,238	105,000		88,381	33,143
Motorcycles	693	150,000		1,109	416
Maritime Industries	111,111	270,000		177,777	66,667
Sugar	15,500	60,000		24,800	9,300
Dairy Products	25,000	220,000		40,000	15,000
Meat	11,250	160,000		18,000	6,750
Fish	26,667	21,000		42,667	16,000
Petroleum	43,125	160,000		69,000	25,875
Lead and Zinc	2,233	30,000		3,573	1,340
Totals	981,138			1,569,819	

[a]Data taken from Table 6.1.
[b]I used the more conservative 1.6 to 1 ratio from Baughman and Emrich, *Analysis of the Impact of the Textile and Apparel Trade Enforcement Act of 1985*, rather than the much larger 3.1 to 1 ratio cited in Denzau, *How Import Restraints Reduce Employment*.
[c]Computed by multiplying the numbers in the Jobs Saved column by 1.6.
[d]Computed by subtracting jobs lost from jobs saved.
[e]The difference between jobs saved (981,138) and jobs lost (1,569,819).

Source: Compiled by the author.

extremely high. In the benzenoid chemical industry, for example, protectionism costs more than $1 million per job saved, whereas wages per employee averaged only about $14.90 per hour for the period under study.[17] That is about $29,800 a year, based on a 2,000 hour work year. Therefore, if it costs exactly $1 million to save a $29,800 job, it seems that it would be a better use of resources just to pay laid-off workers their full $29,800 wage and forget about implementing some protectionist measure.

The ratio of cost per job saved to average annual wage in the carbon steel industry would lead a rational policymaker to reach the same conclusion. Each job saved in this industry costs $750,000, and the average hourly wage is $22.21,[18] or $44,420 for a 2,000 hour work year. This conclusion does not change at the lower end of the spectrum. For example, in the rubber footwear industry, it costs $30,000 a year to save a job that pays only $11,460 a year, based on a 2,000 hour work year.[19] Likewise, for the lead and zinc industry, it cost $30,000 a year per job saved, at a time when the average wage was $3.28 an hour, or $6,560 for a 2,000 hour work year.[20]

I am not saying that the government (taxpayers) should pay people not to work, because that would be unfair to those who do work, but it is an interesting comparison.

Thus, protectionism destroys at least 588,681 more jobs than it creates each year. However, this figure is conservative, because it includes only direct job losses and ignores secondary losses. It also excludes industries that have less than $100 million in annual volume. Also, the job loss/gain ratio might be higher than the 1.6 to 1 I used to compute net employment losses in this example. Had we used the 3.1 to 1 ratio from the Denzau paper, the number of jobs lost would have been 3,041,528 and the deadweight loss would have been 2,060,390.[21] So, it is reasonable to expect that the real net loss is somewhat higher than 588,681.

SOCIAL HARMONY COSTS

Protectionism has a social harmony cost. It is a version of class conflict, but rather than pitting the proletariat against the bourgeoisie, it is a conflict of producers versus consumers, and the producers seem to be winning, in the sense that they are able to get their protectionist policies adopted by the legislature, which is elected by the consumers.

However, the situation is not hopeless. Although the special interest groups are well financed and influential with the legislature and the average consumer is disinterested and powerless, in recent years, various special interest groups that stand to be harmed by protectionist measures have surfaced to do battle with the special interest groups that are asking for government protection. For example, in the auto industry, various auto dealerships, which depend on all or a substantial portion of their business from foreign imports, banded together to oppose a domestic content bill in 1982 and 1983.[22] This group can exercise substantial influence if organized, and they were organized, by manufacturer (for example, Toyota). In 1982, there were 4,000 dealerships that sold only imports and there were 7,250 dealers that sold imports as well as domestically made cars — 11,250 in all — compared with 14,450 dealerships that sold only domestic cars.[23] The AIADA also joined in the fight against domestic content legislation.

Other counterbalancing groups at times assert their views when special interests call for protection. The International Longshoremen's Association opposed sugar quotas in the late 1970s.[24] Other groups that stand to lose by restrictions on sugar imports, such as soft drink bottlers, ice cream makers, and the Coalition to Resist Inflated Sugar Prices, have also been vocal.[25] Importers, represented by the American Association of Exporters and Importers, have also made their views known.[26] Destler and Odell conducted a major study to determine which groups fought various protectionist measures the hardest for a number of protectionist pieces of legislation.[27] The most vigorous opponents in these areas were the following:

Autos
American Honda Motor Co.
American International Auto Dealers Association
Auto Importers of America
Chamber of Commerce
Coalition of 22 associations
National Auto Dealers Association
Nissan Motor Corp., USA
Toyota Motor Sales USA Inc.

Copper
Chile, government of
National Electrical Manufacturers Association

Footwear
European Community
Footwear Retailers of America
South Korea, government of
Volume Footwear Retailers of America

Steel
Canada, government of
Caterpillar Tractor
European Community
South Korea, government of

Sugar
Consumers against Sugar Hikes
Sugar Users Group
U.S. Cane Refiners Association

Textiles
American Association of Exporters and Importers
American Free Trade Council
China, government of
Hong Kong, government of
Retail Industry Trade Action Coalition
Wheat growers

Another negative aspect of protectionism that reduces social harmony is the possibility of retaliation by a trading partner who feels it is being punished or treated unfairly. Retaliation resulting from the Smoot-Hawley Tariff caused the 1930s depression in the United States to deepen, and the threat of retaliation still rears its ugly head from time to time.[28]

REDUCED CHOICE

Another nonmonetary cost is the reduction in choice that results from protectionist policies. Although this cost is intangible, it is a cost, nonetheless. If consumers have to settle for their second or third choice, they lose utility. The measure of this loss is the difference between what they would have chosen had they been able to make their first choice and the product or service they must settle for because their first choice is unavailable, due to some quota or tariff or other restriction.

RIGHTS VIOLATIONS

An often overlooked nonmonetary cost of protectionism is the reduction in political and economic freedom that results when some government makes a policy that results in reducing the number of contracts that consenting adults are able to enter into or raising the cost of entering into such contracts. For example, if the price of a certain foreign auto is $2,000 more than it would be in a free market, then government is forcing consumers to transfer $2,000 of their wealth to someone else, either to a domestic or a foreign producer or to the government, as a condition of entering into a contract to purchase an auto. If an import quota prevents consumers from even obtaining the automobile of their choice, a property right is also violated, because property rights include the right to trade the fruits of one's labor.

The ethics of this form of redistribution (as with any form of forced redistribution) are also questionable.[29] Tariffs and quotas are hidden forms of redistribution. At least with a direct subsidy, the amount is disclosed in the federal budget (unless it is an off-budget item). The extent to which the consumers are subsidizing some special interest can be put in terms of dollars and cents. Public servants who cry out for full disclosure in any number of other areas say nothing about the morality of hiding the cost of their protectionist actions from the voting public. They even go so far as to argue that their actions are in the public interest, to save jobs, or whatever.

CONCLUDING COMMENTS

Protectionism costs. It has both gainers and losers. Studies that have been done in this area are consistent in their conclusions that the losses exceed the gains, that there is a deadweight loss, not only in terms of reduced standard of living but also in terms of employment. More jobs are lost than are gained by adopting a protectionist policy.

There are other costs as well. Besides the economic costs of higher prices, reduced quality and choice, and lost jobs, protectionism also reduces social harmony and results in property rights violations. Yet the United States and other countries consistently adopt protectionist policies, usually at the behest of the special interest groups that stand to gain by such policies, even though the general population loses. Unless some good reason can be found for adopting a protectionist policy, the logical conclusion seems to be that protectionist policies should never be adopted, because the losses exceed the gains.

This is the conclusion that would be reached from a utilitarian perspective — the greatest good for the greatest number.[30] It can probably be said that the majority of economists are utilitarians, but some are not. Some, like Murray Rothbard, reject utilitarianism on moral grounds, because utilitarianism sometimes results in rights violations.[31] For rights theorists like Rothbard, "the greatest good for the greatest number" is an irrelevant argument. Rights theorists take the position that a particular policy is acceptable if no one's rights are violated and is unacceptable in all other cases. Therefore, the fact that a quota prevents consenting adults from entering into contracts is a violation of rights. If the sole purpose of government is to protect life, liberty, and property, any policy that disparages any of these rights is illegitimate.[32] Because a quota law disparages both property rights and the right to enter into contracts, quotas are illegitimate abuses of governmental power. The fact that the societal benefits may exceed the societal losses is irrelevant.

Another weakness of the utilitarian position is that utility is impossible to measure.[33] In the case of a protectionist policy, for example, the few special interest groups (for example, auto or textile manufacturers) benefit much, and the vast majority of consumers are harmed a little bit. However, there is no way to measure individual gains and losses in terms of utility, so it is not possible to determine whether the total gains from a particular policy exceed the total losses.

However, in the case of protectionism, it does not matter whether one takes the utilitarian or natural rights approach, because the conclusion is the same, although for different reasons. A policy that costs

$135,000 a year for each $12,000 job saved is a bad policy, even from a utilitarian perspective.[34] Also, the policy is bad from a natural rights perspective because the policy violates the rights to property and freedom to contract. Thus, the only conclusion to be drawn, from either a utilitarian or a rights perspective, is that protectionist policies are bad.

NOTES

1. For more on rent-seeking, see Gordon Tullock, *The Economics of Special Privilege and Rent Seeking* (Boston, Mass.: Kluwer Academic Publishers, 1989); Charles K. Rowley, Robert D. Tollison, and Gordon Tullock, eds., *The Political Economy of Rent-Seeking* (Boston, Mass.: Kluwer Academic Publishers, 1988); James M. Buchanan, Robert Tollison, and Gordon Tullock, eds., *Towards a Theory of a Rent-Seeking Society* (College Station, Tex.: Texas A&M University Press, 1980).

2. Laura Megna Baughman and Thomas Emrich, *Analysis of the Impact of the Textile and Apparel Trade Enforcement Act of 1985* (International Business and Economic Research Corporation, 1985), table 4; cited in I. M. Destler and John S. Odell, *Anti-Protection: Changing Forces in United States Trade Politics* (Washington, D.C.: Institute for International Economics, 1987), pp. 54, 56.

3. Arthur T. Denzau, *How Import Restraints Reduce Employment* (St. Louis, Mo.: Washington University, Center for the Study of American Business, 1987).

4. Jose A. Mendez, "The Short-Run Trade and Employment Effects of Steel Import Restraints," *Journal of World Trade Law* 20 (September–October 1986): 554–66.

5. Arthur T. Denzau, *American Steel: Responding to Foreign Competition* (St. Louis, Mo.: Center for the Study of American Business, 1985).

6. Arthur T. Denzau, *The Unlevel Playing Field: How High Steel Prices and Trade Protection Help Deindustrialize America* (St. Louis, Mo.: Center for the Study of American Business, Washington University, 1989), p. 20. Industries that gained from steel protection were mining/petroleum, 13,569 jobs; wholesale/retail, 16,712; other, 7,523. Industries that lost jobs were manufacturing (nondurables), 14,896; manufacturing (durables), 128,813; construction, 50,607; services, 14,313.

7. Denzau, *The Unlevel Playing Field*, p. 22.

8. Presidential candidate Walter Mondale, among others, has warned that unless the United States adopts protectionist measures, the only jobs Americans will be able to get will be flipping hamburgers at McDonald's or sweeping up around Japanese computers. Jagdish Bhagwati, *Protectionism* (Cambridge, Mass.: MIT Press, 1988), p. 64.

9. William R. Cline, *The Future of World Trade in Textiles and Apparel* (Washington, D.C.: Institute for International Economics, 1990), pp. 15, 191, 193.

10. Tariffs and quotas.

11. Cline, *The Future of World Trade in Textiles and Apparel*, p. 193. It should be pointed out that the Cline figures are based on wholesale prices. If these figures were converted to retail prices, the numbers could be as much as 100% higher, because the markup in the retail end of the business is about 100%. Whether these numbers should be doubled, though, depends on what percentage of the profit margin can be passed on to consumers, because in the absence of protection, the increased competition might force some sellers to reduce their profit margins in order to compete. It would be reasonable to expect that the actual numbers, at retail, would be somewhat higher than the wholesale numbers that Cline reports, but perhaps not 100% higher.

12. Ibid., pp. 15, 193.

13.   Bovard, *The Fair Trade Fraud*, p. 75.

14.   Ibid., pp.75–76.

15.   Ibid., p. 71.

16.   The statistics I am using to expand upon and extrapolate are scattered throughout Gary Clyde Hufbauer, Diane T. Berliner, and Kimberly Ann Elliott, *Trade Protection in the United States: 31 Case Studies* (Washington, D.C.: Institute for International Economics, 1986), pp. 14–15.

17.   Ibid., p. 59.

18.   Ibid., p. 177.

19.   Ibid., p. 75. The cost per job saved in the fish industry was even lower — $21,000. The annual or hourly wage for employees in this industry was not reported by Hufbauer, Berliner, and Elliott.

20.   Ibid., p. 358.

21.   Jobs lost = 981,138 x 3.1 (jobs saved) = 3,041,528; deadweight loss = 3,041,528 − 981,138 = 2,060,390.

22.   Destler and Odell, *Anti-Protection*, p. 53.

23.   Ibid.

24.   Ibid., p. 50.

25.   Ibid., p. 46.

26.   Ibid., p. 50.

27.   Ibid., pp. 143–74.

28.   Joseph P. Kalt, "The Political Economy of Protectionism: Tariffs and Retaliation in the Timber Industry," in *Trade Policy Issues and Empirical Analysis*, ed. Robert E. Baldwin (Chicago, Ill.: University of Chicago Press, 1988), pp. 339–64.

29.   For more on this point, see Bertrand de Jouvenel, *The Ethics of Redistribution* (Cambridge: Cambridge University Press, 1952).

30.   For one of the classic works on this topic, see John Stuart Mill, *Utilitarianism and Other Writings* (New York: New American Library, 1962).

31.   For Rothbard's critiques of utilitarianism, see Murray N. Rothbard, *For a New Liberty* (New York: Libertarian Review Foundation, 1978), pp. 15–16, 26–27, 30, 40; Murray N. Rothbard, *The Ethics of Liberty* (Atlantic Highlands, N.J.: Humanities Press, 1982), pp. 10–11, 210–13; Murray N. Rothbard, *Man, Economy and State* (Los Angeles, Calif.: Nash Publishing, 1970), pp. 260–68.

32.   Some philosophers would argue that the purpose of government should not be limited to the defense of life, liberty, and property but should also extend to redistribution, taking some people's property and giving it to others. For a moral critique of this view, see Jouvenel, *The Ethics of Redistribution*.

33.   Rothbard, *Man, Economy and State*, pp. 260–68, points this out.

34.   According to Cline, *The Future of World Trade in Textiles and Apparel*, p. 194, it costs $134,686 annually to save a job in the textile industry that pays $12,000 a year.

III

ANTIDUMPING POLICY

7

Antidumping Policy in the United States: Theory and Practice

ECONOMIC AND LEGAL BACKGROUND

Antidumping laws have been on the books in the United States, in one form or another, for decades. Perhaps the first major antidumping law in the United States was included in the Revenue Act of 1916,[1] which is sometimes referred to as the Antidumping Duty Act of 1916.[2] This law was passed in response to alleged German predatory dumping during World War I,[3] and it made it a crime to import foreign products for prices that were less than wholesale or actual market value.[4] Because it was a criminal statute, perpetrators could be found guilty only upon a finding that there was an intent to harm or destroy an industry in the United States or to prevent such an industry from being formed.

Although this law has not yet been repealed, it was not used much until Zenith and National Union Electric Corporation filed charges against Japanese television manufacturers in 1974.[5] The prohibition portion of the act reads as follows:

It shall be unlawful for any person importing or assisting in importing any articles from any foreign country into the United States, commonly and systematically to import, sell or cause to be imported or sold such articles within the United States at a price substantially less than the actual market value or wholesale price of such articles, at the time of exportation to the United States, in the principal markets of the country of their production, or of other foreign countries to which they are commonly exported after adding to such market value or wholesale price, freight, duty, and other charges and expenses necessarily incident to the importation and sale thereof in the United States: *Provided*, That such act or acts be done with the intent of destroying or injuring an industry in the United States, or of preventing the establishment of an industry in the United States, or of restraining or monopolizing any part of trade and commerce in such articles in the United States.[6]

Because this law is a criminal statute, it has a penalty provision. That provision reads as follows:

Any person who violates or combines or conspires with any other person to violate this section is guilty of a misdemeanor, and, on conviction thereof, shall be punished by a fine not exceeding $5,000, or imprisonment not exceeding one year, or both, in the discretion of the court.

Any person injured in his business or property by reason of any violation of, or combination or conspiracy to violate, this section, may sue therefor in the district court of the United States for the district in which the defendant resides or is found or has an agent, without respect to the amount in controversy, and shall recover threefold the damages sustained, and the cost of the suit, including a reasonable attorney's fee.[7]

Because the Antidumping Duty Act of 1916 was a criminal statute and had an intent requirement, it was difficult to convict anyone of dumping. Thus, the need was seen for another antidumping law, civil in nature, that would lower the level of proof needed to convict. The Antidumping Act of 1921 was passed to fit this purpose.[8] Curiously, though, the various Congressional hearings and investigations that were held at this time were unable to uncover much dumping.

In all the hearings that we had before the Committee on Finance there was not in any instance any showing of any dumping of foreign goods into this country. . . . The price of almost every manufactured commodity is so much higher in the United States than anywhere else in the world that it is not necessary for the exporter from a foreign country to export it into this country at a less price than the same article is sold for in the markets of the producing country.[9]

The Antidumping Act of 1921 is conceptually and institutionally similar to present-day antidumping law.[10] For example, it established the sanction of an offsetting duty that is equal to the adjusted price differential of the goods that are dumped and a two-pronged legal process whereby one government agency (originally the Treasury Department but now the Department of Commerce) decided whether a product was being dumped and another government agency (originally the Tariff Commission but now the U.S. International Trade Commission [ITC]) decided whether the dumping caused injury.[11] Foreign manufacturers could not sell their products in the United States for less than fair value, which was defined as the price charged for the product in the home market. If a domestic industry was materially injured by the sale by the foreign company, the import was subjected to a duty that was equal to the difference between the price charged in the United States and the foreign market value of the product. For example, if the product sold in the foreign country for $10 and in the United States for $7, the duty would be $3. The Antidumping Act of 1921 was subsequently amended by the Trade Act of 1974,[12] which was later superseded by the Trade Agreements Act of 1979.[13]

The Tariff Act of 1930, also known as the Smoot-Hawley Tariff,[14] affected trade in a different way, by placing penalties on foreign producers who received export subsidies from their governments. The Smoot-Hawley Tariff is generally recognized as deepening the depression in the United States by closing off the U.S. borders to foreign trade and causing other countries to retaliate by raising trade barriers of their own.[15] U.S. foreign trade dropped by more than 50% the year after the Smoot-Hawley Tariff was passed.[16] The Trade Agreements Act of 1979 added sections 731–40 to the Tariff Act of 1930. Most provisions of the Antidumping Act of 1921 were later merged into the Tariff Act of 1930 as well.[17]

Antidumping investigations became relatively infrequent after passage of the Reciprocal Trade Agreements Act of 1934. Between the beginning of 1934 and October 1, 1954, only 146 dumping cases were brought against foreign companies, and only 7 of them resulted in the imposition of dumping duties. In the next 27 months, only 1 of the 52 cases the Treasury examined found both dumping and injury.[18]

The Trade Agreements Act of 1979 incorporated the 1930 Tariff Act's dumping provisions and extensively amended the antidumping law in an attempt to improve its application and procedures.[19] It took effect January 1, 1980, the same day the GATT Antidumping Code entered into force in the United States.[20] The one major change brought about by the 1979 Act was the addition of an injury test[21] for countervailing duty cases. To determine whether an investigation should proceed, the ITC looks to see whether there is a reasonable indication that an industry in the United States is materially injured or is threatened with material injury or if the establishment of an industry in the United States is materially retarded by imports. If not, the investigation is terminated.[22]

Previously, subsidized imports were subject to a countervailing duty automatically. However, since the passage of the 1979 Act, countries are entitled to an injury test[23] for subsidized imports if they signed the GATT Subsidies Code or subscribe to rules equivalent to those of GATT. Countries that do not fall into this category are still subject to a countervailing duty automatically.[24] A minor revision brought about by the 1979 Act resulted in giving domestic industries a greater interest in administrative procedures and increased court access.[25]

The present antidumping law in the United States is based on the 1979 Act, with minor modifications, the most important of which is a 1984 amendment that requires injuries to be assessed by cumulating imports from competing countries that are subject to investigation.[26] Ever since 1967, when a number of industrial countries signed the Antidumping Code[27] as part of the Kennedy Round of GATT, the

United States has enacted numerous trade laws and regulations aimed at preserving "fair" competition or protecting various domestic industries from "unfair" competition.

The government's attitude toward dumping has grown more protectionist in recent years. The 1979 revision to the antidumping laws made them more protectionist, and Congress shifted the administration of the antidumping laws from the Treasury Department to the Commerce Department mainly because it wanted to see foreign companies get hit with more dumping penalties.[28]

ADMINISTRATION OF THE ANTIDUMPING LAWS

Imagine a system of civil litigation in which a party serves a massive discovery request, consisting of interrogatories and requests for production of documents. Imagine further that the serving party has the sole authority to prescribe the time within which response must be made and the format (such as to require multiple copies and translation into English of all requested documents originally prepared in a foreign language). Imagine still further that the serving party is the sole judge of the adequacy of the response and of the merits of all objections as to relevancy or burdensomeness of the request; that the serving party also is the imposer of sanctions for failure to comply, and the ultimate decision-maker in the underlying matter for which the information is sought.

Such a system would be intolerable in the state or federal courts of the United States. It would raise serious questions of due process in a system of administrative law that separates the investigative from the judicial function within a single agency. But this is the inquisitorial system that was ordained by Congress for the administration of the antidumping and countervailing duty provisions of Title VII of the Tariff Act of 1930. Torquemada, no doubt, would be right at home with it. But this is hardly a recommendation for the system. It should be changed.[29]

One problem with the present system is the short period of time in which to conduct and complete the investigation. The law calls for the Commerce Department to make a preliminary determination within 160 days from the time the petition is filed and to reach a final determination 75 days after that, for a total of 235 days from the date the petition is filed until the matter is finally determined.[30] The Commerce Department may extend a preliminary antidumping investigation for 50 more days and the final determination for 60 days under certain circumstances.[31]

That might be sufficient time if the Commerce Department just asked for a few bits of basic information, and the short time deadlines would speed up the process. However, it demands much more than just a few pieces of information. The standard questionnaire demands information covering all U.S. sales as well as sales in the company's home market for a six-month period. The data must be in a mandatory computer tape format. It will accept only IBM-compatible computer tapes.[32] Much of what it demands is not useful but is demanded so as to avoid criticism from the petitioner for not being thorough enough.[33] If the target of the investigation thinks that the requirements being imposed by the Commerce Department are too onerous, there is no effective appeal, because the Commerce Department determines what is enough, when it should be presented, and in what format it should be presented. Of course, the target company can go to the Court of International Trade,[34] but that is costly and time-consuming, and the Commerce Department can exclude any information the target company wishes to present as not being in conformity with its own administrative requirements.[35]

However, the time element is not the main problem. It is the way the Commerce Department administers the antidumping laws, especially the demands for data that it places on foreign producers, which are sometimes unreasonable.

In one case, it imposed a 115.82% dumping duty on uranium imports from six republics of the former Soviet Union.[36] The prices the Commerce Department looked at were from the period before these republics came into existence.[37] In effect, they were being punished for Soviet pricing behavior.

As part of its investigation, the Commerce Department sent the six governments a 66-page questionnaire — in English, of course — that demanded detailed information regarding their uranium operations. It violated U.S. law by failing to provide them with copies of the full petitions that were filed by the domestic producers and a labor union that initiated the proceedings. The six countries of the Confederation of Independent States (CIS) were found guilty of dumping because they failed to provide the thousands of pages of documentation demanded. The information could have been obtained, theoretically, from the Soviet Ministry of Atomic Power and Industry. However, that ministry was abolished a few months previously, and much of the information would have been top secret, anyway.

The Commerce Department arrived at the 115% figure by taking some unsubstantiated numbers offered by the parties who filed the petition and determining what their costs would have been if they had used Portuguese electricity and Namibian labor costs and performed the work with Canadian efficiency. In arriving at its calculation, the Commerce Department assumed that because Canadian uranium miners are four times as efficient as Czech miners and because Czechoslovakia is also a nonmarket economy, then CIS miners must be only 25% as efficient as Canadian miners. Thus, they require four times as much labor, so the Commerce Department computed CIS labor costs accordingly. Bovard estimates that keeping uranium from CIS countries out of the United States will cost the 50 million U.S. consumers of nuclear power up to $300 million more a year for electricity.[38]

The information demanded (not requested) by the Commerce Department can be overly burdensome, and companies that refuse to supply it do so at their own risk, because the Commerce Department has no qualms about pulling numbers out of the air to construct estimated figures if the company involved will not provide them. The average antidumping questionnaire is more than 70 pages long, single spaced. Companies have 45 to 60 days to reply. Before they can reply, however, they must translate the questionnaire into their language, distribute it to numerous company employees who will be working on various aspects of the questionnaire, determine what information has to be reported, then gather it, read it, and digest it. It is only then that they will be able to respond to the Commerce Department's demands for data.[39]

The Commerce Department can demand practically an infinite amount of information — and any refusal to comply is taken as a confession of guilt, after which it imposes the highest possible dumping margins. The Commerce Department collects vast amounts of confidential information from foreign businesses and has frequently allowed this information to fall into the hands of American competitors.[40]

Matsushita withdrew from an antidumping case involving small business telephone systems,[41] thereby abandoning more than $50 million in export sales, because of the onerous requirements imposed by the Commerce Department.[42] On a Friday afternoon, it received a demand by the Commerce Department to translate 3,000 pages of Japanese financial documents into English by the following Monday morning.

If the company in question does not provide the information the Commerce Department wants, the Commerce Department will construct the numbers it needs, using the "best information available."[43] However, in many cases, this information is not very close to what the actual numbers would have been. In many cases, the Commerce Department uses data that are provided by the very companies that filed the petition, which means it has a high probability of being biased against the foreign producer. In fact, because of the way the Commerce Department can construct imaginary prices, it is entirely possible that it can find dumping even when prices are the same worldwide.[44]

The Commerce Department placed a particularly onerous and burdensome reporting requirement on SKF, a Swedish bearings manufacturer. Commerce demanded, and SKF supplied, information on more than 100 million separate sales. The first submission weighed three tons, was more than 150,000 pages in length, and included more than 4 billion pieces of information.[45] As might be expected, there were a few mistakes in the data, which the company put together in about a week, the amount of time the Commerce Department gave it to respond.

About 1% of the data from its German sales were in a form that was not suitable to the Commerce Department, so it ignored all the data the company supplied and worked up its own numbers, using the best information available. The result was a 180% dumping margin.

Another criticism that can be made of the way the Commerce Department administers the antidumping laws is the way it determines what data to use to compute a dumping margin. It usually examines just the data for the larger companies and uses those data to determine what the dumping duty should be for smaller companies in the same country.[46] These small companies can defend themselves by offering information on their own costs, but the Commerce Department does not have to consider these responses and can reject this information for any reason. In an action filed by the National Knitwear and Sportswear Association against Hong Kong sweater manufacturers, hundreds of Hong Kong companies were assessed a 5.86% duty because one company earned less than 8%.[47]

Some small companies in Taiwan have also felt the wrath of the Commerce Department because they were not able to supply the information required. In one case, the Commerce Department demanded that the companies respond to a 100-page questionnaire, written in English, that required more than 200,000 pieces of information. The management of one of these companies consisted of a husband and wife team, but the Commerce Department found that lack of sufficient management was no excuse for not responding to the questionnaire.[48] The Commerce Department imposed a duty on another Taiwanese company because it did not supply information; the fact that its factory had burned down and its records were destroyed was not a sufficient excuse for failure to provide information. As a result of these and other cases, many Taiwanese sweaters now have a 21.94% dumping duty that, coupled with a 34% tariff, makes it very difficult, if not impossible, for Taiwanese sweater manufacturers to compete in the U.S. market. Within a year after the Commerce Department started its investigation of the Taiwanese acrylic sweater industry, more than two-thirds of the Taiwanese companies that produce acrylic sweaters went out of business.[49] As a result of the investigation, the United States imported 40 million fewer acrylic sweaters from Taiwan, Korea, and Hong Kong in 1990 than in 1989.

Another criticism that has been made of the way in which the antidumping law is administered has to do with the fact that it is administered by both the Commerce Department and the ITC. Sometimes there is a dispute about which agency is to do what.[50] The Tariff Act bifurcated, or split, the duties for administering the antidumping law between these two agencies. The Commerce Department initiates antidumping and countervailing duty investigations, determines whether there has been dumping or subsidization, and publishes whatever orders result. The ITC determines whether a domestic industry has been materially injured or threatened with injury or whether the growth of a domestic industry is being materially retarded. But which agency has the authority to decide whether a petitioner has standing to petition for relief? This issue is by no means clear and comes up when it comes time to decide whether an investigation should be terminated for lack of standing.[51]

COMPUTATIONAL PROBLEMS

There are a number of problems with the way that dumping duties are computed. Many of the computations the Commerce Department uses violate generally accepted accounting principles, the principles companies have to use with their published financial statements. However, the government does not have to follow generally accepted accounting principles, because these rules are promulgated by private groups, such as the American Institute of Certified Public Accountants and the Financial Accounting Standards Board. Some of the computations the Commerce Department uses to arrive at a dumping decision violate common sense as well. Below is a discussion of some of the major problems.

Shifts in Exchange Rates

In order to compare the foreign price with the domestic price, the foreign price has to be converted into dollars. The method used to make this conversion sometimes results in a charge of dumping.[52] It is a problem that cannot be avoided by the foreign seller, because exchange rates cannot be predicted in advance, and even if they could, it would not always be possible to avoid a charge of dumping, as we shall see.

Let's take the case of the German mark. If the exchange rate at the time the contract is signed is DM2.0 equals $1 and the price of the product in Germany is DM2.0 and in the United States is $1.00, then there is no dumping, because the product sells in each market for the same price. However, if the price of the Deutsche mark appreciates against the dollar to 1.6, then there is dumping, because the product then sells on the German market for DM2.0, which is now the equivalent of $1.25, which is $0.25 higher than the price in the United States. Thus, it appears that the German company is selling in the United States for a lower price than on the German market.[53]

In 1989, General Chemical de Puerto Rico, Inc., initiated an antidumping suit against a Venezuelan company for exporting aluminum sulfate to the United States for less than fair value.[54] A weighted average dumping margin of 259.17% was arrived at by using the official exchange rate of 14.5 bolivares to the dollar rather than the 39.5 free market rate. In effect, the Venezuelan government's unrealistic exchange rate policy led to the expulsion from the United States of one of its companies. That is not to say that the Commerce Department was justified in what it did, because it should not have used the official exchange rate, because it deviated so drastically from the market rate.

Companies in countries that have hyperinflation can be especially hard hit by the Commerce Department's methodology.[55] In one dumping case involving a Brazilian company that made steel wheels, the Commerce Department computed the selling price in the United States using the exchange rate in effect at the sale date but based the company's cost of production on the rate that existed when the product was exported, several months later.[56] Such methodology can result in a major distortion when the exchange rate declines rapidly as a result of hyperinflation.

What seems unfair about the Commerce Department's methodology is that foreign companies can be hit with a dumping charge even if there was no intent to dump. The number of dumping cases can increase if the Federal Reserve Board takes actions that result in driving down the value of the dollar in comparison with other currencies. In effect, the Commerce Department has delegated the exchange rate determination to the Federal Reserve Bank, a private organization (nominally, at least).[57] Also, the Commerce Department adjusts its exchange rates only once each quarter, so the rates it uses may be much different than those actually used in the marketplace. If companies purchase currency futures contracts to protect themselves against fluctuations in exchange rates, the Commerce Department may impute a foreign exchange loss even though no loss has occurred.[58] As a result, price comparisons can be distorted. This was the result in the case brought by the Floral Trade Council against a fresh cut flower exporter from Colombia.[59]

N. David Palmeter points out an inherent flaw in the Commerce Department's methodology:

The main problem . . . the regulation requires conversion from foreign currency into U.S. dollars, rather than *vice versa*. Conversion into dollars is necessary for valuation purposes, but it makes no sense in antidumping proceedings.

Theoretically, if the proper exchange rate is chosen, the result should be the same, but in practice it rarely, if ever, is chosen: in the real world it rarely, if ever, can be chosen. One problem lies in the notion that any single exchange rate will permit an accurate dollar-to-dollar comparison. Elements of the dollar-denominated export price, such as insurance and freight, are normally incurred in the exporter's currency, and consequently must also be converted into dollars. However, these items are likely to be contracted and paid for some time after the sales agreement for the exported merchandise. The Department's regulation calls for use of a single conversion rate for all elements of the transaction, i.e. the one in effect the day the exported merchandise was sold. Because a different rate was probably in effect on the day arrangements were made for insurance and freight, the practice is inherently distortive.

Even if this frequent problem is not present in a particular case, realistically it is not possible for the rate determined by the Federal Reserve to be the "proper" rate in any event; consequently, the claim that use of a proper rate prevents distortion collapses in the face of reality.[60]

The Commerce Department departs from the quarterly rate only if there is a fluctuation of 5% or more between the daily rate and the pre-set quarterly rate. However, in order to be liable for a dumping penalty, a company's price need be only 0.5% lower than the home market price, or one-tenth the exchange rate fluctuation. Therefore, it is possible for the Commerce Department to find that a product has been dumped solely on the basis of its exchange rate computation, which is not sufficiently precise, given the narrow acceptability band used to determine the presence or absence of dumping.[61]

The courts have had problems with the Commerce Department's exchange rate methodology.

It is not reasonable for Commerce to find dumping by a firm with only ten relevant home market sales during the period of the investigation solely because of Commerce's use of quarterly exchange rates. In this case the purpose of the antidumping laws would be violated if Commerce found a dumping margin based on the use of quarterly rates, while no margin would result if Commerce were to use the rates prevailing at the time of transactions.[62]

A more equitable approach would be to ignore price differentials that result merely from exchange rate fluctuations.

Computing the Cost of Production

In 1974, Congress added a cost of production test to determine whether dumping was taking place. For the first few years, this test was seldom used, but its use has increased since 1980, when the Commerce Department took over the responsibility for investigating dumping allegations. Now, about two-thirds of all dumping investigations involve looking into a company's cost of production.[63] The Commerce Department allows a foreign company to charge a price that is high enough to cover its cost of production plus allow for a "reasonable profit," which it considers to be 8%.[64] Companies that charge this price are considered to be charging a fair price. Anything less is considered unfair. Interestingly enough, many U.S. companies do not make an 8% profit and would feel lucky if they could.

To arrive at this fair price, the Commerce Department begins by estimating the material production cost,[65] then it adds 10% for administrative overhead.[66] The Commerce Department will not penalize companies that have an administrative overhead of more than 10%, but if the overhead is less than 10%, they could be in trouble. In effect, the more efficient a company is, the greater are its chances of being penalized for keeping its administrative overhead low.[67]

After adding 10% for administrative overhead, the Commerce Department adds an 8% profit margin.[68] It then adds the cost of all containers and coverings of whatever nature and all other expenses that are incidental to placing the product in condition, packed ready for shipment to the United States.[69] If the resulting total is higher than the price the company actually charges for its product in the United States, it will be punished for selling at a loss. Companies that charge a lower price are considered to be selling at lower than production cost. So if a company makes a 6% profit, the Commerce Department considers it to be incurring a 2% loss.

This methodology can be criticized on several counts. For one thing, the 10% overhead allocation is totally arbitrary and has nothing to do with the overhead cost a particular company might incur. Ironically, companies that have an overhead of significantly more than 10% might actually be selling at a loss in the U.S. market, although the Commerce Department figure might show them making a profit, and companies that keep their overhead low are penalized for being efficient. Also, the Commerce Department will ignore the evidence if a company attempts to show that it is actually making a profit if the Commerce Department's computations show that it is taking a loss.[70]

The 8% profit requirement also can be criticized on several counts. For one thing, it is totally arbitrary. Profit margins are different for different industries, but the Commerce Department does not take that into account. Many of the top U.S. companies listed in the Fortune 500 do not make that high a return. The Big-3 automakers often make a negative return, in the sense that they lose hundreds of millions or even billions of dollars in some quarters.

The Commerce Department uses several questionable accounting techniques as well, which sometimes result in inflating a foreign company's cost of production. For example, if a foreign company is able to reduce its labor costs by using part-time labor for the product being investigated, the Commerce Department might decide to compute the company's labor cost by using a company-wide weighted-average labor cost, which tends to inflate the labor cost figure.[71] In effect, companies are penalized for cutting their costs by using part-time labor if the Commerce Department thinks they are using too much of it.

The method the Commerce Department uses to compute production costs in agriculture also is much different from the method an accounting firm would use. Rather than averaging such costs, it computes production cost by using the costs incurred in a single year. Its rationale is that yields are unpredictable and depend on many variables.[72]

Its costing methods are far from scientific. It determined the production cost for red raspberries by taking a random sample of ten Canadian farmers, but an ITC study found that raspberry production costs for U.S. farmers varied by nearly 100%.[73] Part of the wide variance depended on how the farmer financed the business. Mortgage interest was included in the cost of production if the farm had a mortgage, but if there was no mortgage, interest would not be imputed on the farm property. Because of this inconsistent practice, two farmers selling raspberries for the same price could wind up with different results from a Commerce Department investigation. The farmer with the mortgage could get hit with a dumping charge, while the farmer without a mortgage, and, therefore, with lower production costs, would not be liable for dumping. However, if they sell their raspberries for the same price, how can it be said that one is selling at a fair price and the other is not?

The Commerce Department also artificially boosts the farmers' cost of production by imputing wages that are never paid. Farmers do not earn anything until the end of the season; their income consists of whatever they have left after paying expenses. However, the Commerce Department imputes a wage expense to them anyway — the farmer plus family members — then adds a 10% overhead figure and an 8% profit. This methodology raises their production cost (on paper) and enhances the possibility that they will be found guilty of dumping, because the definition of dumping is selling for less than the cost of production plus an 8% profit.[74]

The Commerce Department sometimes includes other unlikely items into the cost of production. For example, it included Suzuki's costs of defending itself against charges by the U.S. Consumer Product Safety Commission that it made unsafe all-terrain vehicles. It included in production costs the donations that two Korean sweater manufacturers[75] made to local charities, claiming that it was part of the cost of making sweaters.[76] Any certified public accountant who made such classifications could be sued for malpractice.

Another problem with the Commerce Department's methodology is that it is not consistent. Its cost accounting has been known to shift from case to case, and even within the same investigation. When it investigated some Brazilian companies, it used more than ten different approaches to measure their cost of production.[77] A problem with using so many different methods is that the company trying to avoid a dumping charge never knows in advance which method will be used, which makes it difficult to plan. Even if the company uses one of the cost accounting methods that the Commerce Department uses, it may still have to defend itself because the Commerce Department investigator decides to use a different method for that particular investigation.

Another flaw in the Commerce Department's methodology is that it sometimes compares the cost of production for one period with the price charged in another period. For example, in one semiconductor case, it compared the sales price currently being charged with cost of production figures for semiconductors that were made three months previously.[78] For some industries, a three-month lag would not be significant, but for the semiconductor industry, it was, because the cost of production declined rapidly for the period being investigated. Between 1984 and 1985, the average variable cost of producing semiconductors dropped by 66% — from $8.0313 to $2.7376 — and from 1985 to 1986, the costs were estimated to drop by another 52%, from $2.7376 to $1.2989.[79] Thus, the cost of production was substantially overstated, thereby enhancing the probability that the company in question would be found guilty of dumping for selling below production cost (plus 8%).

A further criticism of the Commerce Department's cost of production methodology is its emphasis on total costs rather than variable costs. For a particular project, companies measure whether they can make a profit by comparing the selling price (variable revenue) with variable cost (the cost of making one additional unit). Production and sale decisions are made on the basis of variable data. However, the Commerce Department measures profit for a particular project on the basis of total cost, which includes both fixed and variable cost. Yet companies ignore fixed costs when they compute the viability of making their next sale, because fixed costs will remain constant regardless of which decision they make and are, therefore, irrelevant to the outcome of the decision.

For example, if a company's fixed costs are $100 million a year and it is faced with the decision of whether to sell an additional 100 units of product at $5 each, it will decide to make the sale if its variable unit cost is $4, and it will decide not to sell if its variable unit cost (the cost to make an additional unit) is $7. The fact that its fixed cost is $100 million is irrelevant as far as making the sell/not sell decision is concerned. Of course, over the long run, all fixed costs must be recouped, but fixed costs are ignored when making decisions regarding an individual sale/production decision. Indeed, they must be ignored. Otherwise, companies would sometimes make the wrong decision, because they would be comparing marginal revenue to marginal cost plus a portion of fixed cost.[80] In cases where the marginal profit (the excess of marginal revenue over marginal cost) is small, adding a portion of fixed cost to the cost figure being used in the comparison might make it appear that the company would be selling at a loss when in fact it might make a small profit. Corporate accountants would never include fixed costs in their determination of the profit calculation for an individual project, but the Commerce Department does it routinely.

Some industries are more adversely affected than others by this questionable policy of adding fixed costs to the production cost of a particular project. For example, in high-tech industries like semiconductors, the variable cost may constitute only 25% of the total aggregate cost of production.[81] Allocated fixed cost represents the other 75% of

total cost, although unit fixed cost is a meaningless number for deci-
sion-making purposes. "Irrelevant future costs include fixed costs that
will be unchanged by such considerations as whether Machine X or
Machine Y is selected, or whether a special order is accepted . . . fixed
costs . . . can be relevant. . . . Fixed costs are relevant whenever they
differ under the alternatives at hand."[82]

Fixed costs are irrelevant in the case of sell/not sell decisions
because the fixed costs will remain the same regardless of the decision
made. Only on rare occasions will fixed costs change and, therefore,
become relevant. For example, if a company is already operating at full
capacity and could not produce even one additional unit without adding
to plant capacity, then the individual in charge of making the sell/not
sell decision would have to consider fixed costs in determining whether
it would be profitable to expand plant capacity in order to fill an additional order.

Many other problems are also involved when an attempt is made to
allocate fixed costs. There are a number of arbitrary decisions that
must be made for any fixed cost allocation. For example, let us say that
a company purchases a machine for $17,000 on September 30, 1992.
The machine is expected to last for five years, after which it can be sold
for $2,000. It is also expected to produce 10,000 units of product over its
useful life. In 1992, it actually produces 800 units. How much of the
machine's cost should be allocated to depreciation in 1992? At least
seven arbitrary decisions must be made before this question can be
answered.

1. What will the salvage value be in five years? In this example, the
salvage value is $2,000, but that is just a guess. It is impossible to accu-
rately determine how much the machine will be worth in five years. A
new machine may make this machine obsolete well before five years
elapses, especially if the machine is a computer. Its value five years
down the road is also determined by how much the machine is used
over that time span and how well it is maintained. If it is beaten into
the ground, it will be worth less than if it is well-kept and -maintained.
Also, the more it is used, the more value will be lost. The machine may
well fall apart long before the five years is up.

2. How long will the machine be used? The five years in this example is an arbitrary number. There is no way to tell in advance how long
the company will use a particular machine. The company itself may no
longer be around in five years, the machine could fall apart before the
end of five years, or the company may decide to keep it for more than
five years. However, the estimate has to be made and made soon,
because depreciation has to be reflected in each year's financial statements. If the company's accounting year ends on December 31, it must
determine how much depreciation to report within three months of purchase, because it was acquired on September 30 in this example.

3. How many units will the machine crank out over its useful life? In this example, the answer is 10,000, but that is only an estimate, a guess that is almost totally arbitrary. Perhaps the average machine of this sort is capable of cranking out 10,000 units of product before it falls apart. But what if the company only gets orders for 8,000 units? If the machine is well-maintained, it may be able to produce more than 10,000 units.

4. Which depreciation method should be used to compute annual depreciation?[83] There are any number of possibilities. Someone has to make an arbitrary decision to determine which method to use in this particular case. Below are four possibilities that are commonly used and discussed in standard accounting texts.

Straight-line Method: ($17,000 − $2,000)/5 x 3/12 = $750.
   Depreciation for the first year using the straight-line method is $750. Under this method, salvage value is subtracted from cost then divided by 5 to arrive at an annual depreciation charge. However, this machine was acquired on September 30, so depreciation can be taken for just three months in 1992 — October 1 through December 31.

Sum of the Years Digits Method: ($17,000 − $2,000) x 5/15 x 3/12 = $1,250.
   Using this method results in a depreciation charge of $1,250. This is one of several accelerated depreciation methods that are in keeping with generally accepted accounting principles. The "15" in the denominator is arrived at by adding 1 + 2 + 3 + 4 + 5 = 15. Depreciation of five-fifteenths is taken in the first 12 months of the asset's life, in the second 12 months, it is four-fifteenths, and so forth.

Double Declining Balance Method: $17,000 x 2/5 x 3/12 = $1,700.
   Depreciation using this method is $1,700. The depreciation rate used — two-fifths — is twice the straight-line rate of one-fifth. Thus, the name "double declining balance." Salvage value is not subtracted, although the asset may not be depreciated below salvage value.

Units of Production Method: ($17,000 − $2,000) x 800/10,000 = $1,200.
   The depreciation allowed using this method is $1,200.

A review of these four methods illustrates that there are at least four possibilities (there really are many more) that may be used to determine annual depreciation. Which method is chosen is more or less arbitrary. Many accountants choose to use the straight-line method because it is the easiest, even though the double declining balance method may better reflect the decline in the asset's value.

Another problem inherent in choosing a depreciation method involves how the resulting expense should be treated — as fixed or variable. Although most methods treat depreciation as a fixed cost, because the expense is the same regardless of volume, depreciation expense can also be treated as a variable expense, as when the units of production method is used. The more units that are produced, the higher is the depreciation expense. Thus, depreciation is a variable rather than fixed cost in this case. Therefore, even the decision as to whether depreciation expense should be treated as fixed or variable is arbitrary in some cases, because the answer depends on the depreciation method chosen.

5. Another arbitrary decision that must be made is when to start depreciating the asset. In the above example, depreciation was taken based on when the asset was purchased, but that is not the only possibility. Some companies take six months' depreciation in the year of acquisition, regardless of when the asset is purchased. Other companies take a full 12 months if the asset is placed in service before July 1 and take no depreciation the first year if it is placed in service after June 30. It all averages out, so none of these methods distorts the financial statements.

6. Another arbitrary decision must be made if the machine in question produces more than one product. How should total depreciation be allocated (or even computed)? On the basis of units? Raw material cost? Time used to make each product? Relative market value of each unit produced multiplied by the number of units?

7. Another arbitrary decision that must sometimes be made is whether depreciation should be treated as a product cost or a period cost. If it is treated as a period cost, it is deducted at the end of the accounting period. If it is treated as a product cost, it is built into the cost of the product and deducted as part of the cost of goods sold when the product is sold, which might not be until the next accounting period.

Computing the cost of production involves many such arbitrary decisions, and there is no way around it.

Comparing Apples with Oranges

Comparing Prices of Dissimilar Products

Another problem with the Department of Commerce methodology is that it sometimes compares products that are not all that similar. For example, an Italian company was found guilty of selling woodwind musical instrument pads for 1.16% less than fair value.[84] The Commerce Department computed the dumping margin by comparing the cost of smaller pads sold in the United States with larger pads sold in Italy. Naturally, the larger pads would cost more than the smaller pads, all other things being equal, but that did not make any difference to the Commerce Department. It treated the smaller pads and the larger pads as identical for computation purposes. It explained away its position by stating that the Commerce Department has unlimited discretion to make or not make adjustments for differences in merchandise.[85]

The Commerce Department sometimes disregards the differential quality of products when it computes its dumping margins. For example, it has compared grade B Canadian raspberries sold in the United States to make juice with grade A raspberries that are sold in Canada to make jam. The grade B raspberries were harvested by machine, whereas the grade A raspberries were harvested by hand. The cost of hand harvesting is twice the cost of machine harvesting, yet the Commerce Department denied any adjustment for the difference in harvesting cost,[86] and assessed a dumping duty because of a 0.002% price differential, which amounts to less than 1 cent per 500 pounds of raspberries.[87]

In the 1986–87 fresh flowers cases involving Colombia,[88] the Netherlands,[89] Kenya,[90] Chile,[91] and Ecuador,[92] the Commerce Department basically considered the price of a fresh flower in Amsterdam and the price of a wilted flower in New York to be equivalent.[93] At the end of the day, flower mongers were faced with the choice of either selling their rapidly wilting flowers for whatever price they could get or throwing them away and receiving nothing. However, if they sold a wilting flower in the United States, the price they got was compared with the price they would get for a fresh flower sold in the country of origin.

The Commerce Department also compared the selling price of new forklift trucks in Japan and forklift trucks in the United States that were three years old.[94]

Comparing Prices in Dissimilar Markets

The Commerce Department sometimes compares the prices the exporting company receives in the U.S. market with those it receives in some third country market. Such comparisons are often made when the exporting country does not have much of a home market for its product. It penalized some Korean sweater companies because they sold their sweaters in the U.S. market for a little less than what they sold for in foreign markets. One company sold its sweaters for 1.20% less in the United States than in Mexico. Another company sold for 1.11% less in the United States than in Canada. A third company was found guilty for selling its sweaters for 0.73% less in the United States than in the United Kingdom.[95] In arriving at its guilty verdict, the Commerce Department conveniently ignored several facts — that each shipment of sweaters was a custom order and that there were significant differences in the sweaters the companies shipped to different countries. It merely assumed the sweaters were identical. Also, of course, it ignored any cases where the price in the United States was higher than the price in another country, which had the effect of understating the average U.S. price.[96]

This different market comparison is especially questionable when the product involves a nonmarket economy,[97] where prices cannot be determined with any degree of accuracy and the exchange rate calculation involves a currency that is not recognized beyond its own borders. For example, Polish golf carts were the subject of an antidumping investigation in 1975.[98] Whether they were being sold in the United States at a fair price could not be determined with reference to the prices charged in Poland (which has no golf courses[99]) or a third country because the carts were sold only in the United States. So, the investigator computed what it would cost a Canadian company to make similar golf carts and determined that Poland was dumping its golf carts in the U.S. market. A problem arose when the Canadian producer whose costs were being used in the computation went out of business the next year, because no other company made golf carts that could be used for comparison purposes with the Polish golf carts. Therefore, the investigator constructed some costs that would have existed if a producer in another country at about the same stage of economic development as Poland would have made carts (Spain was chosen). It was then determined, using these new cost calculations, that the Polish carts were not being dumped, with the result that the earlier antidumping finding was revoked in 1980.[100]

The use of surrogate countries to assess "fair value" is a dubious process, because countries at similar levels of economic development have differing relative prices and comparative advantage. In an AD case against potassium chloride imports from East Germany, the US Department of Commerce made a preliminary assessment, based on West German prices, of a 112 percent duty, but in the final assessment, based on Canadian prices, a zero margin was calculated and the case dismissed. In the Polish golf cart case the two surrogates led to opposite findings, illustrating the potentially arbitrary outcome of AD cases using this approach.[101]

This problem is inherent in any nonmarket economy. With the change in recent years of many nonmarket economies into market economies, one might think that this problem would be reduced, but the problem is not limited to nonmarket economies. Comparing prices and costs in one economy with those of another will always produce skewed results, because different economies have different comparative advantages. What might be relatively inexpensive to produce in one country might be relatively expensive to produce in another, even if the two countries are at the same level of economic development.

Another facet of this problem emerges if you pretend you are the foreign producer and are trying to determine what price to charge in the U.S. market. If you think that the Commerce Department might compare your prices and costs with those of another country, how can you determine which country it will choose, so you can make the correct pricing decision? Obviously, it is impossible. Who would have guessed that Canada (or Spain) would have been chosen as the surrogate country in the Polish golf cart case? Also, even if one could guess which country would be chosen as the surrogate, it would still be impossible to determine which costs the Commerce Department will choose to look at. The mere use of this questionable surrogate test increases instability into the international market.

Gary Horlick, who was Deputy Assistant Secretary of Commerce for Import Administration from 1981 to 1983, described the process to the Senate Finance Committee: "I can tell horror stories about how one goes about choosing a surrogate; it is usually done about 10 at night when one has run out of any reasonable alternative. Just to take an example, for Chinese shop towels we went through in order: Pakistan, Thailand, Malaysia, Hong Kong, the Dominican Republic, Colombia, and wound up with a hypothetical Chinese factory in India. It just doesn't make any sense."[102]

With such arbitrariness, it would be very easy for Commerce Department officials to choose a surrogate country that would result in the assessment of a dumping duty. "Selection of the surrogate country provides boundless opportunity for biasing the outcome, and there is more than a little evidence that Commerce has availed itself of this opportunity on several occasions."[103]

The Chinese manhole cover case provides an illustrative example of how attempts by a manufacturer to comply with U.S. law can be thwarted.[104] In 1986, the Commerce Department computed a dumping duty of 11% on Chinese manhole covers. It arrived at the 11% figure by comparing Chinese manhole cover prices with those of Belgium, Canada, France, and Japan. As a result, China raised its prices so that it would avoid future problems. However, in 1990, the Commerce Department reviewed its work, changed its methodology, and decided to retroactively raise the duty to 97%. It arrived at this figure by comparing Chinese prices with the imaginary price that would be charged in the Philippines. It ignored the fact that labor costs in the Philippines are much higher than those in China. As a result of this changed figure, Chinese companies were effectively banned from the U.S. market and faced with millions of dollars in dumping duties.

Another aspect of comparing costs in different countries is the quality or reliability of the data. In the case that Tinker Company initiated against a Hungarian manufacturer of tapered roller bearings and parts,[105] the Commerce Department chose Portugal as the surrogate country and got its cost data on Portugal from a telephone call someone at a U.S. consulate made to a Portuguese engineer, who gave an estimate of the Portuguese production cost for steel pipes, small motors, and steel hand tools. The embassy official also passed on the rumor he heard that factory material overhead in Portugal was between 40% and

45% and labor overhead was between 30% and 33%.[106] The final weighted average dumping margin was determined to be 7.42%.

The same day that Tinker initiated an action against Hungary, it initiated actions against Italy,[107] Japan,[108] the People's Republic of China,[109] Romania,[110] and Yugoslavia.[111] It determined the dumping margins in each case to be: Italy, 124.75%; Japan, various, on a case-by-case basis; People's Republic of China, 0.97%, on average; Romania, 8.7%, on average; Yugoslavia, 33.61%, on average. The Commerce Department got a 100% conviction rate, although its evidence was based on questionable data.

Comparing U.S. Wholesale and Foreign Retail Prices

Another criticism of the Commerce Department's pricing methodology is that it has been known to compare U.S. wholesale prices with foreign retail prices. Such comparisons often result in the appearance of dumping when none exists in fact. Motorola initiated an antidumping action against Toshiba for selling cellular mobile telephones and subassemblies for less than fair value.[112] When Toshiba sold in the Japanese market, it sold to small local dealers directly, but when it sold in the U.S. market, it sold to a single purchaser, who then resold to distributors. However, the Commerce Department did not take this fact into account in computing the appropriate dumping duty.

Disregarding Volume Discounts

It is standard practice for companies to give volume discounts for large purchases. Yet the Commerce Department has been known to disregard this fact when determining whether dumping has occurred. If a company charges a lower price for a large sale in the United States than for a small one in its own country, it can be found guilty of dumping. In an antidumping action initiated by the Specialty Tubing Group,[113] the Commerce Department compared the prices a Swedish company, Avesta, charged for small purchases of stainless steel pipe and tubing in Sweden with those charged for large purchases in the United States.[114] More than two-thirds of the sales in Sweden were for quantities of less than 500 kilograms. On small sales such as this, the company charged an average of over 22% more than for sales of quantities between 501 and 5,000 kilograms, and it charged more than 60% more for sales of less than 500 kilograms than for sales of over 5,000 kilograms. The company was found guilty of selling in the United States for less than fair value. The Commerce Department's reason for disregarding such differences is that such adjustments are not easy to make.[115]

Classifying Costs as Direct or Indirect

The classification of costs as direct or indirect has long been a problem for accountants. For example, depreciation expense may be treated as a direct product cost if the units of production method is used and as an indirect cost if the straight-line method is used. If a company has two identical machines, one depreciated under the units of production method and the other under the straight-line method, the depreciation for one machine will be treated as a direct cost and the other as an indirect cost, even though the machines perform the exact same function.

Accountants use cost accounting techniques to make management decisions, such as pricing, break-even points, profit margins, and so forth. One problem, which cannot really be overcome completely, is the problem of determining whether a particular cost is direct or indirect. Determining whether a particular cost is direct or indirect sometimes involves a certain amount of arbitrary decision making. However, when a particular company decides how a particular cost should be classified, whether direct or indirect, it usually treats the cost consistently throughout its operations. It does not treat it as direct for Department A and indirect for Department B or direct in one year and indirect in the next. This approach is in keeping with the basic accounting principles of consistency and comparability.

The Commerce Department is not bound by such rules. In arriving at a decision of whether a particular price is fair for antidumping purposes, an initial determination must be made regarding which costs are to be included in the price and which should be omitted. One criticism that has been made of the Commerce Department's approach to this calculation is that it often subtracts the sales costs a company incurs when it computes the U.S. sales price but includes similar sales costs when it computes the foreign market value.[116] Thus, the price in the United States is consistently understated whenever this approach is used.

The Commerce Department often imputes a cost for various reasons, for example, when the cost data are not available. In one case, it imputed the cost of carrying Brother typewriters in inventory in the United States but did not impute inventory carrying costs for Brother typewriters that were sold in Japan.[117] It justified not imputing an inventory cost for the Japanese market because it did not have any information with which to quantify the adjustment, but it did make an inventory carrying cost adjustment for the typewriters sold in the United States even though it had no information on that market, either. In another case, it subtracted the cost of shipping the product to regional warehouses in the United States from the U.S. price but did not subtract similar shipping costs incurred in Japan from the Japanese price; it reasoned that the Japanese costs were not attributable to specific sales under consideration.[118] In a case initiated by American Telephone and Telegraph Company and Comdial, Inc.,[119] the Commerce Department deducted from the U.S. price the cost of inland freight for Korean small business telephone systems sold in the United States but did not make a reduction for similar costs incurred in Korea.[120]

The companies initiating the antidumping actions sometimes try to convince the Commerce Department to adjust downward the U.S. price in order to create or increase a dumping duty. For example, in the suit initiated by Zenith against several Japanese television companies, Zenith tried, unsuccessfully, to convince the Commerce Department that it should subtract the Japanese companies' legal defense costs from its U.S. selling price, thus increasing the dumping charge. In effect, this would have resulted in making the Japanese U.S. prices increasingly unfair as they continued to incur legal defense costs.[121]

Another inconsistency is in the way the Commerce Department classifies warranty costs. Foreign companies that contract out their warranty costs have them classified as direct selling expenses, but companies that provide their own warranty services have their warranty expenses split between direct (allowable) and indirect (nonallowable) costs. Both the Court of International Trade and the General Accounting Office have called this practice unfair.[122]

Using Average Prices

Merely selling a product in the United States for the same price it sells for at home is not sufficient to avoid a dumping charge. The Commerce Department can allege dumping anyway because of the way it computes selling price. One common methodology it uses is to compute the average foreign price over a six-month period with individual domestic prices. It's another way to compare apples with oranges.

It is rare for a company to sell a particular product at the same price in all locations at all times during a 6- or 12-month period. It is far more common to find a range of prices. However, if a company sells *any* product in the United States at a price that is below the average foreign price for the period under investigation, it will give the Commerce Department the ammunition it needs to compute a dumping margin.[123] Also, if the price charged for a product is not uniform — if it varies — the chances are that about half of the units sold will be below average in price and, thus, subject to penalty. The use of average prices to determine the existence of dumping is inherently unfair.[124]

In the 1989 Tokyo Juki investigation, the Commerce Department found that the company sold a few typewriters for less than "fair value," although the vast majority of typewriters were sold for more than "fair value" (which leads to an interesting question — why would anyone buy something for more than fair value?). The Commerce Department saw fit to ignore the vast majority of sales that were above the minimum (safe) price and assessed a 0.0004% dumping margin on the company, which amounts to less than a tenth of a cent difference between the price charged for a typewriter in Japan and that charged in the United States. Usually, the Commerce Department's band of tolerance is 0.5%, but that figure applies only to initial investigations. Because Tokyo Juki was previously investigated for dumping, the 0.5% tolerance did not apply.[125]

The Commerce Department's average pricing method has been controversial. The General Accounting Office has criticized the method because it tends to increase existing margins or create margins where none previously existed.[126] The Court of International Trade has said that the Commerce Department's price comparison method is not reasonably fair.[127]

When Congress amended the 1979 provision to authorize Commerce under § 1677f-1 to average both U.S. price and foreign market value in making comparisons, Congress did not direct Commerce to apply a stricter set of prerequisites when ascertaining the U.S. price. Legislative history discloses that by extending the use of averaging with respect to the U.S. price, the lawmakers wanted to "expand the instances in which the administering authority may use sampling and averaging techniques." H.Rep. No. 725, 98th Cong., 2d Sess. 45, *reprinted* in 1984 U.S. Code Cong. & Admin. News 5127, 5172 (1984). Despite this, it appears that Commerce almost universally averages only the foreign market value. The Court questions whether the impact of Commerce's current averaging policy relieves administrative burden to the extent that it leads to "loss of reasonable fairness in the results."[128]

The method the Commerce Department uses to average prices results in a consistent bias that tends to increase the dumping margin. Rather than comparing average prices in the United States with average prices in some foreign country, it compares the average foreign country market value with the price at which each sale is made in the United States. When sales are made at a price above fair value, it treats them as if made at fair value and assigns a less than fair value amount of zero rather than a negative value. Therefore, when it combines sales made at less than fair value with those made at more than fair value, it skews the statistical result in favor of a higher dumping margin.[129] In some cases, the result is a dumping margin where none should exist.

NOTES

    1.   Revenue Act of 1916, chap. 463, §§ 800–1, 39 Stat. 798, codified at 15 U.S.C. §72. Richard Dale points out that the Sherman Antitrust Act (1890) and section 73 of the Wilson Tariff Act of 1894 could have been applied to dumping situations. See Richard Dale, *Anti-dumping Law in a Liberal Trade Order* (New York: St. Martin's Press, 1980), p. 12.

2.   Michael S. Knoll, "United States Antidumping Law: The Case for Reconsideration," *Texas International Law Journal* 22 (1987): 265–90.

3.   Dale, *Anti-Dumping Law in a Liberal Trade Order*, p. 12; Jacob Viner, *Dumping: A Problem in International Trade* (Chicago, Ill.: University of Chicago Press, 1923), pp. 242–46.

4.   15 U.S.C. §72.

5.   This is pointed out in Note, "Managing Dumping in a Global Economy," *George Washington Journal of International Law & Economics* 21 (1988): 511. The case in question was *Zenith Radio Corp.* v. *Matsushita Elec. Indus. Co.*, 513 F. Supp. 1100, 1120 (E.D. Pa. 1981), 723 F.2d 238 (3d Cir., 1983), 475 U.S. 574 (1986). Michael S. Knoll states that there was only one (unsuccessful) prosecution under the 1916 Act for the first 50 years. Knoll, "United States Antidumping Law," p. 268. A. Paul Victor, "Antidumping and Antitrust: Can the Inconsistencies Be Resolved?" *N.Y.U. Journal of International Law and Politics* 15 (1983): 339–50, gives a history of prosecutions under this act and reviews the relationship between the U.S. antitrust and antidumping laws.

6.   15 U.S.C. § 72 (emphasis in original).

7.   15 U.S.C. § 72.

8.   Antidumping Act of 1921, Pub. L. No. 67-10, 42 Stat. 11, codified as amended at 19 U.S.C. §§ 160–71.

9.   Congressional Record, May 4, 1921, p. 1021, quoted in James Bovard, *The Fair Trade Fraud: How Congress Pillages the Consumer and Decimates American Competitiveness* (New York: St. Martin's Press, 1991), p. 113.

10.   Knoll, "United States Antidumping Law," p. 269.

11.   Ibid.

12.   Trade Act of 1974, 19 U.S.C. § 160 (1976).

13.   Trade Agreements Act of 1979, Pub. L. No. 96-39, tit. I, § 106(a), 93 Stat. 193, codified at 19 U.S.C. §§ 1673–73i, 19 U.S.C.A. §§ 1673–73i (1980 & 1992 Supp.).

14.   The Smoot-Hawley Tariff Act of 1930, Pub. L. No. 71-361, 46 Stat. 590, 19 U.S.C. §§ 1671–77g, 19 U.S.C.A. §§ 1673–73i (1980 & 1992 Supp.).

15.   Hans F. Sennholz, *Age of Inflation* (Belmont, Mass.: Western Islands, 1979), pp. 52, 128; Murray N. Rothbard, *America's Great Depression* (Los Angeles, Calif.: Nash Publishing, 1963, 1972), pp. 213–15; Christian Saint-Etienne, *The Great Depression 1929–1938: Lessons for the 1980s* (Stanford, Calif.: Hoover Institution Press, 1984), p. 29.

16.   James Bovard, *The Farm Fiasco* (San Francisco, Calif.: ICS Press, 1989), p. 23.

17.   See S. Rep. No. 249, 96th Congress, 1st Session, pp. 60–61, reprinted in *1979 U.S. Code Cong. & Admin. News*, pp. 446–47.

18.   Bovard, *The Fair Trade Fraud*, p. 114.

19.   Note, "Managing Dumping in a Global Economy," p. 512.

20.   Ibid., p. 513.

21.   For a discussion of the injury test as applied to actual antidumping and countervailing duty cases between 1980 and 1984, see A. Paul Victor, "Injury Determinations by the United States International Trade Commission in Antidumping and Countervailing Duty Proceedings," *New York University Journal of International Law and Politics* 16 (1984): 749–70.

22.   19 U.S.C.A. 1671b(a) (1980 & 1992 Supp.).

23.   19 U.S.C. § 1671(b), 19 U.S.C.A. §§ 1671b (1980 & 1992 Supp.).

24.   19 U.S.C. § 1303(a)(1); 19 U.S.C.A. §1303(a)(1) (1980 & 1992 Supp.); Knoll, "United States Antidumping Law," p. 269.

25.   Knoll, "United States Antidumping Law," p. 269; Victor, "Antidumping and Antitrust," pp. 347–48.

26. Knoll, "United States Antidumping Law," pp. 269–70.

27. Agreement on the Implementation of Article VI of the General Agreement on Tariffs and Trade, June 30, 1967, art. 2, 19 U.S.T. 4348, 4348–49, T.I.A.S. No. 6431, pp. 3–4, 651 U.N.T.S. 320, 322, 324.

28. Bovard, *The Fair Trade Fraud*, p. 114.

29. N. David Palmeter, "Torquemada and the Tariff Act: The Inquisitor Rides Again," *International Lawyer* 20 (1986): 641.

30. 1930 Tariff Act, §§ 733 and 735, 19 U.S.C. § 1673b, 19 U.S.C.A. § 1673b (1980 & 1992 Supp.).

31. The procedure actually can be a bit more complicated than that, and the final determination by the ITC may be made as late as 420 days after the petition is filed. For the specifics, see U.S. International Trade Commission, *Summary of Statutory Provisions Related to Import Relief* (Washington, D.C.: U.S. International Trade Commission, n.d.), pp. 8–16.

32. Palmeter, "Torquemada and the Tariff Act," p. 644.

33. Ibid., p. 646.

34. At least one commentator has called for the abolition of the Court of International Trade because the multilayer review process that results from its existence is too time-consuming and costly. He suggests that its duties can be performed just as well by administrative law judges and regular district courts, with appellate review. See Kevin C. Kennedy, "A Proposal to Abolish the U.S. Court of International Trade," *Dickinson Journal of International Law* 14 (1985): 13–37.

35. Palmeter, "Torquemada and the Tariff Act," pp. 646–47.

36. James Bovard, "U.S. Protectionists Claim a Russian Victim," *Wall Street Journal*, June 8, 1992, p. A-10. For more on the antidumping investigation that was filed in November 1991 against Soviet uranium importers by U.S. mining interests, see U.S. General Accounting Office, *Uranium Enrichment: Unresolved Trade Issues Leave Uncertain Future for U.S. Uranium Industry*, GAO/RCED-92-194, June 19, 1992; U.S. International Trade Commission, *Uranium from the U.S.S.R.*, Investigation 731-TA-539, Publication No. 2471, December 1991.

37. U.S. International Trade Commission, *Uranium from the U.S.S.R.*

38. Bovard, "U.S. Protectionists Claim a Russian Victim." Some of this information is also reported in the Federal Register, Vol. 56, No. 234, December 5, 1991, pp. 63711–12, reproduced in U.S. International Trade Commission, *Uranium from the U.S.S.R.*

39. Bovard, *The Fair Trade Fraud*, p. 135.

40. James Bovard, "No Justice in Anti-Dumping," *New York Times*, January 28, 1990, p. F13.

41. Investigation 731-TA-426, listed in I. M. Destler, *American Trade Politics* (Washington, D.C.: Institute for International Economics, 1992), p. 393.

42. Bovard, *The Fair Trade Fraud*, p. 136.

43. Tariff Act of 1930, §776, 19 U.S.C. 1677e, 19 U.S.C.A. §§ 1677e (1980 & 1992 Supp.).

44. Knoll, "United States Antidumping Law," p. 280.

45. Bovard, *The Fair Trade Fraud*, p. 137.

46. Ibid., p. 138.

47. Ibid., pp. 138–39, listed in Destler, *American Trade Politics*, p. 396. Investigation 731-TA-448, filed September 22, 1989. More information on this investigation may be found in U.S. International Trade Commission, *Sweaters*, Publication No. 2312 (1990) and *Sweaters (Hong Kong, Republic of Korea, Taiwan)*, Publication No. 2311 (1990).

48. Bovard, *The Fair Trade Fraud*, p. 139.

49. Ibid., p. 155.

50.　For example, see *Algoma Steel Corp.* v. *United States*, 865 F.2d 240, 241 (Fed. Cir.), cert. denied, 492 U.S. 919 (1989).

51.　At least two commentators take the position that the Commerce Department has the sole statutory power to make standing determinations. See Edwin J. Madaj and Charles H. Nalls, "Bifurcation without Direction: The United States International Trade Commission and the Question of Petitioner Standing in Antidumping and Countervailing Duty Cases," *Law & Policy in International Business* 22 (1991): 673–88. Curiously, both authors of this article are employees of the ITC.

52.　For more on this point, see N. David Palmeter, "Exchange Rates and Antidumping Determinations," *Journal of World Trade* 22 (1988): 73–80.

53.　If 1.6DM =$1, then 1.0DM =$0.625 (1.0/1.6) and 2.0DM = $1.25 (2 x $0.625).

54.　Investigation No. 731-TA-431, initiated March 29, 1989. Bovard, *The Fair Trade Fraud*, pp. 116–17; Destler, *American Trade Politics*, p. 394; U.S. International Trade Commission, *Dry Aluminum Sulfate from Sweden*, Publication No. 2174 (March 1989).

55.　It has been suggested that a different methodology would be more appropriate when there is hyperinflation. See Gilbert B. Kaplan, Lynn G. Kamarck, and Marie Parker, "Cost Analysis under the Antidumping Law," *George Washington Journal of International Law and Economics* 21 (1988): 357–418.

56.　Bovard, *The Fair Trade Fraud*, p. 117.

57.　Palmeter, "Exchange Rates and Antidumping Determinations," raises this point. The present author was unable to find anything in the literature that explores the legality of the Commerce Department's delegation of authority to the Federal Reserve Bank. An exploration of this issue would make an interesting article.

58.　Bovard, *The Fair Trade Fraud*, pp. 117–18.

59.　731-TA-329, initiated May 21, 1986. Bovard, *The Fair Trade Fraud*, p. 118; Destler, *American Trade Politics*, p. 374; U.S. International Trade Commission, *Fresh Cut Flowers*, Publication No. 2119 (1988).

60.　Palmeter, "Exchange Rates and Antidumping Determinations" (italics in original).

61.　Ibid., p. 77, raises this point.

62.　*Luciano Pisoni Fabrica Accessori* v. *United States*, 640 F. Supp. 255, 260-61 (CIT 1986).

63.　Kaplan, Kamarck, and Parker, "Cost Analysis under the Antidumping Law," p. 358.

64.　19 U.S.C.A. § 1677b(e)(1)(B)(ii) (1980 & 1992 Supp.).

65.　19 U.S.C.A. § 1677b(e)(1)(A) (1980 & 1992 Supp.).

66.　19 U.S.C.A. § 1677b(e)(1)(B)(i) (1980 & 1992 Supp.).

67.　Bovard, *The Fair Trade Fraud*, p. 126.

68.　19 U.S.C.A. § 1677b(e)(1)(B)(ii) (1980 & 1992 Supp.).

69.　19 U.S.C.A. § 1677b(e)(1)(C) (1980 & 1992 Supp.).

70.　Bovard, *The Fair Trade Fraud*, p. 127.

71.　Kaplan, Kamarck, and Parker, "Cost Analysis under the Antidumping Law," p. 394.

72.　Bovard, *The Fair Trade Fraud*, p. 128.

73.　U.S. Department of Commerce, Administrative Hearing, Certain Red Raspberries from Canada, Investigation No. A-122-401, March 22, 1985, p. 33, cited in Bovard, *The Fair Trade Fraud*, pp. 128, 164 .

74.　Ibid., pp. 128–29.

75.　This investigation (731-TA-449) was initiated by the National Knitwear and Sportswear Association on September 22, 1989. Reported in Destler, *American Trade Politics*, p. 396.

76. Bovard, *The Fair Trade Fraud*, p. 129.

77. Ibid.

78. Ibid., p. 130.

79. Ibid.

80. Charles T. Horngren and Gary L. Sundem, *Introduction to Management Accounting* (Englewood Cliffs, N.J.: Prentice-Hall, 1987) pp. 98–99.

81. This 25% figure was arrived at by Motorola in the Commerce Department's 1985–86 investigation of the semiconductor industry. See Bovard, *The Fair Trade Fraud*, p. 130.

82. Horngren and Sundem, *Introduction to Management Accounting*, pp. 136–37.

83. The depreciation chapter of any good financial accounting or intermediate accounting text will illustrate several acceptable depreciation methods, including the ones discussed here. Taxation texts also discuss this topic at length.

84. This investigation is discussed in Bovard, *The Fair Trade Fraud*, p. 119.

85. *Luciano Pisoni Fabrica Accessori Instrumenti Musicali* v. *United States*, 640 F.Supp. 255 (CIT 1986).

86. Bovard, *The Fair Trade Fraud*, pp. 119–20.

87. Ibid., p. 121.

88. 731-TA-329, initiated May 21, 1986, by the Floral Trade Council. Destler, *American Trade Politics*, p. 374.

89. This investigation was not listed in Destler, *American Trade Politics*, as an antidumping investigation. However, Destler does list antidumping investigations taken against Canada, Costa Rica, Mexico, and Peru by the Floral Trade Council on May 21, 1986, on pp. 374–76 and does list the Netherlands and several other countries as being on the receiving end of countervailing duty investigations initiated by the Floral Trade Council on May 21, 1986, on pp. 315–17.

90. Investigation 731-TA-332, initiated May 21, 1986, by the Floral Trade Council. Destler, *American Trade Politics*, p. 375.

91. Investigation 731-TA-328, initiated May 21, 1986, by the Floral Trade Council. Destler, *American Trade Politics*, p. 374.

92. Investigation 731-TA-331, initiated May 21, 1986, by the Floral Trade Council. Destler, *American Trade Politics*, p. 375.

93. Bovard, *The Fair Trade Fraud*, p. 120.

94. Ibid. This investigation (731-TA-377) was initiated by Hyster Co. of Portland on April 22, 1987; reported by Destler, *American Trade Politics*, p. 383.

95. Bovard, *The Fair Trade Fraud*, p. 121. These investigations (731-TA-449) were initiated by the National Knitwear and Sportswear Association on September 22, 1989. Destler, *American Trade Politics*, p. 396.

96. Bovard, *The Fair Trade Fraud*, pp. 121–22.

97. For a discussion of the measurement problems involved with a nonmarket economy, see Kaplan, Kamarck, and Parker, "Cost Analysis under the Antidumping Law," pp. 410–14.

98. Richard Pomfret, *International Trade: An Introduction to Theory and Policy* (Oxford: Basil Blackwell, 1991), p. 133. Polish golf carts were also the subject of a case, *Outboard Marine Corp.* v. *Pezetel*, 461 F. Supp. 384 (D. Del. 1978).

99. Victor, "Antidumping and Antitrust," p. 343, makes this point.

100. In *Outboard Marine Corp.* v. *Pezetel*, 461 F. Supp. 384, 409–10 (D. Del. 1978), the judge reasoned that in applying the 1916 Antidumping Act [15 U.S.C. § 72], the law requires that the import price must be compared with some *actual* foreign market price in order to establish whether dumping had occurred. Because there was no home market for the Polish golf carts and because they were sold only in the

United States, there was no foreign price to compare with the U.S. price. Therefore, there could be no dumping.

101. Pomfret, *International Trade*, p. 133.

102. Bovard, *The Fair Trade Fraud*, p. 132, quoting U.S. Congress, Senate Committee on Finance, *Nonmarket Economy Imports Legislation*, May 7, 1984 (Washington, D.C.: Government Printing Office, 1984), p. 18.

103. Bovard, *The Fair Trade Fraud*, p. 132, quoting Ronald A. Cass and Stephen J. Narkin, *Antidumping and Countervailing Duty Law: The United States and the GATT*, Conference on the Commerce Department's Administration of the Trade Remedy Laws (Washington, D.C.: Brookings Institution, 1990), p. 22.

104. Bovard, *The Fair Trade Fraud*, pp. 133–34.

105. Investigation 731-TA-341, initiated August 25, 1986, listed in Destler, *American Trade Politics*, p. 377. The details of this investigation are included in U.S. International Trade Commission, *Tapered Roller Bearings and Parts Thereof and Certain Housings Incorporating Tapered Rollers from Hungary*, Publication No. 2245 (December 1989).

106. Bovard, *The Fair Trade Fraud*, p. 133.

107. Investigation 731-TA-342. Details of the Italy and Yugoslavia investigations can be found in U.S. International Trade Commission, *Tapered Roller Bearings (Italy, Yugoslavia)*, Publication No. 1999 (1987).

108. Investigation 731-TA-343.

109. Investigation 731-TA-344.

110. Investigation 731-TA-345.

111. Investigation 731-TA-346, listed in Destler, *American Trade Politics*, pp. 377–78.

112. Bovard, *The Fair Trade Fraud*, p. 122; Dumping Investigation 731-TA-207, initiated November 5, 1984.

113. Antidumping Investigation 731-TA-354, initiated October 20, 1986, reported in Destler, *American Trade Politics*, p. 379. The Specialty Tubing Group also filed a countervailing duty investigation against Avesta on September 4, 1986 (Investigation 701-TA-281). See Destler, *American Trade Politics*, p. 318. In this investigation, there were affirmative preliminary injury and subsidy determinations, net subsidy 1.24% ad valorem (December 5, 1986); affirmative final subsidy determination, net subsidy 2.18% ad valorem (February 26, 1987); negative final injury determination (April 3, 1987). Also see U.S. International Trade Commission, *Stainless Steel Pipes and Tubes*, Publication No. 1919 (1986).

114. Destler, *American Trade Politics*, pp. 122–23.

115. Bovard, *The Fair Trade Fraud*, p. 123.

116. Ibid.

117. Ibid., pp. 123–24.

118. Ibid., p. 124.

119. Investigation 731-TA-427, initiated December 28, 1988. AT&T and Comdial initiated similar investigations against Taiwan (731-TA-428) and Japan (731-TA-426) the same day. Reported in Destler, *American Trade Politics*, p. 393; also see U.S. International Trade Commission, *Certain Telephone Systems and Subassemblies Thereof from Korea*, Publication No. 2254 (January 1990).

120. Bovard, *The Fair Trade Fraud*, p. 124.

121. Ibid., pp. 124–25.

122. Ibid., p. 125.

123. Ibid., pp. 120–21.

124. Wesley K. Caine, "A Case for Repealing the Antidumping Provisions of the Tariff Act of 1930," *Law & Policy in International Business* 13 (1981): 681–726, makes this point.

125.   Bovard, *The Fair Trade Fraud*, p. 121.

126.   U.S. General Accounting Office, *U.S. Administration of the Antidumping Act of 1921* 21 (March 15, 1979), mentioned in Bovard, *The Fair Trade Fraud*, pp. 122, 163.

127.   *NAR, S.p.A.* v. *United States*, 707 F.Supp. 553 (CIT 1989), also cited in Bovard, *The Fair Trade Fraud*, pp. 122, 163.

128.   *NAR, S.p.A.* v. *United States*, 707 F.Supp. 553, 559 (CIT 1989).

129.   Knoll, "United States Antidumping Law," p. 278.

8

Some Examples of Dumping

AUTOS

The auto industry is one of the most prominent examples that can be given where special interests (the auto industry and the auto unions) seek the assistance of government to shelter them from the effects of foreign competition. The protection has taken many forms, ranging from tariffs and quotas to allegations of dumping. One of the more recent examples involving allegations of dumping in the auto industry is the case of Japanese minivans. On the basis of a preliminary investigation brought by General Motors, Ford, and Chrysler[1] that alleged dumping margins of between 5.4% and 30.5%,[2] the ITC determined that there was a reasonable indication that a U.S. industry was materially injured because of Japanese minivans that were allegedly sold in the United States for less than fair value. It based its preliminary determination on the basis of the best available information.[3]

The ITC's final determination, though, was that no domestic industry was materially injured or threatened with material injury as a result of Japanese minivan imports,[4] although the ITC found that more than 90% of the home market sales were made at prices below the cost of production.[5] It reached its not guilty finding by comparing U.S. sales of new minivans with fair market value based on constructed value. The computations the ITC used to arrive at its findings were extremely complex and, in some cases, of questionable validity from an accounting standpoint.[6] It is one of the few cases where a foreign producer was found not guilty, but the case is not over yet. General Motors, Ford, and Chrysler have appealed.

Regardless of the legal outcome of the dumping case, Detroit's auto makers believe they've already scored a victory in the market by pressuring Japanese companies to boost the prices of their vehicles. "On dumping, we've already won that one," Chrysler Chairman Lee A. Iacocca said in an interview yesterday. "They [Japanese auto makers] have raised their prices 12%."[7]

This victory snatched from the jaws of defeat means that the Big-3 automakers will feel less pressured to compete on price because the Japanese minivan makers feel compelled to raise their prices in order to avoid being hit with an antidumping penalty. The only loser is the U.S. consumer, who must now pay 12% more for a Toyota minivan or somewhat more for a U.S.-made minivan.[8]

There have been several other investigations of dumping in the auto industry. For example, Southampton Coachworks, Ltd., initiated an investigation of Canadian limousine dumping.[9] The ITC found the weighted average dumping margin to be 5.78%. Polaris Industries initiated an investigation against Japanese manufacturers of all-terrain vehicles. Although the ITC determined that the vehicles were being sold for less than market value, no injury to a U.S. producer was found.[10]

STEEL

Foreign imports of steel and steel products have been subject to many dumping investigations in recent years. Bethlehem Steel Corporation initiated an antidumping investigation against Canadian producers of new steel rail.[11] The ITC found a preliminary weighted average dumping margin of 2.72% and a final injury and determination margin of 38.79%. Wyman-Gordon Corporation initiated investigations against Brazilian,[12] German,[13] Japanese,[14] and United Kingdom[15] manufacturers of forged steel crankshafts. The ITC found dumping margins and injury in some cases but not in others. The dumping margins ranged from 1.9% to 14.67%. Several steel companies initiated an antidumping investigation against Chinese,[16] Polish,[17] and Yugoslavian[18] manufacturers of steel wire nails. A dumping margin of 6.3% was found against the Chinese companies; the other two cases were withdrawn. Several steel companies also initiated investigations against Polish,[19] Portuguese,[20] and Venezuelan[21] manufacturers of carbon steel wire rod. The preliminary investigations revealed that a U.S. company was injured. All three cases were later terminated. The ITC also terminated three investigations initiated by U.S. Steel Corporation against Austrian,[22] Romanian,[23] and Venezuelan[24] manufacturers of oil country tubular goods. Numerous other examples could be given.

In one recent example, the ITC reached a preliminary determination to continue 76 of the 84 cases it had opened on imported flat-rolled steel. These cases involve 6.5 million tons of steel having an annual value of almost $3 billion.[25] Of the 21 countries under investigation, only Taiwan has been cleared. The cases the ITC decided to drop represented only 5% of the imports listed in the petitions, based on tonnage and dollar value. These cases originated on June 30, 1992, when 12 U.S. flat-rolled steel producers filed 48 antidumping petitions and 36 countervailing duty petitions, alleging serious and material injury. The companies were feeling pressure from the foreign producers partly as a result of the lapsing of voluntary restraint agreements a few months previously[26] and from the collapse of discussions to form a Multilateral Steel Agreement. A final determination of injury could lead to tariffs of between $600 million and $900 million on foreign steel.

Two of the six commissioners told the steel companies that the evidence presented was weak and that their cases would have to be stronger in the future. However, even though the cases of dumping are weak, they may still be having some effect. As USX Chairman Charles Corry said, "If you're going into my hen house and stealing my eggs, and I accuse you of that before a magistrate, probably you're not going to keep going into my hen house tonight and next week and next week."[27] The mere fact that a dumping action has been instigated will probably place a chilling effect on the foreign steel companies. Many of them may decide to raise their prices just to avoid future antidumping investigations, even if they are found innocent this time. The probability that they will engage in aggressive price competition will be greatly reduced. Even if the foreign steel producers do not raise their prices, domestic steel prices might increase anyway. According to John Jacobson, a steel industry consultant, these antidumping actions might reduce steel imports by as much as 19%, which could boost prices by 5% to 10%.[28]

Filing of the petition is having some adverse effects on the domestic steel industry. Although the petitioners refrained from filing petitions against their Korean and Japanese joint venture partners, the partners are irritated by the antidumping action. A spokesman for Korea's Pohang Iron & Steel Company said the petitions put its California joint venture with USX in jeopardy. As a result, hundreds or, perhaps, thousands of jobs could be at stake. The filings could also lead to retaliation. The Canadian government is starting to investigate retaliatory complaints. Companies that use steel also stand to lose, because their raw material prices are likely to increase, making them less competitive on world markets and possibly leading to job losses.

TEXTILES

The U.S. textile industry is known for filing dumping petitions. The National Knitwear and Sportswear Association has filed petitions against sweater manufacturers in Hong Kong,[29] Korea[30] and Taiwan.[31] In all three cases, dumping was found. Century Martial Arts Supplies, Inc., filed a petition against martial arts uniform manufacturers in Taiwan. The ITC found that the uniforms were being sold in the United States for less than fair value but did not find any injury to a domestic producer.[32] The Headwear Institute of America initiated an investigation against sewn cloth headgear from the People's Republic of China. It was determined that the product was sold for less than market value, although no injury to a U.S. producer could be proven.[33]

One major development in the textile industry in 1990 was the large decline in the number of sweater shipments. Sweater imports fell by more than 20% in volume and value (by $573 million) based on 1989 levels.[34] The decline was attributed to a soft sweater market, a shift in fashion to other knit goods, and the antidumping petitions that were filed against sweater manufacturers in Hong Kong, Taiwan, and Korea. Sweater imports from these three countries fell substantially — by 41% in 1990 — and their share of imports slid ten percentage points, to 44%. However, although there have been a number of antidumping and countervailing duty actions initiated against foreign textile companies, most of the trade restrictions that have been placed on the textile industry have been from tariffs and quotas rather than from dumping and subsidy actions.[35]

AGRICULTURAL PRODUCTS

Frozen Concentrated Orange Juice

In 1986, Florida Citrus Mutual brought an antidumping action against a Brazilian company for dumping frozen concentrated orange juice on the U.S. market.[36] The company was found guilty of dumping it on the market for 1.96% less than fair value (the price it sold for in Brazil). What was curious is how the Commerce Department arrived at the 1.96% figure, because the sales price was at least 45% higher in the United States than in Brazil. In order to arrive at the unfairly low selling price in the United States, the Commerce Department subtracted the 40% tariff that is imposed on orange juice, the Brazilian government's 3.5% export tax, and a few percentage points for shipping, freight, and insurance.[37] Therefore, even though the selling price in the United States was at least 45% higher than the price in Brazil, the company was found guilty of dumping.

Pistachio Nuts

In 1985, the California Pistachio Commission initiated an action against an Iranian company for selling in-shell pistachio nuts in the United States for less than fair value.[38] The Commerce Department computed the dumping margin to be 317%, which means that the Iranians sold $4.17 worth of nuts for $1 in the U.S. market. The only problem was that the Commerce Department used the official Iranian exchange rate of 90 rials to the dollar when it made its computation, whereas the real-world exchange rate was 600 rials to the dollar. The U.S. Court of International Trade concluded that the official rate was irrelevant and threw out the case.[39]

Kiwifruit

Imports of kiwifruit from New Zealand are also under attack. On April 25, 1991, the Ad Hoc Committee for Fair Trade of the California Kiwifruit Commission and several individual California kiwifruit growers filed a petition with the ITC,[40] alleging that an industry in the United States was materially injured or threatened with material injury because of New Zealand fresh kiwifruit being sold for less than fair value.[41] Most of the growers who completed the ITC questionnaire said that the large shipments of kiwifruit from New Zealand in December 1990 caused a delay of their kiwifruit sales and resulted in lower prices for kiwifruit. Of the 67 responding U.S. growers, 64 said that they anticipated a negative impact from New Zealand kiwifruit imports.[42] In its preliminary investigation,[43] the ITC determined that there was a reasonable indication of injury.

It arrived at its preliminary conclusion by using a constructed value methodology.[44] The petitioners based their estimates of U.S. prices on actual invoices and customer orders. They then adjusted the U.S. price for foreign inland freight, foreign brokerage and handling, ocean freight, marine insurance, U.S. Customs user fees, U.S. brokerage and handling charges, U.S. inland freight, and U.S. selling expenses, such as advertising, financing, marketing, and other selling expenses.

The petitioners claimed that evidence of less than fair market value prices was present regardless of whether U.S. prices are compared with home market prices, third country prices, or constructed value. However, they claimed that home market prices could not be used as the basis for estimating foreign market value because the home market was not viable; the majority of the kiwifruit sold in the home market was not of comparable quality and was, therefore, not similar to that exported to the United States; and home market sales of kiwifruit of comparable quality were made at prices below the cost of production. The petitioners also argued that third country prices should not be used to compare with U.S. prices because they, too, are below the cost of production. At this point, any rational individual might question how an industry could stay in business if it sold its product at prices below the cost of production both in the home market and abroad. One might also ask how consumers are harmed if this is true. However, such questions have no place in an ITC investigation.

The petitioners based their dumping margin estimates on constructed value, which consists of the cost of production, general expenses, packing, and profit. They obtained cost of production figures from various studies and reports published by the New Zealand Ministry of

Agriculture and Fisheries and the New Zealand Kiwifruit Marketing Board. To arrive at constructed value, the petitioners added the statutory 10% for selling, general, and administrative expenses to the cost of production and an 8% profit margin.[45] They then subtracted packing, principal repayments, and general expenses from grower costs and added general expenses from one of the New Zealand studies because they exceeded the statutory 10%. They then added the 8% profit margin and the packing expenses that were deducted from the grower costs.

On the basis of these calculations, the petitioners arrived at a dumping margin of 255.02%. Some ITC adjustments whittled that margin down to 220%. With such high dumping margins, one might wonder how the industry could stay in business year after year. One might question the accuracy of such a high figure. However, the ITC did not question its accuracy; it decided to move forward with its investigation.

The final investigation found that fresh kiwifruit from New Zealand was being, or was likely to be, sold in the United States at less than fair value.[46] It determined the dumping margin to be 98.6%.[47]

The data upon which the grower information was based were from the responses to questionnaires that were sent to 204 of the 572 domestic kiwifruit growers, selected as a stratified random sample.[48] Packers, cold storers, and handlers also received questionnaires.[49] The Hayward variety of kiwifruit was the only variety compared, because the Hayward variety is the only variety that is grown on a commercial basis worldwide. It is the kind grown both in New Zealand and California, so the products being compared were similar, although some purchasers who returned the ITC questionnaire indicated that the New Zealand variety was often superior to the U.S. product in terms of size, shape, color, consistency, and shelf life.[50]

New Zealand kiwifruit represents about 90% of all kiwifruit imports to the United States.[51] About 600 farmers grow kiwifruit in California, which represents 99% of U.S. production.[52] About 79 firms pack kiwifruit in California, and roughly 50 handlers are active in the California kiwifruit trade.[53] It was these three groups — growers, packers, and handlers — that stood to be injured as a result of New Zealand imports.

The methodology the ITC used in its final determination was somewhat different from that used in the preliminary investigation. For example, it decided to use a third country market for comparison purposes, a methodology that it rejected at the preliminary stage of the investigation. The country it chose was Japan.[54] It decided to use the best information available to determine cost of production because it did not receive all the information it requested from New Zealand growers. From an examination of the cost of production data, the ITC determined that between 10% and 90% of the respondent's sales were at prices above the total cost of production.[55] (The only respondent was the New Zealand Kiwifruit Marketing Board [NZKMB]).

A number of criticisms could be made about the way in which the dumping margin was determined.[56] For example, NZKMB argued that Germany, rather than Japan, should have been used as the third country market for comparison purposes because the German market has more in common with the U.S. market than does the Japanese market. It said that German sales are a closer match because they provide more matches by time period, count size, and packing type. Furthermore, the Japanese and U.S. markets have different pricing mechanisms, organization, and levels of development, and NZKMB does not control sales from cool stores in Japan as it does in the United States. The market organization in Japan has a significant effect on Japanese kiwifruit prices. NZKMB has an earlier upstream exit from the sales process in Japan, whereas in Germany and the United States, the first unrelated sale takes place farther downstream, after importation. Japan also has higher retail prices, which allows it to charge a higher price to importers. The ITC chose Japan because it was New Zealand's largest third country market. It found that the differences between the German and Japanese markets were not significant.

The NZKMB contended that the ITC should only compare U.S. sales with contemporaneous Japanese sales — those within six days of the U.S. sale or, at least, within the same month or pricing period — because kiwifruit is perishable. As support for its position, it cited the Mexican vegetable case,[57] the Canadian white potato case,[58] and the Norwegian salmon case,[59] where the ITC compared prices for the same time period.

The NZKMB wanted the ITC to exclude from its computations the U.S. sales that were shipped from the Pioneer Reefer. It wanted these sales to be classified as distress sales, because the fruit was in danger of rotting and had to be sold at a deep discount. The ITC responded that although it had the authority to exclude aberrational sales from the comparison, it had no obligation to do so.

The NZKMB argued that because kiwifruit is a perishable product, the Commerce Department should disregard sales that are below the cost of production only if such sales exceed 50% of total sales volume. To support its argument, it cited the Canadian potato case, in which the 50% ratio was used. The Ad Hoc Committee argued that a 10% threshold is appropriate for kiwifruit. It supported its position by pointing to the Mexican vegetable case, where the Commerce Department allowed below cost sales of up to 50% for products for which the sellers were unable to control output or storage and for which below cost selling is a normal part of operations. It pointed out that in the Norwegian salmon case, the Commerce Department determined that the 10% threshold was appropriate because salmon farmers could control the time of the sale of their output. Because kiwifruit is storable and the NZKMB exercises control over the distribution and price of its product, the Commerce Department argued that the 50% threshold was not appropriate in the case of kiwifruit. The ITC decided that the 10% threshold was more appropriate. Although it acknowledged that kiwifruit has much in common with potatoes, it said that there was no clear rationale for departing from the 10% threshold and that the decision to apply the 50% threshold in the potato case could not serve as a basis for decision in the kiwi case.

The Ad Hoc Committee argued that the expenses the NZKMB incurred in hiring a Japanese advertising agency to conduct a survey of Japanese consumer attitudes toward kiwifruit should not be classified as a direct advertising expense. The NZKMB said that it should be classified as a direct advertising expense. The ITC categorized it as an indirect selling expense.

The Ad Hoc Committee convinced the ITC to reduce the NZKMB's indirect selling expenses in Japan because the amount reported incorrectly included corporate general and administrative expenses and an amount miscategorized as unrecovered Japanese shipping expenses, which actually were related to a shipment that was eventually sold in the United States. It wanted the misclassified general and administrative expenses to be added to the costs that would be used in determining the cost of production. The NZKMB had argued, unsuccessfully, that the Auckland office administrative expenses were allocated to the sales division, which mostly serves the Japanese market, and should, therefore, be treated as a direct cost of selling in the Japanese market. It pointed out that similar costs were reported as an indirect selling expense for U.S. sales. It also argued that unrecovered shipping costs were directly related to Japanese sales, because they consisted of the costs incurred for the Pioneer Reefer, which was originally bound for Japan.

Because the NZKMB could not document a reported rebate for one preselected sale, the Ad Hoc Committee asserted that all rebates reported on Japanese sales should be disallowed. The ITC agreed that all such rebates should be disallowed. It concluded that because the sale in question was the only one selected for verification in which a rebate was reported, the assumption must be made that the rebates were incorrectly reported for all sales. Such an assumption is highly debatable, but there is no appeal from the holding.

The NZKMB argued that the stratified sample the Commerce Department used to compute the cost of production was not representative or based on generally recognized sampling techniques. It pointed out that 80% of U.S. exports came from New Zealand's Bay of Plenty region, and only farms greater than two square hectares in size are real businesses. Anything smaller than that is a hobby farm. There also was some miscategorization of farms by size or region in the database that was used to make the sample selection, but it was held that the selection was reasonable.

Some growers did not respond to the questionnaire. In other cases, their responses could not be verified. The NZKMB argued that these growers should not be factored into the Commerce Department's cost of production calculation. It argued that the NZKMB had cooperated in the investigation and had done its best, so the Commerce Department should not use adverse or punitive best information available for uncooperative or unverifiable growers over which it had no control, because doing so would be unfair to the NZKMB and would further distort the sample. The Ad Hoc Committee contended that the Commerce Department must use adverse best information available, because the use of verified growers' costs as best information available would reward the uncooperative growers. It was determined that, based on 19 CFR 353.37, the Commerce Department is required to use best information available when information is not reported.

Accounting for capitalized cultivation costs was another disputed issue. The Ad Hoc Committee argued that the cost of support structures and shelter belts should be amortized over the actual useful life of these assets, not over the life of the kiwifruit vines. The NZKMB argued that capitalized cultivation costs should be allocated over a minimum of 45 years and pointed out that a properly maintained orchard has an indefinite useful life and that capitalized cultivation costs should not be amortized at all because the land's value has been permanently enhanced. The Commerce Department decided that amortization should be over 20 years, which, it determined, was the life of a kiwi vine.

Allocation of most general expenses was also debated. The Ad Hoc Committee took the position that allocating most general expenses on the basis of area is not appropriate, because most of these expenses bear no relationship to farm area. The Ad Hoc Committee suggested that it would be more appropriate to allocate costs based on the cost of sales. The NZKMB contended that allocating costs on the basis of area is the best and most reasonable method to apportion costs among different products. The Commerce Department sided with the Ad Hoc Committee, for the most part.

With all these issues in dispute, it is easy to see that there can be much arbitrary judgment involved in a dumping investigation. Even reasonable accountants and economists might disagree on how to resolve some of these issues. However, the issues become even more complex when one adds the confrontational dimension, as is the case with all antidumping petitions. The petitioner wants to clobber the respondent, and the respondent wants to be cleared of all charges at minimal cost. The Commerce Department and ITC have near-absolute power and need not be concerned with due process because they are exempted from the due process rules. Many Commerce Department officials consider it a goal to find a dumping margin, and this mindset biases their judgment and leads to a finding of dumping where none exists.

What is the likely effect of this holding on the marketplace? New Zealand kiwifruit growers anticipate a 25% to 30% drop in sales to the United States.[60] The antidumping holding forced them to raise their prices by 20% or more. Before the dumping order, they charged $15 to $18 for a three-tray equivalent. After the dumping order, they are charging between $19.50 and $22.50.

New Zealand farmers are mad. They say it is unfair to force them to sell their fruit for more than their Chilean and California competitors. Chilean farmers are gobbling up market share in the United States by selling their kiwifruit at prices that are far lower than any price ever charged by New Zealand growers — between $8 and $12 for a three-tray equivalent. Chilean sales of kiwifruit in 1992 are expected to be more than 400% higher than they were in 1991. New Zealanders are also upset because the Chileans are gaining market share without having to spend anything to promote their product. Historically, New Zealanders have borne 80% of the worldwide cost of promoting kiwifruit.

TELEVISIONS

The U.S. television industry has often used the antidumping laws to protect itself from foreign competition. During the 1980s, U.S. manufacturers either went out of business or shifted their production overseas. As its share of the U.S. market diminished, what remained of the U.S. television industry began to accuse Japanese, Taiwanese, and Korean television manufacturers of dumping their products on the market in violation of the antidumping laws.[61] In one case, a Japanese company had its dumping margin increased because it gave some television sets to charity; the Commerce Department treated the televisions as having a selling price of $0.00 in the U.S. market. Companies also have had their dumping margins increased by selling damaged televisions at a discount or giving their employees a discount.[62]

A classic case in this area is *Matsushita v. Zenith*.[63] The facts in this case are as follows: In 1974, Zenith and several other companies brought an action in the federal district court,[64] alleging that Matsushita and 20 other Japanese manufacturers and/or sellers of consumer electronic products had illegally conspired over a 20-year period to drive U.S. firms from the market by engaging in a scheme to fix and maintain artificially high prices for television sets sold by the Japanese companies in Japan and, at the same time, to fix and maintain low prices for the sets they exported and sold in the United States. The action was brought under §§ 1 and 2 of the Sherman Antitrust Act, §2(a) of the Robinson-Patman Act, and § 73 of the Wilson Tariff Act. In holding that Matsushita and the other companies were not guilty of predatory pricing, the Supreme Court stated:

A predatory pricing conspiracy is by nature speculative. Any agreement to price below the competitive level requires the conspirators to forgo profits that free competition would offer them. The foregone profits may be considered an investment in the future. For the investment to be rational, the conspirators must have a reasonable expectation of recovering, in the form of later monopoly profits, more than the losses suffered.[65]

The court also pointed to the empirical evidence uncovered by a number of commentators over the years, namely, that predatory pricing conspiracies almost never occur, and when they do, they are almost never successful. Further, the facts in Matsushita showed that the company did not drive competitors out of business and that its market share remained about constant over the 20-year period in question, which made it impossible to charge monopoly prices. Even if Matsushita had attained monopoly power, the opposition was not able to prove that entry barriers were high enough to prevent other competitors from entering the market.

The Matsushita case did have some interesting effects on the market, though. Between 1971 and 1991, the inflation-adjusted price of television sets dropped by 25.6%.[66] While U.S. companies continued to build large televisions that doubled as living room furniture, the Japanese built the small televisions that U.S. consumers wanted. While U.S. producers were investing their resources in politics and lawsuits, the Japanese were investing in better quality control and improved technology. The U.S. antidumping laws forced the Japanese to raise their prices, adding to their profits, which played a major role in financing their VCR production, according to the Organization for Economic Cooperation and Development.[67]

NOTES

    1.   Federal Register, Vol. 56, No. 111, June 10, 1991, 26694, reprinted in U.S. International Trade Commission, *Minivans from Japan*, Publication No. 2402, July 1991, p. B-3.
    2.   Federal Register, Vol. 56, No. 123, June 26, 1991, 29221, reprinted in U.S. International Trade Commission, *Minivans from Japan*, Publication No. 2402, July 1991, p. B-11.
    3.   Investigation 731-TA-522. The preliminary findings are reported in U.S. International Trade Commission, *Minivans from Japan*, Publication No. 2402, July 1991.
    4.   U.S. International Trade Commission, *Minivans from Japan*, Publication No. 2529, July 1992, p. 1.
    5.   Federal Register, Vol. 57, No. 101, May 26, 1992, 21938.
    6.   The adjustments the ITC made are outlined in the Federal Register, Vol. 57, No. 101, May 26, 1992, pp. 21937–58, reproduced in U.S. International Trade

Commission, *Minivans from Japan*, Publication No. 2529, July 1992, pp. B-5–26.

7. "Big Three Auto Firms Move to Appeal Decision on Sales of Toyota Minivans," *Wall Street Journal*, August 7, 1992, p. B-3.

8. The mischief of the Big-Three U.S. auto companies is not limited to the United States; they have also been known to initiate antidumping investigations in other countries. For example, in Canada, General Motors and Ford (but not Chrysler) caused the Canadian government to initiate an antidumping action against the Hyundai Motor Company. Curiously, Chrysler did not join in this petition, perhaps because at the time, it owned a 25% interest in Mitsubishi Motors, which owned 15% of Hyundai. For more on this case, see Matthew S. Kronby, "Kicking the Tires: Assessing the Hyundai Antidumping Decision from a Consumer Welfare Perspective," *Canadian Business Law Journal* 18 (1991): 95–117.

9. Investigation 731-TA-438, initiated July 24, 1989. These investigations are reported in I. M. Destler, *American Trade Politics* (Washington, D.C.: Institute for International Economics, 1992), pp. 326–403.

10. Investigation 731-TA-388, initiated February 9, 1988.

11. Investigation 731-TA-422, initiated September 26, 1988.

12. Investigation 731-TA-350, initiated October 9, 1986.

13. Investigation 731-TA-351, initiated October 9, 1986.

14. Investigation 731-TA-352, initiated October 9, 1986.

15. Investigation 731-TA-353, initiated October 9, 1986.

16. Investigation 731-TA-266, initiated June 5, 1985.

17. Investigation 731-TA-267, initiated June 5, 1985.

18. Investigation 731-TA-268, initiated June 5, 1985.

19. Investigation 731-TA-256, initiated April 8, 1985.

20. Investigation 731-TA-257, initiated April 8, 1985.

21. Investigation 731-TA-258, initiated April 8, 1985.

22. Investigation 731-TA-249, initiated February 28, 1985.

23. Investigation 731-TA-250, initiated February 28, 1985.

24. Investigation 731-TA-251, initiated February 28, 1985.

25. Rose Gutfeld and Dana Milbank, "U.S. Steel Firms Get Early Boost in Import Fight," *Wall Street Journal*, August 11, 1992, p. A-2.

26. The Voluntary Restraint Agreements limiting imports lapsed March 31, 1992.

27. Gutfeld and Milbank, "U.S. Steel Firms Get Early Boost in Import Fight."

28. Gutfeld and Milbank, "U.S. Steel Firms Get Early Boost in Import Fight." Jacobson estimates that the preliminary ITC determination could shrink foreign steel imports from the 1991 level of 16 million tons to between 13 and 14 million tons.

29. Investigation 731-TA-448, initiated September 22, 1989.

30. Investigation 731-TA-449, initiated September 22, 1989.

31. Investigation 731-TA-450, initiated September 22, 1989.

32. Investigation 731-TA-424, initiated November 23, 1988.

33. Investigation 731-TA-405, initiated May 26, 1988.

34. U.S. International Trade Commission, *U.S. Imports of Textiles and Apparel under the Multifiber Arrangement: Annual Report for 1990*, Publication No. 2382, May 1991, p. iii.

35. William R. Cline, *The Future of World Trade in Textiles and Apparel* (Washington, D.C.: Institute for International Economics, 1990), p. 59.

36. Destler, *American Trade Politics*, p. 373; Dumping Investigation 731-TA-326, initiated May 9, 1986, resolved April 22, 1987.

37. Bovard, *The Fair Trade Fraud*, p. 115.

38. Investigation No. 731-TA-287, initiated September 26, 1985.

39.   Bovard, *The Fair Trade Fraud*, p. 116; Destler, *American Trade Politics* p. 366, lists the average duty at 192%. N. David Palmeter, "Exchange Rates and Antidumping Determination," *Journal of World Trade* 22 (1988): 73–75, also discusses this investigation.

40.   Investigation 731-TA-516.

41.   Certain other domestic industries, such as those involved in the importation of kiwifruit, tend to be helped by such imports, but the ITC does not look at this side of the coin when making its determinations of damage.

42.   U.S. International Trade Commission, *Fresh Kiwifruit from New Zealand*, Publication No. 2394, June 1991, p. B-9.

43.   U.S. International Trade Commission, *Fresh Kiwifruit from New Zealand*, Publication No. 2394, June 1991, p. 1.

44.   The methodology used is described in the Federal Register, Vol. 56, No. 98, May 21, 1991, pp. 23273–74, reprinted in U.S. International Trade Commission, *Fresh Kiwifruit from New Zealand*, Publication No. 2394, June 1991, pp. B-3–4.

45.   It should be kept in mind that the 10% overhead charge and the 8% profit margin might have nothing to do with reality in the kiwifruit industry, either in the United States or in New Zealand, but they are the percentages the law allows for any industry, regardless of circumstances or location.

46.   Federal Register, Vol. 57, No. 75, April 17, 1992, 13695, reprinted in U.S. International Trade Commission, *Fresh Kiwifruit from New Zealand*, Publication No. 2510, May 1992, p. A-4. Information for the next few paragraphs is taken either from Publication No. 2510 or from Federal Register pp. 13695–706, reproduced in Publication No. 2510 pp. A-4–15.

47.   Federal Register, Vol. 57, No. 75, April 17, 1992, 13706, and Publication 2510, p. I-3.

48.   Publication No. 2510, p. 7.

49.   Ibid., p. I-16.

50.   Ibid., p. I-4.

51.   Ibid., p. I-9.

52.   Ibid., p. I-10.

53.   Ibid., p. I-11.

54.   57 Federal Register 13696.

55.   57 Federal Register 13697.

56.   Information for this section was obtained from 57 Federal Register 13697–706, reproduced in Publication 2510, pp. A-6–15.

57.   45 Federal Register 20512 (1980).

58.   48 Federal Register 51669 (1983).

59.   Ibid.

60.   Ai Leng Choo, "New Zealand Braces for Loss in Kiwi Sales," *Wall Street Journal*, July 20, 1992, p. A10B.

61.   Note, "Managing Dumping in a Global Economy," *George Washington Journal of International Law & Economics* 21 (1988): 503, 506.

62.   Bovard, *The Fair Trade Fraud*, p. 120.

63.   *Matsushita Electric Industrial Co. Ltd. et al.* v. *Zenith Radio Corp. et al.*, 475 U.S. 574 (1986).

64.   513 F.Supp. 1100 (ED Pa. 1981).

65.   475 U.S. 574, pp. 588–89 (1986).

66.   Bovard, *The Fair Trade Fraud*, p. 157.

67.   Organization for Economic Cooperation and Development, *Costs and Benefits of Protection* (Paris: OECD, 1985), p. 11, cited in Bovard, *The Fair Trade Fraud*, pp. 157, 168.

9

Harmful Effects of Antidumping Policy

THE CHILLING EFFECT ON COMPETITION

A strong case can be made that antidumping law, rather than promoting competition, actually impedes it. The cost of entering and competing in the U.S. marketplace might be too high if the foreign producer stands a good chance of being hit with an antidumping action. As a result, some foreign producers rationally decide not to enter the U.S. market rather than face the risk of an antidumping action, which could spawn numerous lawsuits that take years to settle.[1] As soon as an antidumping case is filed, customers and importers face an unknown liability and price for an indefinite future period. Because U.S. importers could get hit with dumping penalties, they hesitate to do business with a foreign supplier that has an outstanding dumping investigation or one that has been found guilty of dumping, because the liability could increase and shift to them with no warning or due process.[2] The possibility of being hit with large unknown liabilities somewhere down the road also reduces importers' ability to borrow or make new commitments.[3] The antidumping laws are exempt from the Administrative Procedures Act, which would guarantee due process. In effect, the antidumping laws punish U.S. importers for doing business with foreign suppliers.

Another aspect of the chilling effect that antidumping laws have on trade is the possibility that an accused foreign supplier will have to reveal cost of production data. Although such disclosures are supposed to remain confidential, the information foreign suppliers provide often winds up in the hands of their U.S. competitors.

HIGHER PRICES

Antidumping policy results in higher prices for several reasons. For one, foreign producers have a tremendous incentive to raise their prices in order to lower the probability of being hit with an antidumping action. Also, the chilling effect that antidumping policy has on competition results in reduced competition, and where there is reduced competition, there are higher prices.

Initiating an antidumping action allows domestic producers to increase their own prices and profit margins. In the case of foreign imports of antifriction bearings, for example, industry profits increased by $20 million for each 1% increase in price. Torrington Corp., which initiated the dumping action, alleged that dumping margins were as high as 50%, which would have increased its share of profits due to price increases of $250 million[4] — all for the price of a postage stamp, because Torrington did not have to pay anything to prosecute the case; the government picked up the entire cost of prosecution.

Another effect antidumping policy has is to weaken U.S. competitiveness. If U.S. companies cannot get the products they want at a reasonable cost, it raises their cost of production. Automakers have to pay more for steel. Company cars cost more, as do raw materials for numerous industries. Retail clothing stores have to pay more for textile products. As a result, profit margins are squeezed and companies make less profit, which means they have less to invest in research, development, expansion, and job creation. Antidumping policy amounts to a form of price control that affects hundreds of billions of dollars in imports each year.

THE EFFECT ON EMPLOYMENT

The relationship between antidumping legislation and employment might not seem obvious at first glance. However, antidumping laws do have an effect on employment. On the positive side, a certain number of jobs can be saved by making it difficult for foreign producers to sell in the domestic market. If Japanese automakers, for example, had to increase the price of their cars by $3,000, they would sell fewer cars and the Big-3 domestic auto manufacturers would be able to sell more cars. Also, the domestic producers would be able to raise their prices, because the Japanese would not be competing as aggressively on price.

However, antidumping laws also destroy jobs. Slapping on antidumping duties has the same effect as slapping on a tariff or imposing import quotas. Foreign producers that decide to sell in the U.S. market anyway, even in the presence of antidumping laws, will merely raise their prices, which has the same effect on consumers as if the government imposed a tariff. However, in the case of raising prices to avoid antidumping duties, the foreign producers receive more cash, thereby strengthening their bottom line, whereas in the case of a tariff, the government gets the money. So, from a domestic producer point of view, antidumping laws are actually more harmful than a tariff, because antidumping laws strengthen the financial position of their foreign competitors. For foreign competitors that decide to stay away from the U.S. market rather than risk the possibility of an antidumping action, the effect is similar to a quota, in the sense that fewer units of product enter the country.

Several studies have found that the number of jobs saved by imposing tariffs or quotas is less than the number of jobs lost. There is a net decrease in welfare and employment because of tariffs and quotas. Every steel job saved costs $113,622 annually.[5] Saving a textile job costs $134,686 a year.[6] Each dairy job saved costs $220,000 a year.[7] Were the money spent where it would be more productive, it is reasonable to expect that more jobs would be created than those lost.

Some studies that have been done in this area attempt to measure the job gains and losses. For example, imposing voluntary restraints on the steel industry in 1984 actually destroyed more jobs than it saved — 16,900 steel production jobs saved versus 52,400 jobs lost in industries that use steel.[8] Another study estimated that the passage of a certain trade bill would save 36,000 apparel manufacturing jobs but destroy 58,000 apparel retailing jobs.[9]

One particularly enlightening example where antidumping laws destroy jobs is the case of flat panel display screens.[10] In this case, the ITC found that Japanese companies were dumping flat panel display screens, which are used in laptop computers, on the U.S. market.[11] The ITC recommended a 62.7% dumping duty. As a result of this ruling, U.S. computer manufacturers were unable to get the flat panel displays they needed to manufacture laptop computers. Therefore, Toshiba's production facility in Irvine, California, decided to shut down its plant and move back to Japan. Apple Computer abandoned plans to make laptop computers in Colorado and decided to make them in Ireland, instead. IBM said it was also considering moving its production facilities to another country. What is really irrational is the fact that there were no domestic suppliers for the panel in the first place. The two U.S. companies that manufactured the screens were both small and had the U.S. government as their only customer. U.S. computer manufacturers decided not to give their business to the two U.S. producers because they concluded that the U.S. suppliers could not give them the product and service they required. Therefore, the Japanese suppliers could in no way be considered to have harmed the domestic industry. Yet, the ITC saw fit to impose an antidumping duty on the Japanese suppliers.

A Brookings Institution study estimated that one particular technical amendment to the 1987 trade bill would destroy 880,000 jobs in the import portion of the wholesale and retail distribution industries.[12] This amendment, which would have artificially lowered U.S. prices by subtracting selling expenses from U.S. sales prices but not from foreign sales prices and deducting a subsidiary's profit from the U.S. sales price, would make it appear that there was dumping where in fact there was none. This amendment also was estimated to reduce domestic living standards by $39 billion and increase affected import prices by 20%. The chilling effect the amendment would have on direct foreign investment also would endanger 2.7 million jobs that are provided by foreign affiliates.

Antitrust enforcement is another area that may be compared with antidumping. In both cases, the market becomes less efficient.[13] To avoid charges of predatory pricing (in antitrust) or dumping (in antidumping), companies raise their prices, which means that the consumers of their products have reduced standards of living. They must spend more for the product in question, so they have less to spend on other things. One study in the antitrust area estimated that for every 1% increase in enforcement, 7,000 jobs were destroyed.[14]

Although coming up with exact numbers to measure the job gains and losses of a particular policy may be difficult, it is not too difficult to see that implementing a policy that results in higher prices reduces total welfare and employment. If consumers have to spend an extra $3,000 for a Japanese (or U.S.) car, they will have $3,000 less to spend on something else. They will not be able to buy the motorboat they want because they will have to spend the $3,000 on the car. What is seen is the automobile purchase; what is not seen is the boat, which cannot be bought — or even made — because of the policy to raise auto prices. The company that manufactures motorboats, the retailer who sells them, and the sales person who works for the retailer all lose because the boat is not purchased, but they do not even know they are losing, because they have no way of knowing that the consumer who bought the car would have also bought a boat if only there had been enough money to buy both.[15]

It is easier to identify the jobs that will be lost by a particular policy than the jobs that will be gained by not adopting the policy, because job losses are visible. All one need do is count the number of people on the unemployment line. Auto companies can see that adopting a certain policy will save X number of jobs in their industry, and they lobby accordingly. However, the people who stand to gain by rejecting a protectionist policy aimed at saving jobs in the auto industry do not see how the policy will affect them. The boat manufacturer and dealer do not see that they stand to increase their sales if the protectionist auto policy is not adopted.

Another phenomenon that has a built-in bias in favor of the protectionists is the relative cost and benefit of doing anything to protect your interests. For example, a textile manufacturer may stand to gain millions of dollars if Congress passes a particular trade bill that might result in raising the cost of a shirt by $5. It is in the textile manufacturer's interest to spend time, effort, and money to see that such a bill becomes law. However, the individuals who wear shirts, even if they are aware that the pending legislation will cost them $5 a shirt, tend not to do anything about it. For a mere $5, it is not worth their while to take time off from work and travel to Washington to lobby their elected representatives. For them, the cost exceeds the benefit. Thus, there is a built-in bias in favor of the concentrated special interests and against the consumers.

EFFICIENCY LOSSES

The antidumping laws result in efficiency losses because companies that are under attack must shift their resources from productive activities to defensive, asset-protecting activities. Efforts shift from income producing activities to income redistribution activities. The dozens or hundreds of individuals who must compile data for the Commerce Department cannot spend their time performing wealth creating activities. Research and development, planning, and any other number of activities must receive fewer resources when resources are drained away for compliance. The funds that are spent for attorneys and accountants cannot be spent for engineering or marketing. Colombian flower growers, for example, spent more than $1 million just in legal fees between 1987 and 1989 to defend themselves against a charge of dumping. Ecuadorean flower growers spent more in legal fees than the entire value of the contested flowers they exported to the United States.[16] Productivity suffers, making the company less competitive.

NOTES

1.   Wesley K. Caine, "A Case for Repealing the Antidumping Provisions of the Tariff Act of 1930," *Law & Policy in International Business* 13 (1981): 700.

2.   James Bovard, *The Fair Trade Fraud*, (New York: St. Martin's Press, 1991), pp. 147–48.

3.   Caine, "A Case for Repealing the Antidumping Provisions of the Tariff Act of 1930," p. 701.

4.   Bovard, *The Fair Trade Fraud*, p. 155.

5.   D. Tarr and M. Morkre, "Aggregate Costs to the United States of Tariffs and Quotas on Imports," Bureau of Economics Staff Report to the Federal Trade Commission, December 1984.

6.   William R. Cline, *The Future of World Trade in Textiles and Apparel* (Washington, D.C.: Institute for International Economics, 1990), p. 194.

7.   Gary Clyde Hufbauer, Diane T. Berliner, and Kimberly Ann Elliott, *Trade Protection in the United States: 31 Case Studies* (Washington, D.C.: Institute for International Economics, 1986), p. 15.

8.   Arthur T. Denzau, *How Import Restraints Reduce Employment* (St. Louis, Mo.: Center for the Study of American Business, Washington University, 1987), p. 5.

9.   I. M. Destler and John S. Odell, *Anti-Protection: Changing Forces in United States Trade Politics* (Washington, D.C.: Institute for International Economics, 1987), p. 56.

10.   U.S. International Trade Commission, *Certain High-Information Content Flat Panel Displays and Display Glass Thereof from Japan*, Publication No. 2413, August 1991, Investigation 731-TA-469.

11.   This case is also discussed in Bryan T. Johnson, *A Guide To Antidumping Laws: America's Unfair Trade Practice*, (Washington, D.C.: Heritage Foundation, 1992), pp. 11–12.

12.   The Brookings Institution study was conducted by Robert Lawrence and is reported by Mary Alexander, "No Dumping on Consumers," *Houston Post*, November 24, 1987; also see Mary Alexander, "Antidumping Amendment Dumps on Consumers," *Citizens for a Sound Economy*, November 5, 1987.

13.   For more on the inefficiency of antitrust laws, see Robert H. Bork, *The Antitrust Paradox: A Policy at War with Itself* (New York: Basic Books, 1978); Dominick T. Armentano, *Antitrust and Monopoly: Anatomy of a Policy Failure* (New York: Holmes & Meier, 1990). Basically, the argument goes like this: The antitrust laws do not prevent monopoly, they encourage it. They reduce competition because companies keep their prices high enough to avoid being prosecuted for predatory pricing. Antitrust laws raise barriers to entry rather than reduce them, thus reducing competition and economic efficiency.

14.   The Shughart-Tollison study, "The Employment Consequences of Antitrust," covered the 1947–81 period. This study, in manuscript form, was cited in Robert D. Tollison, "Public Choice and Antitrust," *Cato Journal* 4 (Winter 1985): 914.

15.   This idea is not new. Frédéric Bastiat wrote about it in the mid-nineteenth century in France. See Frédéric Bastiat, "What Is Seen and What Is Not Seen," in Frédéric Bastiat, *Selected Essays on Political Economy* (Irvington-on-Hudson, N.Y.: Foundation for Economic Education, 1964), pp. 1–50.

16.   Bovard, *The Fair Trade Fraud*, p. 149.

10

The Philosophy of Antidumping Policy

The philosophy behind antidumping policy is a curious one. Those who advocate antidumping policy do so for a number of reasons. Some advocates support antidumping on the basis of fairness; they subscribe to some variation of the "fair trade" theory and honestly believe that there is such a thing as fair trade, just as medieval scholars believed that there was such a thing as a fair price. For example, when Congress was debating the merits of what was to become the Trade Agreements Act of 1979, an antidumping advocate said that antidumping laws were "vital to the maintenance of fair trade because they deter and offset the value of predatory dumping and subsidization in the United States market by foreign governments or exporters."[1]

Other advocates support antidumping because they find it useful as a club, a threat that they can use against countries that have trade barriers (perceived or real) against the importation of U.S. products or services. They advocate using the antidumping laws as a bargaining chip. Another group favors antidumping laws because they see that jobs are being lost to foreigners who sell their products at such low prices that U.S. companies cannot compete. Then there are the special interest groups, the rent-seekers, who want to use the antidumping laws to increase their profits and reduce the competition that is causing their companies to lose sales and market share, even if it means that consumers will have to pay higher prices for lower quality products.

On the other side of the coin are the free traders, who see antidumping laws as an impediment to economic growth and/or individual freedom. James Bovard sees the antidumping laws as a "sword of Damocles" that hangs over every foreign country that exports to the United States and says that the Commerce Department views cheap foreign products as Trojan horses that insidiously try to undermine the U.S. economy.[2]

THE PREDATORY PRICING ARGUMENT

The predatory pricing argument is an especially curious one, curious in the sense that the economic literature of the past few decades seems to conclude that predatory pricing either does not exist, because such behavior is irrational, or if it does exist, it has usually or always failed when tried.[3] James Bovard points out that although the fear of predatory pricing permeates the dumping laws and regulations, there are no known cases in the past hundred years where a company has dumped its products on the U.S. market, bankrupted U.S. producers, and then driven up prices and squeezed consumers for a long period of time.[4] Yet much of the theory upon which antidumping policy is built takes for granted that predatory pricing both exists and is widespread. Along with the notion that predatory pricing exists is the belief that predatory pricing is somehow evil. At least one federal judge believes that dumping is inherently evil and involves some element of wrongdoing.[5] U.S. trade representative Clayton Yeutter has called dumping a "predatory pricing practice condemned under U.S. law."[6] The evidence seems to suggest that allowing companies to charge low prices benefits consumers without leading to monopoly. The only ones harmed are inefficient producers who cannot meet the competition's price. One might even go so far as to call predatory pricing a victimless crime, in the sense that no one's rights are violated by it.[7]

When is pricing predatory? Perhaps never. The economic theory underlying the prohibitions against predatory pricing is that an established company can price its product below cost (whatever that is) until competitors are driven from the marketplace. It can then raise its prices above the market price because there is no competition. The strategy is considered effective if the predatory pricer gains more after competitors have been purged from the market than it lost in its attempt to drive them away.

There are several problems with this argument. For one thing, a company that prices below cost loses money on every sale. If its price is lower than that of its competitors, it will gain market share, so every sale it makes will push it closer to bankruptcy. Even if its price cutting does force all competitors from the market, the former competitors' assets do not just vanish when they go out of business. Someone purchases the assets at fire-sale prices, which makes the purchaser a low-cost competitor. Therefore, companies that resort to predatory pricing harm themselves on two counts: they lose money on every sale, and they help create new, low-cost competitors. Even if the predator buys competitors' assets at 10% of market value, it must still worry about new competition, which will enter the market if the predatory company's prices are high enough. In almost no case are the barriers to entry so high that new competitors cannot enter the market, unless some government denies a license or prohibits entry in some other fashion.

The predatory pricing argument is especially weak when applied to antidumping. When applied to domestic antitrust, the predatory pricing argument might have some superficial plausibility, because the domestic market in widgets or whatever might consist of just a few competitors that dominate the market. In the United States, for example, there are just three major auto manufacturers, General Motors, Ford, and Chrysler, so it might be possible to argue that General Motors might resort to predatory pricing in an attempt to drive Ford and/or Chrysler out of business, leading to the conclusion that the antitrust laws should prohibit such activity. Although there is no evidence to support this position, and because such behavior would be irrational, as was pointed out above, the predatory pricing argument, even in the case of domestic industry, is a weak one that will not stand up to analysis.

When the predatory pricing argument is applied to international markets, the argument becomes even weaker. As long as trade barriers are low or nonexistent, it is impossible to drive out all competitors and capture the market. Even if General Motors were able to bankrupt Ford and Chrysler, it would capture only a small portion of the domestic market for autos. Foreign auto manufacturers like Honda, Toyota, Nissan, Fiat, Hyundai, Mercedes Benz, Volkswagen, and Volvo would still maintain a strong position in the U.S. market, unless the government prevented their products from entering the United States (quotas) or unless it raised tariffs so high that foreign autos were priced out of the market. The antitrust literature of the past few decades seems to conclude that it is impossible to achieve a monopoly position or to maintain it without receiving protection from government against foreign competition.[8] Therefore, the real threat to consumers is not that some foreign company will capture a market but that the U.S. government will assist some inefficient and high-cost domestic producer in capturing a market that would not be possible in the absence of such support.

When one looks at the rationale behind the antidumping laws — predatory pricing — and then looks at a list of the companies, industries, products, and countries that have been the subject of antidumping actions, the predatory pricing argument for having antidumping laws becomes a mockery. Often, the target of an antidumping action is some company or product in an industry that has a very small share of the U.S. market. Sometimes the target is in the third world and poses little or no threat of bankrupting U.S. companies. The antidumping suits are invariably filed by some U.S. company or companies that want to use government as a tool to keep competitors from chipping away at their market share.[9] Table 10.1 contains a few examples of the products, countries, and initiators.

TABLE 10.1
A Sampling of Antidumping Actions 1979–90

Product	Country	Initiator
Melamine in crystal form	Austria Italy Netherlands	Melamine Chemicals, Inc.
Sodium hydroxide in solution	Germany France Italy United Kingdom	Linden Chem. & Plastics
Carbon steel plate	Belgium France Germany Italy United Kingdom	Lukens Steel Company
Carbon steel plate	Czechoslovakia Germany Hungary Poland Venezuela Finland	U.S. Steel
Carbon steel plate	Romania	U.S. Treasury
Certain carbon steel products	Belgium Germany France Italy Luxembourg Netherlands United Kingdom	U.S. Steel Corp.
Frozen winter vegetables	Mexico	S.W. Florida Winter Vegetable Growers Assn.
Natural or synthetic menthol	People's Republic of China	Haarman and Reimar Corp.
Cotton shop towels	People's Republic of China	Milliken Industries, Inc.
Cotton print cloth	People's Republic of China	American Textile Manufacturers Institute
Canned mushrooms	People's Republic of China	Four "H" Corp.
Certain iron metal castings	India	Pinkerton Foundary, Inc.
Truck trailer axle-and-brake and parts	Hungary	Rockwell International Assemblies Corp.
Tapered roller bearings and parts	Hungary	Tinker Co.
Carbon steel wire rod	Poland Argentina Mexico Spain	Six domestic steel producers
Fresh cut roses	Colombia	Roses, Inc.

Table 10.1, continued

Product	Country	Initiator
Certain fresh cut flowers	Canada Chile Colombia Costa Rica Ecuador Kenya Mexico Peru	Floral Trade Council
Hot-rolled carbon steel plate	Belgium France Italy Luxembourg Netherlands Romania United Kingdom Germany	U.S. Steel, Bethlehem Steel, and other steel corporations
Hot-rolled carbon steel sheet	Finland Hungary Romania Venezuela	U.S. Steel
Cold-rolled carbon steel sheet and strip	Belgium France Italy Luxembourg Netherlands United Kingdom Germany	U.S. Steel, Bethlehem Steel, and other steel corporations
Cold-rolled carbon steel sheets and plates	Austria Czechoslovakia Germany Finland Romania Venezuela	U.S. Steel
In-shell pistachio nuts	Iran	California Pistachio Commission

Source: Compiled by the author.

It is unlikely that the United States is about to be overrun with Romanian carbon steel plate[10] or Chinese cotton shop towels. Fresh cut flowers hardly pose a threat, either. It would be interesting to delve into the reasoning behind the argument to keep Iranian nuts out of the United States. Also, it appears that the various domestic steel producers have made a concerted effort to bring antidumping charges against just about anyone that tries to sell steel products in the domestic market. However, can it honestly be said that any of these foreign producers are engaged in predatory activity, or do they just want to sell their products in the U.S. market?

USING THE LAW AS A CLUB TO BATTER THE COMPETITION

The United States has imposed more antidumping penalties on low-priced foreign goods than has any other government,[11] and the rules are so biased that nearly all the foreign companies that were investigated for dumping between 1980 and 1989 were found guilty.[12] So, as a practical matter, it is only a matter of time between the time the petition is filed and the foreign company is found guilty. Even if the company is ultimately exonerated, the time, money, and hassle involved in settling the case can bankrupt a small or medium-sized company and can make even a large company think twice about doing business in the U.S. marketplace. Thus, the antidumping laws have a definite chilling effect on foreign competitors.

Domestic companies are aware of this situation and sometimes use the antidumping laws to punish foreign competitors or scare them away from the U.S. market. It is a classic case of rent-seeking, the term Public Choice economists use to describe situations where individuals or special interest groups seek special privileges or protection from government or get someone else to pay for their benefits.[13]

Rent-seeking activity is likely to pop up whenever the cost is low and the potential benefits are great. Rent-seeking activity has been common in the area of antitrust, where a private company accuses a competitor of some anticompetitive practice and the government conducts the prosecution at its own expense. If the government wins the case, the accusing company can collect up to three times the amount of damages that can be proven. The accuser does not have to spend anything except the cost of a postage stamp or telephone call. The accused has to spend years, and perhaps millions of dollars, to defend itself in court. Even if the accused is able to win the case, its resources will be strained and it will be a weaker competitor for the experience. With this kind of low downside risk and high potential gain, it is no wonder that more than 90% of all the antitrust cases filed in recent years were started by a private company rather than by the federal government.[14]

The ratio of antidumping cases initiated by private parties is also more than 90% of all the antidumping cases filed.[15] Also, as is the case with antitrust, the government pays all the costs of prosecution, so the company that starts the proceeding does not incur any cost but stands to gain much if a competitor either can be bloodied by the Commerce Department and forced to raise its prices or exits the U.S. market altogether, reducing the competition and the need to keep prices low.

Nearly all of the antidumping petitions that U.S. companies file with the Commerce Department result in an investigation — 96% according to a General Accounting Office study.[16] Companies are never penalized for submitting incorrect or knowingly false information.[17] However, once a company is convicted of dumping, it can be penalized for perhaps a decade or more, even though the dumping may have occurred just once.[18]

William Baumol and Janusz Ordover wrote an article titled "Use of Antitrust to Subvert Competition."[19] If we were to substitute the word "antidumping" for "antitrust," much of what Baumol and Ordover said would still be true. The same is true of the following quote:

> There is a specter that haunts our antitrust institutions. Its threat is that, far from serving as the bulwark of competition, these institutions will become the most powerful instrument in the hands of those who wish to subvert it. More than that, it threatens to draw great quantities of resources into the struggle to prevent effective competition, thereby more than offsetting the contributions to economic efficiency promised by antitrust activities. This is a specter that may well dwarf any other concern about the antitrust processes. We ignore it at our peril and would do well to take steps to exorcise it.[20]

The antitrust laws and the antidumping laws are basically mechanisms for wealth redistribution — from strong, competitive companies to weaker, inefficient companies that want government to protect them from the competition. Robert Bork calls this phenomenon "predation through government processes."[21] I prefer to call it "using government as a club" to batter your opponents and get what you want. William Shughart has also written about this phenomenon at length.[22]

Whatever label you wish to attach to it, it is just a case where interest groups lobby government for privileges. Companies, industries, or trade groups are sufficiently concentrated and have sufficient interest to make the investment necessary to lobby government for favors. They use government to increase their wealth at the expense of others — consumers, in this case — who are not mobilized to lobby government. The special interest groups gain at the expense of the consumers, who have to pay higher prices and who have a reduced choice of products, because some foreign manufacturers are driven out of the U.S. market by the antidumping laws. These lobbyists will continue to invest resources into lobbying efforts as long as the return they receive is more than the cost of their efforts.[23] This phenomenon is not new, and it will persist as long as the people who elect government officials continue to elect people who think that this kind of activity is a legitimate function of government.

One case in particular where using the antidumping laws as a weapon proved to be profitable involved the investigation started by Timkin against Koyo Seiko and several other Japanese tapered roller bearing exporters.[24] The Treasury Department investigated Koyo Seiko for dumping as far back as 1969. The initial investigation, which concluded in 1971, found no evidence of dumping. However, Timkin Company, one of Koyo Seiko's major competitors, convinced the Treasury Department to investigate Koyo Seiko and other Japanese roller bearing exporters again in 1973. Three years later, the Treasury Department found Koyo Seiko to be guilty of dumping and imposed a 3.2% dumping penalty, although only one of its tapered roller bearing models was found to have been sold for less than fair value, and even that model was sold below fair value for just one month. As a result of the investigation, Koyo Seiko adjusted its tapered roller bearing prices so that it would be able to avoid future dumping penalties.

Between then and 1989, six different investigators at either the Treasury Department or the Commerce Department continued to work on the Koyo Seiko case in an attempt to find more evidence of dumping. Over that time span, Koyo Seiko had to comply with more than 50 different requests for data. Various government officials paid visits to the company's headquarters in Japan nine times in order to verify the data supplied by the company. After these repeated examinations, the government imposed no dumping duty deposits on the company's imports, which indicated that it could not find evidence of dumping.

However, in 1982, it was told that the investigation, which ended in 1979, had found some dumping margins of up to 2%. Curiously, the Commerce Department never published its findings, because a Commerce Department bureaucrat thought that it would be advisable not to make the findings public until the Commerce Department was able to resolve all points of contention, due to Timkin Company's intense interest in the case.

A year later, in 1983, Timkin Company alleged that the sales Koyo made in its home market were below its cost of production. Because of that allegation, the Commerce Department demanded Koyo's cost of production information starting as far back as 1978. Upon examining the data, the Commerce Department could find no evidence of dumping, and in the summer of 1985, it said that it would close the case within 45 days unless someone protested. As a result, Timkin protested and urged the Commerce Department to start another investigation of Koyo's bearing exports as far back as 1974.

In July 1986, the Commerce Department announced that it would conduct a new investigation of Koyo and said that it would issue its findings within a year. However, the following month, the Commerce Department announced that it was changing its methodology and expanding its investigation to include additional bearing models. As a result, it would require much new data. However, in response to the previous investigations, Koyo had adjusted its prices so that it could avoid future liability for dumping under the old methodology. Because of the change in the Commerce Department's methodology, 17 years of experience (1973 to 1986) in adjusting prices to conform to Commerce Department requirements was rendered useless. In June 1987, the Commerce Department changed its methodology again and greatly expanded the number of bearing models under investigation.

In March 1989, the Commerce Department announced its findings. It determined that Koyo's dumping margin for its exports for the 1974–79 period was as high as 22.9%. It later raised that margin to 35.9%. As a result, Koyo faced an antidumping penalty in the millions of dollars, which was perhaps more than the total value of the bearings it sold in the United States during the mid- and late-1970s.[25]

The means by which the Commerce Department arrived at its dumping duty figure is especially enlightening, because it illustrates how the system works in practice. The Commerce Department found minor discrepancies among the vast quantities of data that Koyo provided — information that had been verified over and over again by both Treasury and Commerce Department officials over the years — and used the discrepancies as an excuse to reject much of the data and substituted its own data instead, based on the best information available. It treated Koyo's vast quantities of data as though they had never been filed. In fact, in some cases, it appears that the Commerce Department was unaware that it had the information it was requesting. As a result, the Commerce Department sometimes constructed the information it needed, which involved much guesswork, even though it already had received precise data from Koyo.

To make matters worse, Koyo no longer retained much of the data it needed to defend itself against the Commerce Department's dumping charges. U.S. tax law generally requires companies to retain financial data for just three years, and although many companies retain such information a little longer than that, there is seldom any legitimate business reason for keeping data much longer than five years, because most information is no longer relevant by then. Therefore, it is not surprising that Koyo did not retain information that was as much as 15 years old. Even if it did retain the information, the Commerce Department ignored it, for the most part, and relied on the best information available, which, as previously discussed, often consists of highly inaccurate information that is taken either out of thin air or from the competitor that called for the investigation in the first place.

To make matters worse, shortly after the Commerce Department announced the dumping penalties, Timkin took the opportunity to inform Koyo's customers that Koyo would soon file for bankruptcy and attempted to get Koyo's customers to switch their business to Timkin.[26]

Using the antidumping laws as a club does not take much of an investment on the part of the petitioning company, and the Commerce Department is very sensitive to any allegations made by a domestic company or industry, regardless of the truth or quality of information. Administrative reviews can be continued even after no wrongdoing is found. All it takes is a letter from a company that might stand to be harmed by a foreign competitor. Also, because the government pays for the full cost of the investigation (by this I mean that Timken did not have to pay anything, although Koyo incurred considerable expense), the present policy encourages domestic companies to use the system to batter their competitors at the expense of consumers.

THE ETHICS OF USING THE ANTIDUMPING LAWS AS A WEAPON

Are there any ethical issues to be discussed in connection with using antidumping laws as a weapon to reduce competition? I think there are, although the literature has ignored this point. In fact, a cursory search of the literature failed to reveal a single article that has been written about the ethics of initiating an antidumping investigation.

The management of a company has a fiduciary duty to its shareholders. Indeed, some commentators would say that their only duty is to the shareholders.[27] Friedman would say that the only responsibility of the board of directors and corporate officers is to increase shareholder wealth. However, there are ethical ways to increase shareholder wealth, and there are unethical ways. Ethical means would consist of things like acting diligently and making products that consumers want in the most efficient manner available. Unethical ways would consist of stealing and putting the proceeds into the corporate checking account.

Under which category, ethical or unethical, would using the antidumping laws to batter the competition fall? Clearly, using the antidumping laws against a competitor tends to weaken the competitor, which benefits the shareholders of the company that instigates the antidumping action. Competitors must expend perhaps millions of dollars to accumulate the information the Commerce Department requests, which means that resources must be taken away from other areas, such as research and development, product enhancement, quality control, and the search for more cost-effective ways of doing business. Rather than using their resources to create wealth, competitors that are under the Commerce Department's microscope must expend resources merely to protect what they already have.

There are ethical ways to batter the competition, and there are unethical ways. An ethical way to batter the competition would be to sell a better product at a lower price. An unethical way to batter the competition would be to blow out the kneecaps of the competitors' board members. Using the antidumping laws to batter the competition is akin to asking the government to blow out the competitors' kneecaps.

A good rule of thumb to use to determine whether conduct is ethical would be to determine whether anyone's rights are violated or whether anyone's property is being taken without the consent of the owner. In the case of antidumping laws, the company initiating the antidumping investigation is clearly causing the competitor to expend assets in an inefficient manner, to preserve resources rather than to create shareholder wealth. If the competitor is violating some right of the company instigating the antidumping action, such action could be justified on the part of the instigating company. However, if no rights of the instigating company are violated, then the company instigating the action is merely using the force of government to dissipate a competitor's assets, which, in effect, is not much different than burning down the competitor's warehouse or destroying its property.

Are the instigating company's rights violated when a competitor sells a product to a consumer who might otherwise buy the instigator's product? I think not. Clearly, the instigating company is harmed, in the sense that the competitor is causing it to lose profits, but being harmed is not the same as having rights violated. The competitor has the right to sell to anyone who will buy. If the instigating company uses force, or the threat of force, to prevent the competitor from making the sale, then it is the instigator, not the competitor, who is acting unethically. Asking the Commerce Department to initiate an antidumping investigation against a competitor is resorting to force or the threat of force to block a competitor's right to sell, because the Commerce Department has the power to block the competitor from entering the market or can force the competitor to pay a fee — a dumping duty — for offering consumers a product at a better price than the instigating company.

Therefore, it appears that it is not the dumping company that is acting unethically; it is the company that initiates the antidumping investigation. Of course, "companies" cannot act unethically, any more than companies can eat, sleep, breathe, or walk up stairs. Only individuals can act ethically or unethically, so it is the individuals at the company initiating the antidumping action who are acting unethically, not the company itself. The individual or individuals who do anything to move the antidumping investigation forward are acting unethically, just like anyone who takes part in the planning or torching of the competitor's warehouse is acting unethically. Just because the damage is done with a telephone call or letter rather than a match does not change the unethical nature of the act.

ANTIDUMPING AS SILLINESS

When looked at rationally, antidumping laws are really silly. In effect, they protect consumers from low prices. But do consumers really need such protection? If consumers wanted higher prices, all they would have to do is tell the sellers that their prices are too low, and the sellers would gladly meet the consumer's needs by raising them.

However, the antidumping laws have nothing to do with consumers. Antidumping laws are advocated by producers and are made for their benefit, at the expense of consumers. In effect, the Commerce Department works for the benefit of producers and at the expense of consumers. Public Choice economists would say that the special interests have "captured" the Commerce Department because it is they, the special interests (producers), who control policy.

Dumping, when it actually exists, is merely an exercise in price discrimination, selling the same product in different markets at different prices, which is rational economic behavior. It is a policy that, when properly followed, maximizes a company's profits. Yet when it is done across national borders, it is considered sinister or evil. Antidumping laws reward companies that sell 100 units at an 8% profit and punish companies that sell 1 million units at a 7.9% profit. Antidumping laws twist rational economic behavior by making it more attractive to earn a higher unit profit than a higher total profit. It is better to sell many units at a lower unit profit than a few units at a higher unit profit. Antidumping laws reward companies for raising consumer prices.

Another aspect of price discrimination that is often overlooked by antidumping enthusiasts is that price discrimination can actually enhance competition. One reason a company may engage in price discrimination is so that it can gain a foothold in a new market. It can facilitate entry by dropping its profit margin. Another procompetitive feature of price discrimination is that it can help to erode the cohesiveness of collusive pricing arrangements,[28] yet this fact is often overlooked, perhaps because the intent of antidumping laws is to protect domestic producers, not to enhance competition.

A RIGHTS APPROACH TO ANTIDUMPING

So far, the discussion has taken a utilitarian approach to antidumping policy, for the most part. It tries to answer questions like "Does antidumping policy do more good than harm?" or "Does antidumping policy provide the greatest good for the greatest number?" Really, such questions are beside the point. They were addressed because economists tend to speak in terms of utilitarianism. However, utilitarianism is not the only approach that can be taken to the policy of antidumping. Indeed, it is not even the best approach that can be taken.

Utilitarianism suffers from several weaknesses. For example, it is impossible to measure whether the good to be gained by a particular policy exceeds the bad,[29] so it is impossible to tell whether a policy would result in the greatest good for the greatest number. Jacob Viner merely assumes that dumping laws generally do not result in the greatest good for the greatest number. He must make the assumption, because there is no way to prove it mathematically. One strength of Viner's position, though, is that he looks at both sides of the coin — consumers as well as producers. Many commentators on the antidumping laws just look at the effect the laws have on producers and ignore consumers.

It should not be necessary to elaborate on the proposition that a gain to the consumer is by so much a gain to the country as a whole, and that cheap imports are an advantage to the importing country provided the injury to domestic industry is not as great as the gain to the consumer. . . . From the point of view of the importing country as a whole, there is a sound economic case against dumping only when it is reasonable to suppose that it will result in injury to domestic industry greater than the gain to consumers. Only on the crudest of protectionist reasoning can it be argued that the desirability of allowing the importation of dumped goods should be decided with reference solely to its effect on domestic producers and without taking into account its benefit to consumers.[30]

Another weakness of utilitarianism is that it tends toward majoritarianism. Because it cannot measure the degree of utility or disutility each individual receives in a particular case, there is a tendency to assume, out of necessity, that all individuals receive equal utility, and it then becomes a question of how many individuals are harmed and how many are helped by a particular policy. For example, if 50,000 steelworkers will lose their jobs if a particular policy is adopted but 250 million consumers will be able to buy steel products at lower prices, the conclusion might be that the policy should be adopted that will aid consumers even though steelworkers will lose because of the concept of the greatest good for the greatest number. However, the steelworkers lose a lot and the average consumer gains only a little.[31] Although the correct policy might be adopted, it might be adopted for the wrong reason. There is no way to measure the extent of gain or loss in individual cases, yet these individual gains and losses must somehow be added together to determine whether the policy results in the greatest good for the greatest number.

Perhaps the greatest weakness of the utilitarian approach is that it sometimes disparages individual rights. When choosing the policy that will result in the greatest good for the greatest number, it sometimes becomes necessary to violate someone's rights. If two wolves and one sheep vote on what's for dinner, the wolves will win, but only at the expense of the sheep's rights.

A property and contract rights approach to antidumping avoids problems like this because majoritarianism never enters into the discussion. In the case of dumping, the question is not "Who is harmed?" or "Who is helped?"; the question is "Do consenting adults have the right to trade or do they not, and if they do not, who has the right to prevent them from doing so and where does this authority come from?"

Being harmed is not the same as having rights violated. A U.S. textile manufacturer might be harmed if Chinese or Korean textile manufacturers are permitted to sell their products in the U.S. market, but it does not follow that U.S. producers are having their rights violated by allowing foreigners to sell in the United States. U.S. producers have a right to sell their products to anyone who is willing to buy, and so do Chinese manufacturers. The right to life, liberty, and property includes the right to sell the fruits of your labor.[32] Preventing people from selling the fruits of their labor is a violation of their rights, and preventing such sales also violates the rights of anyone who might buy the product if it were available for sale. The fact that some majority (or the majority's elected representatives) might approve of limiting sales of foreign products does not change the fact that rights are being violated, because rights do not come from governments or majorities, they are inherent. That is the strength of the rights position and the weakness of the utilitarian position.

Antidumping laws are a form of theft because they prevent individuals from doing with their property as they see fit. Although it may not be the property itself that is being stolen, the right to acquire, trade, or dispose of property is being hindered or prevented in order to protect some group that has no right to protection. Which brings us to another question — What is the legitimate function of government?

ANTIDUMPING LAWS AND THE LEGITIMATE FUNCTIONS OF GOVERNMENT

One aspect of antidumping law and policy that is rarely discussed is the relationship between antidumping laws and the legitimate functions of government. Most commentators just assume that governments can legitimately pass antidumping laws if they want to. Although the scope of this book precludes a detailed discussion of the legitimate functions of government, a few preliminary points should be made in order to open up this aspect of the topic to further discussion.

Many believers in liberal democracy believe that government should do whatever individuals cannot do for themselves. This view is widespread, at least in the United States, and is generally not challenged. However, reflection on this view of the legitimate functions of government would reveal that the argument is flawed, because it ignores the possibility that some functions that cannot or would not be performed by individuals or groups of individuals on their own should not be performed by governments, either. For example, it is unlikely that private individuals would willingly spend their own money to build multimillion dollar monuments or subsidize the activity of some foreign government, but it does not logically follow that government should do it just because individuals will not voluntarily do it on their own. In fact, if there is no market demand for building a particular monument or subsidizing a particular activity, a strong argument can be made that that particular expenditure should not be made, because consumers have determined that the value of funding the activity is less than the value of using the funds for some other purpose.[33]

Others believe that government has no legitimate functions.[34] Still others believe that government should become involved to a certain extent in the redistribution of wealth.[35] Utilitarians believe that the government should work toward the greatest good for the greatest number.

Another view on the legitimate scope of government argues that government should be limited to the defense of life, liberty, and property. This view has been expressed by John Locke[36] and, more recently, by Harvard philosopher Robert Nozick.[37] The Locke and Nozick views are based on natural rights. This view of government has been referred to as "minimal government" or the "nightwatchman state."

Frédéric Bastiat, a nineteenth-century French political economist and antiredistributionist in the broad sense of the term, expresses his view on the legitimate scope of government as follows:

See if the law takes from some persons what belongs to them, and gives it to other persons to whom it does not belong. See if the law benefits one citizen at the expense of another by doing what the citizen himself cannot do without committing a crime.

Then abolish this law without delay, for it is not only an evil itself, but also it is a fertile source for further evils because it invites reprisals. If such a law — which may be an isolated case — is not abolished immediately, it will spread, multiply, and develop into a system.[38]

Based on the Bastiat definition of the legitimate scope of government, it appears that many present-day government functions that are taken for granted are actually illegitimate. Strictly speaking, any government action that redistributes income would fall into this category. Unfortunately, the scope of this book precludes exploring this concept in depth.

Ludwig von Mises, the Austrian/U.S. economist and philosopher, took a different approach. He believed that a particular government policy is good if it enhances social harmony and cooperation and bad if it reduces such harmony and cooperation.[39] His approach is based in utilitarianism but does not go so far as to advocate the greatest good for the greatest number, because Mises realized that majoritarianism can sometimes be in conflict with social harmony and cooperation.

Western democracies incorporate all of these views into their governments to a certain extent, although these views are in conflict with each other. How do antidumping laws measure up when using any of these viewpoints as the standard?

Antidumping laws definitely are illegitimate from the anarchist perspective, because all laws having less than 100% approval fail the anarchist test.[40] However, anarchist views are not mainstream views in modern liberal democracies, and if such ideas are discussed at all, it is only as a benchmark against which to measure and compare other views.

Antidumping laws are redistributionist in that they transfer wealth from consumers to producers. Consumers have to pay higher prices because of antidumping laws. Foreign producers raise their prices so that they can avoid running afoul of the antidumping laws, and domestic producers can get away with charging higher prices because the antidumping laws reduce the downward pressure on prices that would result if competition were more free and unrestrained. Some foreign producers are precluded from even entering the U.S. market, which also reduces competition and reduces the downward pressure on prices.

However, the antidumping laws do not fit the traditional redistributionist model, because the redistribution — the transfer of wealth — goes in the other direction. Rather than going from the rich to the poor, the wealth transfers are from consumers to producers, which, in many cases, means from the poor and middle class to the rich. Therefore, antidumping laws cannot be justified on traditional redistributionist grounds either, because the redistribution goes in the wrong direction.

Antidumping laws are also outside the legitimate scope of government from the nightwatchman state perspective, because they go beyond the mere protection of life, liberty, and property. Antidumping laws actually violate property rights, because they prevent a willing buyer and a willing seller from entering into a contract at a mutually agreed upon price. Either the price must be raised in order to avoid an antidumping penalty or the transaction cannot take place at all because the foreign producer is not allowed to ship goods into the domestic market. Therefore, rather than protecting property rights, antidumping laws disparage them.

It is also difficult to justify antidumping laws on utilitarian grounds — the greatest good for the greatest number — because a minority is benefiting at the expense of the majority. Although it is true that the minority benefits a lot by antidumping laws and the majority is hurt a little by them, there is no calculus that can measure whether the benefit received by the minority — the domestic producer — outweighs the harm done to the majority — the consumers — who must now pay $5 more for a shirt or $2,000 more for an automobile.

Even the argument that saving 10,000 jobs in the textile industry is worth having consumers pay $5 more for a shirt does not hold up under analysis. The studies that have been done are consistent in finding that there is a deadweight loss, jobwise, when some protectionist measure is allowed to distort the market. If a particular policy can save 10,000 jobs in the steelmaking industry, the policy will also destroy 15,000 or 20,000 jobs in the steel-using industries.[41]

It seems that antidumping laws cannot pass the Misesian version of utilitarianism, either. Mises would say that a policy is good if it enhances social harmony and cooperation. However, the antidumping laws do just the opposite. They pit producers against consumers. Rather than allowing or assisting producers and consumers to enter into mutually beneficial exchange, antidumping laws put barriers in the way, either by raising the prices consumers must pay or by preventing foreign producers from entering into mutually beneficial exchange with domestic consumers at all.

Antidumping laws seem to fit the Bastiat definition of legal plunder — using the law to help you steal — that was quoted above. Antidumping laws benefit one person or group — a particular company or industry — at the expense of others — consumers or foreign producers. It would be a crime for a private individual or group of individuals to use force to prevent a foreign company's product from crossing the border or to threaten to penalize a foreign producer if it did not raise prices, yet when government does it, it is not called a crime, it is called an antidumping penalty.

Because antidumping laws cannot be justified on any theory of liberal democracy or on economic grounds, the logical conclusion is to abolish them, the sooner the better. Economically, antidumping laws result in a deadweight loss. There are more losers than gainers. Rather than being a zero-sum game, antidumping laws are a negative-sum game. Such laws reduce rather than enhance social cooperation and harmony, raise prices, and reduce the standard of living for virtually everyone. Even auto companies, which benefit by having the antidumping laws applied to foreign imports, are harmed when such laws are applied to foreign steel or any of the many other components that go into the making of automobiles.[42]

Although the case for outright and immediate repeal is obvious, antidumping laws not only are still on the books but also are gaining in popularity. More nations are enacting them each year, and those nations that have antidumping laws are strengthening them. The solution — repeal — is clear, but implementing it seems difficult, if not impossible.

For one thing, consumers, for the most part, do not realize that the antidumping laws are reducing their standard of living. Even if they did realize it, they are unorganized and unable to compete against the special interests that have a high stake in keeping the antidumping laws on the books. Also, because consumers also usually work for some company, they might also see that antidumping laws are protecting their jobs, so they are extremely hesitant to call for their repeal. In their view, it is better to pay $5 more for a shirt than to lose their job and not have the $5 extra to spend.

Our political leadership could repeal the antidumping laws, yet they do not, for a variety of reasons. Many of them do not realize that the antidumping laws are a deadweight loss. They fall victim to the widespread economic fallacy of what Bastiat calls "what is seen and what is not seen."[43] What they see is 10,000 jobs being saved if they adopt a certain policy. What they do not see is the 20,000 jobs that will be destroyed or never created if they adopt the policy. Therefore, they adopt the policy because they can see only one side of the coin.

Politicians also fall victim to the various special interest groups — the steel industry, the steel unions, the auto industry and auto unions, the textile industry and unions, various farm lobbies, and so forth — who give campaign contributions or threaten to back their opponent in the next election if they do not support this view or that. There seems to be no easy solution to this dilemma. We must find individuals who understand how the antidumping laws work and who are willing to give up substantial time and effort to become elected so they can be in a position to make the necessary changes. More than just intelligence and energy are required. They must convince voters that they should be elected, which will not be easy, because many of them fear losing their jobs if the antidumping laws are repealed. They must also be honest and able to withstand the onslaught of the many special interest groups that are waiting for them once they get elected. They must somehow get elected without compromising themselves to the special interest groups that are willing and able to give them the funding they need to get elected.

CONCLUDING COMMENTS

After analyzing both the theory and practice of antidumping, there is only one conclusion that can be drawn. The antidumping laws must be repealed, the sooner the better. They serve no public interest but merely protect producers at the expense of everyone else. They result in a deadweight loss to the economy, destroy more jobs than they create, and lower living standards. Reform is not called for, because the goal of antidumping — protecting domestic industry at the expense of everyone else — is not a worthy goal.

The way the antidumping laws are administered is a crime, or would be if they were administered by anyone other than government. There is no due process, because the Administrative Procedures Act exempts the antidumping laws from the due process requirement. The government can ask for any amount of information it wants, relevant or otherwise, and can demand it practically on the spot, and it can choose to ignore, for the flimsiest of reasons, any information a company or industry provides. It can impose penalties without recourse. Investigations can be started easily by competitors who merely want to reduce the pressure of competition. The charges do not have to be well-founded or even accurate. The government absorbs the costs of prosecution, so the initiator gets a free ride at the expense of the target of the investigation and the consumer, who must pay the price in the form of higher prices and reduced choice. Investigations can drag on endlessly and can be restarted after they have been closed. The mere threat of an antidumping action chills commerce, reduces competition, and raises prices.

The antidumping laws are ambiguous and vague. Producers never know by which standard they will be held accountable because there are so many standards. The Commerce Department can choose to use one standard for one case and an entirely different standard for another case involving the same company or industry. It can decide to change standards retroactively, and there is no recourse.

Many of the rules and procedures used to arrive at a conclusion of dumping are irrational. In order to avoid a dumping duty, a company must have an 8% profit, which is often higher than the profit achieved by its domestic competitors. A foreign producer can charge the same price as domestic producers and still be found guilty of dumping.

The way in which a fair price is arrived at is also subject to question because of the way the Commerce Department computes it. It often compares apples with oranges. The method by which the cost of production is sometimes computed could result in a malpractice suit if the computation were done by a certified public accountant. Cost allocations are totally arbitrary and inconsistent from case to case. The Commerce Department can choose to use the best information available and can totally disregard better information that is provided by the target of the investigation. The Commerce Department's methodology punishes rational economic behavior and rewards irrational behavior. It bases its actions on outdated theories such as predatory pricing, which has been discredited for several decades. It looks at only one side of the coin — that of the domestic producer — and totally ignores the other side — how the policy will affect consumers. Most importantly, from a rights standpoint, antidumping laws prevent consenting adults from entering into contracts at a mutually agreed upon price. The law allows producers to unethically use antidumping as a weapon to batter the competition.

Antidumping laws cannot be justified by any theory of liberal democracy. They are not utilitarian because they do not result in providing the greatest good for the greatest number. Indeed, they provide good for the minority (producers) at the expense of the greatest number (consumers). They reduce rather than enhance social cooperation and harmony. They violate rights. Even redistributionists would argue against them because they redistribute income in the wrong direction — from the poor and middle classes to the rich. There is no rational reason why antidumping laws should exist.

NOTES

1. S. Rep. No. 249, 96th Congress, 1st Session 41, reprinted in *1979 U.S. Code Cong. & Admin. News*, p. 427.

2. James Bovard, *The Fair Trade Fraud* (New York: St. Martin's Press, 1991), p. 107.

3. For example, see Ronald H. Koller, "The Myth of Predatory Pricing: An Empirical Study," *Antitrust Law and Economics Review* 4 (Summer 1971): 105–23; John S. McGee, "Predatory Price Cutting: The Standard Oil (N.J.) Case," *Journal of Law and Economics* 1 (October 1958): 137–69; "Predatory Pricing, RIP," *Wall Street Journal*, April 1, 1986.

4. Bovard, *The Fair Trade Fraud*, p. 157.

5. *Algoma Steel Corp. Ltd. et al.* v. *United States*, 865 F.2d 240, 242 (Fed. Cir. 1989); Bovard, *The Fair Trade Fraud*, p. 107.

6. Clayton Yeutter, Speech to American Association of Exporters and Importers, New York, May 21, 1987, cited in Bovard, *The Fair Trade Fraud*, pp. 156, 168.

7. Franklin M. Fisher, "On Predation and Victimless Crime," *Antitrust Bulletin* 32 (Spring 1987): 85–92.

8. D. T. Armentano, *The Myths of Antitrust* (New Rochelle, N.Y.: Arlington House, 1972); Dominick T. Armentano, *Antitrust and Monopoly: Anatomy of a Policy Failure* (New York: Holmes & Meier, 1990); Robert H. Bork, *The Antitrust Paradox: A Policy at War with Itself* (New York: Basic Books, 1978); William F. Shughart II, *Antitrust Policy and Interest-Group Politics* (New York and Westport, Conn.: Quorum Books, 1990).

9. For a listing of the antidumping investigations filed between 1979 and 1990, which includes a listing of the product involved, the date initiated, the country involved, the initiator of the investigation, and the action taken, see I. M. Destler, *American Trade Politics* (Washington, D.C.: Institute for International Economics, 1992), pp.326–403. Destler also gives a listing of countervailing duty investigations filed between 1979 and 1990.

10. U.S. International Trade Commission, *Carbon Steel Products*, Publication No. 1642 (1985).

11. U.S. General Accounting Office, *Use of the GATT Antidumping Code* (July 1990), pp. 3–4; Bovard, *The Fair Trade Fraud*, p. 107.

12. Bovard, *The Fair Trade Fraud*, p. 108. Only 6% of the investigations the Commerce Department conducted between 1980 and 1986 found the accused to be innocent of dumping. See James Bovard, "No Justice in Anti-Dumping," *New York Times*, January 28, 1990, p. F13. For a summary of the investigations taken and the outcomes between 1979 and 1990, see Destler, *American Trade Politics*, pp. 326–403.

13. For more on the theory of rent-seeking, see James M. Buchanan, Robert Tollison, and Gordon Tullock, eds., *Towards a Theory of a Rent-Seeking Society* (College Station, Tex.: Texas A&M University Press, 1980); Charles K. Rowley, Robert D. Tollison, and Gordon Tullock, eds., *The Political Economy of Rent-Seeking* (Boston, Mass.: Kluwer Academic Publishers, 1988); Gordon Tullock, *The Economics of Special Privilege and Rent Seeking* (Boston, Mass.: Kluwer Academic Publishers, 1989).

14. D. T. Armentano, *Antitrust Policy: The Case for Repeal* (Washington, D.C.: Cato Institute, 1986), p. 11. Shughart, *Antitrust Policy and Interest-Group Politics*, p. 139, puts this figure at more than 95%.

15. Destler, *American Trade Politics*, pp. 326–403, lists most (not all) of the antidumping investigations initiated between 1979 and 1990. Only seven of the many hundreds of investigations he lists were initiated by the federal government — six because of the trigger price mechanism for steel and one for semiconductors — so, the actual ratio of suits initiated by private companies might be close to 99%.

16. U.S. General Accounting Office, *Comparison of U.S. and Foreign Antidumping Practices* (November 1990), p. 20; statistics cover the period 1986–89.

17. Bovard, *The Fair Trade Fraud*, p. 139.

18. Ibid., pp. 140–46.

19.   William J. Baumol and Janusz A. Ordover, "Use of Antitrust to Subvert Competition," *Journal of Law and Economics* 28 (May 1985): 247–65.

20.   Baumol and Ordover, "Use of Antitrust to Subvert Competition," p. 247.

21.   Bork, *The Antitrust Paradox*, pp. 347–64.

22.   Shughart, *Antitrust Policy and Interest-Group Politics*, pp. 157–76.

23.   Gordon Tullock, "The Welfare Costs of Tariffs, Monopolies, and Theft," *Western Journal of Economics* 5 (1967): pp. 224–32, discusses this point.

24.   Bovard, *The Fair Trade Fraud*, pp. 143–46.

25.   Ibid., p. 145, makes this comparison.

26.   Ibid., p. 145.

27.   Milton Friedman, "The Social Responsibility of Business," *The New York Times Magazine*, September 13, 1970, pp. 122–26, reprinted in many places, including Kurt R. Leube, ed., *The Essence of Friedman* (Stanford, Calif.: Hoover Institution Press, 1987), pp. 36–42.

28.   Richard Dale, *Anti-Dumping Law in a Liberal Trade Order* (New York: St. Martin's Press, 1980), pp. 22–23, points this out.

29.   For a detailed critique on the weaknesses of the utility concept, see Murray N. Rothbard, *Man, Economy and State* (Los Angeles, Calif.: Nash Publishing, 1970), pp. 260–68.

30.   Jacob Viner, *Dumping: A Problem in International Trade* (Chicago, Ill.: University of Chicago Press, 1923), p. 138.

31.   In practice, it is often the group that has a lot to lose (steelworkers) that wins, at the expense of the larger group that has a little to lose (consumers), because of the special interest effect.

32.   John Locke, *The Second Treatise on Civil Government* (Buffalo, N.Y.: Prometheus Books, 1986), p. 20, discusses this point.

33.   Some economists call it "market failure" when the market does not provide something that they think should be provided. For a critique of this theory, see Tyler Cowen, ed., *The Theory of Market Failure: A Critical Examination* (Fairfax, Va.: George Mason University Press, 1988). A variation on the market failure theme is the idea that some things are public goods and that government must provide them. For a devastating critique that completely dismantles the public goods argument, see David Schmidtz, *The Limits of Government: An Essay on the Public Goods Argument* (Boulder, Colo.: Westview Press, 1991).

34.   Anarchists take this view. For example, see Colin Ward, *Anarchy in Action* (London: Freedom Press, 1988).

35.   John Rawls, *A Theory of Justice* (Cambridge, Mass.: Harvard University Press, 1971). For a critique of Rawls, see Brian Barry, *The Liberal Theory of Justice* (Oxford: Oxford University Press, 1973). For a critique of the ethics of redistribution, see Bertrand de Jouvenel, *The Ethics of Redistribution* (Cambridge: Cambridge University Press, 1952).

36.   Locke, *The Second Treatise on Civil Government*. For a discussion of the relationship between Locke's political views and the structure of the economy, see Karen Iversen Vaughn, "The Second Treatise of Government and the Foundation of Economic Society," in Karen Iversen Vaughn, *John Locke: Economist and Social Scientist* (Chicago, Ill.: University of Chicago Press, 1980), pp. 77–107.

37.   Robert Nozick, *Anarchy, State, and Utopia* (New York: Basic Books, 1974). For critiques of Nozick's views, see Jeffrey Paul, ed., *Reading Nozick: Essays on Anarchy, State, and Utopia* (Totowa, N.J.: Rowman & Allanhead, 1981).

38.   Frédéric Bastiat, *The Law* (Irvington-on-Hudson, N.Y.: Foundation for Economic Education, 1968), p. 21. Originally published in 1850 as a pamphlet, *La Loi*, reprinted in *Sophismes Économiques, I: Oeuvres Complètes de Frédéric Bastiat* (Paris: Guillaumin et Cie, 1878), pp. 343–94.

39. Ludwig von Mises, *Human Action: A Treatise on Economics* (Chicago, Ill.: Henry Regnery Company, 1966), pp. 664–715.

40. For a discussion of the anarchist philosophy from a Public Choice perspective, see Gordon Tullock, ed., *Explorations in The Theory of Anarchy* (Blacksburg, Va.: Center for the Study of Public Choice, Virginia Polytechnic Institute and State University, 1972). James M. Buchanan, the co-founder with Tullock of the Public Choice School of Economics, has also written on the place of anarchy in economic theory; for example, see James M. Buchanan, *The Limits of Liberty: Between Anarchy and Leviathan* (Chicago, Ill.: University of Chicago Press, 1975); James M. Buchanan, *Liberty, Market and State* (New York: New York University Press, 1985), pp. 108–20; James M. Buchanan, *Freedom in Constitutional Contract: Perspectives of a Political Economist* (College Station, Tex.: Texas A&M University Press, 1977).

41. For some specifics, see I. M. Destler and John S. Odell, *Anti-Protection: Changing Forces in United States Trade Politics* (Washington, D.C.: Institute for International Economics, 1987); Gary Clyde Hufbauer, Diane T. Berliner, and Kimberly Ann Elliott, *Trade Protection in the United States: 31 Case Studies* (Washington, D.C.: Institute for International Economics, 1986).

42. James M. Buchanan, "Free Trade and Producer-Interest Politics," in James Buchanan, *Essays on the Political Economy* (Honolulu, Hawaii: University of Hawaii Press, 1989), pp. 52–66, makes this point.

43. See Frédéric Bastiat, *Selected Essays on Political Economy* (Irvington-on-Hudson, N.Y.: Foundation for Economic Education, 1964), pp. 1–50 (originally published in French in 1850). For more on this fallacy, see Henry Hazlitt, *Economics in One Lesson* (New York: Harper & Brothers, 1946).

11

Concluding Comments: Implications for International Trade in Europe

There are two major implications of U.S. protectionism that could have an effect on trade in Europe and elsewhere. The first is the effect that U.S. trade policies will have on the way individual countries, and Europe as a whole, deal with the United States, which is clearly in a protectionist mode and has been for some time. The second implication is the possibility that U.S. trading partners would adopt U.S. trading policies as their own, not to retaliate, but because they think that U.S. policies are somehow better than those of other countries.

POLICY OPTIONS FOR EUROPE

None of the arguments supporting protectionism hold up under analysis. Subsidies actually benefit consumers, as does dumping (if it actually existed, which is questionable). Although jobs are destroyed in the absence of protection, an attempt to protect an industry results in more job losses than if government stayed out of the picture and let consumers buy the products of their choice. The low wage argument, full employment argument, level playing field argument, and so forth have little relation to reality.

Protectionism costs, not only in terms of money, but also in terms of retarded economic growth, less choice, a deadweight employment loss, reduced social harmony, and lessened individual freedom.

The reasons given in favor of protecting this or that industry do not hold up under analysis. Yet the policymakers in Washington do not see that. As a result, U.S. trade policy is being driven by fallacious economic theory. Public Choice economists would see this as no surprise. The special interests have the resources and incentives to push their policies through the legislature, to the detriment of U.S. consumers and our trading partners in Europe and elsewhere.

Our European trading partners have two basic choices: they can retaliate by adopting similar policies of their own, which would be counterproductive, or they can adopt free trade policies and try to convince the U.S. policymakers of the errors of their ways.

One major implication of U.S. protectionism that could have an effect on trade in Europe is the possibility that our trading partners, especially those in emerging democracies, could decide to adopt U.S. trade policies as their own, not in order to retaliate, but because they think that U.S. policies are somehow better than those of other countries. Nothing could be farther from the truth.

There is a tendency in emerging democracies, especially those that are attempting to convert from a centrally planned system to a market system, to look to the policies of Western democracies for guidance. For example, the government of Poland invited representatives of the U.S. Internal Revenue Service to Poland to teach Polish tax collectors how to collect taxes.[1] Many Americans who learned of this invitation were horrified at such a prospect. The Internal Revenue Service is one of the least freedom loving of all government bureaucracies. It has been known to confiscate and destroy or sell assets with little or no due process.[2] Yet Poland and other countries want to copy U.S. policies and methods.

This copycat approach is not all bad, however. There is often no need to reinvent the wheel. Whether adopting another country's policies is good or bad depends on the policy and how it fits into the social and political framework of the country adopting it. What is of the most concern is that European policymakers in countries with emerging market economies will adopt a policy without carefully examining all the implications first. In the area of antidumping, for example, several countries in the past few years have adopted policies similar to those of the United States. Antidumping policy is among the most irrational policies that a country could adopt, but the trend seems to be in favor of expanding antidumping policy rather than abolishing it. That has certainly been the trend of the Uruguay round.

One of the most crucial issues in the Uruguay round of trade talks is also one of the most neglected: dumping. The reason for the neglect is that the negotiators with most muscle, America and the European Community, broadly agree on the subject. Both want to make the anti-dumping code in the General Agreement on Tariffs and Trade (GATT) more effective. But when governments agree so readily, watch out. The consensus on dumping is a grave threat to liberal trade, because when officials say more effective what they really mean is more protectionist.[3]

The rules legitimizing the imposition of antidumping duties were written into the GATT rules during the Tokyo round of the 1970s, and Uruguay round negotiators have been urging that the rules be strengthened rather than repealed, which is a mistake. During the 1980s, almost 80% of the actions instigated against foreign competitors were for violations of the antidumping rules, and two-thirds of the "voluntary" export restraints that were negotiated in that period were in response to antidumping actions.[4]

The only legitimate rationale for bringing an antidumping action is in a case that might involve predatory pricing. Yet, as the literature over the past two decades has shown, either predatory pricing does not exist or, if it does, it has benefitted consumers. Yet more than 50% of the antidumping actions have been instigated against companies whose European Community market share has been less than 5%, and in 90% of antidumping actions, market share was less than 25%. Therefore, it is clear that, in practice, antidumping actions are brought for some reason other than to prevent predatory pricing.[5] "Anti-dumping is the classic case of a 'fair-trade' procedure captured by special interests and turned against the liberal trading system."[6]

One example of where antidumping policy has been used irrationally is the case of Korean dynamic random access memory (DRAM) chips. Korea's rapid rise in the semiconductor industry was heralded by Europeans and Americans as the best chance to break the near stranglehold that Japanese chip makers had on this market. Korea's three major chip makers, Samsung, Goldstar, and Hyundai, quadrupled their capital investment since 1986, with the result that these three Korean companies combined are now second only to Japan's Toshiba Corporation in terms of market share. How did the European Community reward the Koreans for their diligent efforts in breaking the Japanese stranglehold? By slapping them with a punitive antidumping tariff.[7] The action was brought as the result of a complaint by the European Electronic Component Manufacturers' Association, which instigated the action on behalf of Motorola Ltd. of the United Kingdom, Siemens AG of Germany, and SGS-Thornson of Italy.[8] Until the matter is resolved, the Korean companies will have to pay the punitive tax into an escrow account. In the meantime, there is tremendous incentive for them to raise their prices to avoid paying higher penalties. If they do succumb to the pressure to raise their prices, their Japanese and European competitors will feel less pressure to reduce their prices and may actually decide to raise them. The losers in this scenario are those who use computers, because the computer manufacturers must now pay more for their chips, and it is reasonable to expect that they will try to pass on this added cost in the form of higher prices. If computer manufacturers are unable to pass on their costs to consumers, their profit margins will suffer, which means they will not be able to expand production as rapidly and create as many jobs in the computer industry as would otherwise be possible.

There is a very real danger that the emerging democracies in Eastern and Central Europe will feel pressured to adopt antidumping and other protectionist policies like those of the West,[9] especially if they are anxious to join the European Community.[10] This urge must be resisted, because adoption of such protectionist policies will reduce the standard of living and retard economic growth, which is exactly what these emerging democracies do not need. These countries need to adopt policies that are in keeping with the structural changes[11] they are making in converting from centrally planned economies to market economies, and adopting protectionist policies will hinder rather than help their efforts.

OTHER ISSUES

The Effect of Competition on Prices and Efficiency

Eliminating trade barriers will allow resources to flow to their most productive uses. Consumers will be able to buy higher quality products at lower prices. Both theory and practice conclude that removing trade barriers — reducing or eliminating tariffs and quotas — increases competition, which exerts downward pressure on prices and increases the quantity and quality of products available to consumers. Yet practice also shows that, in the case of Eastern and Central Europe at least, the switch from central planning to a market economy has resulted in higher, rather than lower, prices. Is there any way that these two positions — lower prices in theory but higher prices in practice — can be reconciled?

I think that this seeming divergence of theory and practice can be reconciled. Let us say that the price of bread in the former Soviet Union was kept artificially low at 1 ruble per loaf because the Soviet government decided to subsidize bread. After the subsidy was ended and the market was permitted to determine the price of bread, the price rapidly rose to 10 rubles a loaf.[12] A casual observer might, therefore, conclude that allowing the market to determine prices can and does result in higher prices. However, does this mean that lifting trade barriers and increasing competition will result in higher prices? I think not, because these are two separate issues. Removing a subsidy on bread is not the same as removing a barrier to trade, and removing a price subsidy has no effect on competition if all bread factories are owned by the state both before and after the subsidy has been lifted.

Let us look at another example. In Poland and other emerging European democracies, the switch from a centrally planned economy to a market economy led to a rise in prices without a corresponding rise in wages,[13] which resulted in reducing the standard of living. Wage rates are determined by productivity and capital investment, which remain nearly constant over the short run, but prices are determined by supply and demand in a market economy. When price regulations were lifted, prices that had been kept artificially low were allowed to rise to the market level. However, it is not quite accurate to say that the lifting of price restraints, which led to the rise in bread prices from 1 ruble a loaf to 10 rubles a loaf, meant that consumers now have to pay ten times as much for bread as they once did, because under central planning, the true cost of bread and other products was hidden.

Although the price of bread might have been only 1 ruble, the cost of producing it might have been 8 rubles. Consumers paid the full 8 rubles, but only 1 ruble was paid directly; the other 7 rubles were paid indirectly by means of a hidden wealth transfer. The exact means by which wealth is transferred from consumers to producers depends on the system of public finance the state uses to pay for government services. In a system that relies on an individual income tax, the wealth transfer is accomplished by withholding a portion of the workers' pay and using the withheld funds to pay the baker and other suppliers of government services. For example, if a worker who earns 100 rubles is in the 40% income tax bracket, the worker will receive only 60 rubles and the government will take 40 rubles, some of which are used to pay the employees at the state-owned bakery. If there is no income tax system, the worker who contributes 100 rubles worth of production still receives only 60 rubles from his state employer. The other 40 rubles is retained and used to subsidize bread or to pay for other state services. What is seen is the price of bread rising from 1 ruble to 10 rubles. What is overlooked is the fact that the cost of producing a loaf of bread is 8 rubles regardless of how the funds are raised to pay the baker.

If the state bakery monopoly is privatized and subsidies are removed, certain things start to happen. The price system is a signaling mechanism that conveys information. If the state bakery monopoly is replaced with competing, privately owned bakeries, the price system will convey information to these private owners. It will tell them how much consumers are willing to pay for bread, and it will tell them how much it costs them to make the bread, enabling them to determine whether they are producing at a profit or a loss. Also, because the price system enables them to determine what their costs are, it gives them incentives to find ways to reduce costs so they will be able to compete and make a profit. Thus, they will be able to allocate their resources more efficiently than would be possible under a centrally planned regime, where costs are arbitrary and hidden.

Stages of Economic Development

There are a number of theories regarding the relationship between policy and the stages of economic development. The basic question these theories attempt to answer is whether policy should differ depending on the stage of economic development. Although there is not sufficient space in this chapter to fully develop the issues, a few points can be explored.

One issue is whether trade policy between developed countries should be the same as trade policy for developing countries, or whether trade policy between countries of approximately equal development should be the same as for countries in different stages of development. Some economists have taken the position that international trade itself is responsible for underdevelopment.[14] Those who advocate this theory would have us believe that it is acceptable for Canadians to buy shirts made in the United States and vice versa but that it is somehow not acceptable for Americans or Canadians to buy shirts made in some developing Asian country. Those who advocate this "fair trade" rather than "free trade" policy (mostly Canadian and U.S. textile manufacturers) would like to see trade barriers, such as tariffs or quotas, erected to prevent these developing countries from competing against domestic producers that have higher labor costs.[15]

The fundamental problem with this view is the failure to recognize that free, unrestricted trade benefits the vast majority of people. It benefits consumers, who are able to buy from a wide selection of products at lower prices than would be possible under a protectionist regime. The effect of free trade policy — lower prices and wider selection — is the same regardless of the stage of economic development. Those who advocate restrictive trade practices for lesser developed countries do so because they see international trade as a zero-sum game, when, in fact, it is a positive-sum game.[16]

Protectionist regimes erected in developing countries have an especially detrimental effect on economic growth, because the limited resources these countries have are being used to protect inefficient producers at the expense of everyone else. This misallocation of resources cannot help but stifle economic growth, because resources are diverted from their most productive uses.

Although free, unrestricted trade is always the best policy, regardless of the stage of economic development, developing countries can least afford the luxury of closing their borders to trade and, especially, to foreign investment, because their capital base needs to be expanded.[17] The argument that the underdeveloped countries can never catch up with the West is just not true. The experiences of South Korea and Hong Kong are only two examples that could be cited to refute this view. Underdeveloped countries lack a capital base, but they do not need to grow their own capital base. All they have to do is allow unrestricted foreign investment.[18] If they enact legislation to protect property rights[19] and allow foreigners to invest with minimal or no restrictions,[20] capital and technology will flow into the country and produce an economic boom.

A perfect example of where this policy has worked is the United States. In the nineteenth century, the U.S. infrastructure — canals, private roads and railroads — was built primarily with the capital of British investors. The United States did not have much of its own capital to invest, but this difficulty was overcome by allowing unrestricted investment by foreigners. U.S. policymakers did not plan things to happen the way they did; it was the absence of planning that caused the United States to become an economic power during the course of the nineteenth century.

The Irrationality of East European Trade Policy

The present U.S. policy on Eastern and Central European trade is irrational. The International Monetary Fund, the World Bank, and the U.S. government have each given billions of dollars in aid or loans to this region in each of the years since the collapse of the Berlin Wall.[21] The federal government has established Enterprise Funds to promote private sector development in Hungary, Poland, and Czechoslovakia. The U.S. Export-Import Bank is providing loans, guarantees, and insurance for the financing of export sales of U.S. goods and services. The Overseas Private Investment Corporation is also subsidizing U.S. business investment in the region. Eighteen different federal government agencies are engaged in some form of assistance in Eastern Europe. Yet U.S. trade policy is making it difficult or impossible for the emerging democracies in Eastern Europe to sell their products in the United States.

U.S. quota and tariff policies raise the price of textile products from Eastern Europe to the point where their products are uncompetitive in the domestic market. Poland is allowed to sell only 144,000 women's and girls' wool coats in the United States each year. Similar quotas prevent Polish men's and boys' wool suit coats, suits, and other woolen products from crossing the border. Czechoslovakia was allowed to ship only 198,000 men's and boys' wool coats and 160,000 men's and boys' suits to the United States in a single year. Hungary can export only 50,000 women's and girls' wool suits and 155,000 men's wool suits to the United States. Yugoslavia and Bulgaria have similar quotas. The tariff on women's wool suit jackets is 22.3% and is more than 20% on a variety of other textile products coming from Eastern Europe. The effective tariff charge resulting from combined tariff and quota restrictions averages more than 50%.

Voluntary restraint agreements greatly limit the amount of East German, Czech, Polish, and Yugoslav steel and steel products that can come into the United States. These restrictions provide substantial disincentives to foreign investment, because one of the largest markets for these products is partially closed because of artificial barriers.

Trade policies in the U.S. and European Community are stifling the recovery of the agricultural sector in Eastern Europe. Hungary and Poland were formerly agricultural exporters and could be again, but their efforts are being stifled by a trade policy that erects artificial barriers to their products. Eastern European countries are not able to sell a single pound of butter, dry milk, or ice cream to U.S. consumers. Quotas on beef greatly restrict the flow of beef products into the United

States. Bulgaria, the world's fourth largest tobacco exporter and the world's largest cigarette exporter, is faced with a 458.3% tariff on tobacco stem exports to the United States and has to pay a tariff of more than 30% on tobacco and cigarettes. The Hungarian chemical and pharmaceutical sector, which could be a major growth area, is being stifled by U.S. tariffs of more than 20% on hundreds of chemical and pharmaceutical items.

The European Community has not been completely rational in its Eastern European trade policy, either. Although the European Community has signed trade agreements with Hungary, Poland, and Czechoslovakia that are intended to move these countries toward completely free trade with the European Community over a ten-year period, some European Community members have attempted, with varying degrees of success, to stifle competition with the emerging market economies in a number of areas. Portugal attempted to delay a decision on ending textile quotas until after the GATT trade talks. Spain and Italy tried to block steel shipments, and France resisted attempts to open up its market to Polish beef. Eurofer, the European Community steel producers' organization, has threatened to launch antidumping actions of its own to prevent the former Eastern Block from invading the European Community with cheap steel.[22]

A number of dumping actions have been instigated against the countries of Eastern Europe in recent years. Also, U.S. countervailing duty laws stand ready to disrupt the flow of trade between Eastern Europe and the United States for 15 years. These countervailing duty laws penalize foreign producers that receive foreign government subsidies. Nonmarket economies are not subject to these laws, but market economies are.[23] The countervailing duty laws can be applied to subsidies made as far back as 15 years, which means that exporters from newly emerging market economies can be held accountable for subsidies that were made as much as 15 years previously, when they were under a central planning regime.

It seems ridiculous that the U.S. government and its various agencies are willing to spend billions of dollars on aid to Eastern Europe but make it difficult or impossible for their products to enter the United States. What sense does it make to pour capital into the retooling and modernization of their industry when the revitalized factories cannot sell their products in the United States? It would make far more sense to declare an immediate end to all trade barriers for any emerging democracy in Eastern Europe. Such a move would open markets that were previously closed because of quotas and tariff barriers. Also, the filing of antidumping and countervailing duty actions should be prohibited; otherwise, much of the investment that is being poured into these countries will be wasted.

CONCLUDING COMMENTS

The arguments in favor of protectionism being advanced by U.S. policymakers have been refuted for decades. Yet European policymakers often spout the same long-refuted arguments as though they had some validity. They often look to the United States to support their opinions, but even if they do not, the danger is still there that they will adopt policies that are irrational and counterproductive.

Emerging democracies that are converting from a centrally planned economy to a market economy present a special case. Through decades of misallocation of resources resulting from central planning and the absence of a price system, most of their industries are not competitive with those in the West. The best solution to their problem is immediate free and unrestricted trade. The speed with which their industries can be upgraded to compete with the West will be accelerated if they permit unrestricted foreign investment, which will provide the capital and technology needed to make a rapid conversion. The way to maximize efficiency and the standard of living is to dismantle trade restrictions, do what you do best, and trade for everything else.[24] Foreign investment will accelerate the conversion process, and if resources are allowed to flow, they will flow to their most productive uses.

The complete and immediate adoption of free and unrestricted trade is the only approach that is consistent with the "rights" approach to trade. If individual rights are being violated by not allowing individuals to buy the products of their choice at the market price, the only moral solution is to stop these rights violations immediately. Allowing special interests to dictate terms of trade results in allowing the minority (special interests) to benefit at the expense of the majority (consumers).

The same argument was used before and during the U.S. Civil War in the case of slavery. If slavery is immoral, the only solution is to end the practice immediately. The fact that slaveowners will be driven out of business is irrelevant, as is the fact that hundreds of thousands of slaves will become unemployed. An increase in the bankruptcy and unemployment rates is not relevant, either in the case of abolishing slavery or in the case of abolishing protectionism. Viewed from this perspective, questions such as "What would happen if we abolished this policy or that?" are not legitimate questions. If a certain policy violates rights, it does not matter what the consequences would be of righting the wrong and replacing a rights-violating policy with one that does not violate rights. Thus, the rights approach to trade would hold that a conversion to total and immediate free trade is the best solution. However, most economists do not use the rights approach; they use a utilitarian approach.[25]

In the case of centrally planned economies that are converting to a market system, there are at least two versions of the utilitarian approach that can be used, the long-run approach and the short-run approach. We previously concluded that free trade is to be preferred to protectionism regardless of whether the rights approach or the utilitarian approach is taken. Both approaches lead to the same conclusion. However, a complete and immediate switch from protectionism to free trade can lead to traumatic results, especially when an entire economy has to convert from central planning to a market system. If all state-owned or recently privatized industries are left to sink or swim in the international marketplace, many of them will sink, leading to massive bankruptcy, unemployment, and social unrest. To minimize the pain and trauma resulting from rapid conversion, some economists have advocated a gradualist approach. Rights theorists, of course, would be quick to point out that the only policy that is consistent with individual rights is a complete and immediate change from a policy that violates rights to one that does not. In the case of the U.S. Civil War, the conversion from a slave society to a free society was made in a short period of time but at a cost of more than 500,000 dead and the destruction of the plantation system. Some economists have argued that a gradualist approach would be better for practical reasons, because a gradualist approach would ease the transition and reduce the pain of converting from a centrally planned system to a market system. I do not agree with this view, but it might still be worthwhile to explore the question of "If a gradualist approach is held to be a better approach, what form would it take?" An examination of this question makes it possible to see the flaws in the gradualist argument.

Probably the most plausible gradualist approach would be based on the infant industry argument.[26] This approach advocates temporary protection, just long enough to allow the uncompetitive industry to become competitive. Temporary protection would prevent the massive unemployment and social disruption that would otherwise occur. In the case of centrally planned economies that are attempting to convert to a market system, it might also prevent a counterrevolution.

However, there are dangers to the infant industry approach. Historically, there have been problems with this approach. The main problem is that protection that starts out being temporary often becomes permanent. An example is the sugar industry in the United States, which has been protected since 1816,[27] and many other industries have been receiving protection, in one form or another, at least since the 1930s. The auto industry in the United States has been receiving government protection since at least 1981, when a voluntary import restraint agreement took effect. At that time, Japanese automakers had a 20.5% share of the market. As of 1991, ten years later, they had a 30.3% share, the same year that the Big-3 automakers in Detroit lost a record $7.5 billion.[28] One reason for the decline in the U.S. auto industry is the fact that the U.S. automakers used the breathing room the protection gave them to invest in other industries rather than plowing capital into modernization of their auto plants. Also, now that Japanese automakers have built auto plants in the United States, it will be even more difficult for the Big-3 to compete, because the import restrictions do not apply to cars made by Japanese companies in the United States.

Even if protection does help one industry, it does so at the expense of others, because resources must be diverted in order to protect it. Thus, other industries are weakened and resources are allocated inefficiently. There is evidence to suggest that the infant industry approach does not work even when it is applied to just one industry,[29] and if it is applied to too many industries, it will not work either, because of the fallacy of composition.[30]

The infant industry or "breathing room" argument is also theoretically unsound. Competition provides incentives to improve quality and reduce costs. Taking away this incentive by insulating an industry from foreign competition retards these improvements. In effect, government restrictions on foreign imports give U.S. producers a monopoly. When there is monopoly, there is far less incentive to innovate, cut costs, and improve quality because consumers have fewer choices in the marketplace. If industry executives know that the legislature will give them protection, they will spend their time and resources getting protection from the legislature rather than tending to their business and satisfying consumer needs.

Some proponents of the infant industry or breathing room argument point to apparent successes to support their position. One example from U.S. experience is the federal government's bailout of Chrysler, one of the Big-3 auto manufacturers in the United States. The federal government gave Chrysler a multi-billion dollar loan at favorable interest rates in order to provide it with the capital it needed to avoid bankruptcy, which seemed imminent. Chrysler was able to turn its operations around and earn a profit, saving thousands of auto jobs. What was seen was the thousands of jobs that were saved by the bailout, but that is only part of the story. Few commentators ask what the funds would have been used for if they had not gone to Chrysler. Had the funds been lent to more creditworthy customers, it is likely that the borrowers would have been able to create even more jobs than what Chrysler stood to lose if it had not received the money. Companies that are already healthy can generally do a better job of creating wealth and employment than can companies, like Chrysler, that are on the verge of bankruptcy. It is likely that the Chrysler bailout actually caused more unemployment than it prevented, although it is impossible to say precisely, because it is not possible to measure the jobs in other industries that were never created because the federal government diverted the funds to Chrysler.

If one wants to protect workers from the ravages of free trade, how can it be done? The protectionist arguments do not hold up under analysis, and even the infant industry argument — the strongest of all the protectionist arguments — is a weak one. All forms of protectionism cause resources to flow down suboptimal paths, retard economic growth, and destroy more jobs than they create.

A viable alternative to protectionism is to make direct payments to those who lose their jobs as a result of free trade. Although this approach is not fair to the taxpayers, who must pay people not to work, it would be less expensive to pay people not to work than to continue a protectionist policy. For example, because of tariff and quota policies, U.S. consumers pay perhaps $40 billion a year —nearly $500 per household — to subsidize the textile and apparel industries.[31] That amounts to $134,686 a year for every textile job saved and $81,973 for each apparel job saved.[32] However, textile and apparel workers earn an average of only $12,000 a year, which means that protectionism costs $11.20 for each $1 of wages paid in the textile industry and $6.80 for each $1 of wages paid in the apparel industry. Therefore, it would be much cheaper just to pay the workers that are displaced than to continue protecting them.

How much should they be paid and for how long? Given these statistics, it would be cost effective to pay them 100% of previous wages each year over their remaining working lives. Making these payments would allow trade barriers to be dismantled, and the gains would far exceed the losses. However, this liberal a policy is not necessary and would not be fair to those who have to pay. Such a policy would also stifle economic growth, because it would take away all incentive for the displaced workers to find other productive work and because the money that taxpayers must pay these workers not to work would not be available for saving or investment.

A U.S. Department of Labor study found that apparel industry workers who lose their jobs are displaced an average of 24.8 weeks and textile workers are displaced an average of 13.3 weeks.[33] When they do find new employment, they tend to earn about as much as they did in their old jobs.[34] Rather than pay these displaced workers 100% of previous wages over their remaining working lives, why not pay them their regular wages, or perhaps a percentage of their previous wages, for just three to six months? By that time, they will find new jobs, the taxpayers will not have to suffer the long-term burden of paying these people not to work, and the displaced workers will retain their incentive to find new productive employment because they know that their idleness will not continue to be subsidized forever.[35]

The economic return on this type of approach is enormous. Rather than paying between $81,973 and $134,686 (in the form of higher prices) *each year* to save one $12,000 job, it would be much cheaper to make a one-time payment to each displaced worker of $3,000 to $6,000 — three to six months' pay. Such an approach would solve the transition problem at minimal cost and would remove the danger of the infant industry approach, which has a tendency of turning temporary protection into permanent protection. Of course, even the direct payment approach is not fair to those who must pay for the idleness of others, but at least it will reduce the total amount they are being forced to pay.

This payment approach could be applied to displaced workers in emerging democracies that are converting to a market system. However, these economies would have problems implementing the approach as outlined above. For example, the average displaced worker might earn $3,600 a year rather than the $12,000 in the above example, so the appropriate one-time payment might be $900 to $1,800, which represents three to six months' pay. The time needed to find a new job in an emerging market economy might not be 13.3 or 24.8 weeks; it might be either longer or shorter. The governments in these countries might find it difficult to pay even these amounts, because they are already running fiscal deficits. The goal under this payment approach should be to provide a short-term cushion that provides sufficient income for a short period of time without taking away the incentive to find new work.

There is a danger in using this approach. As is the case with infant industries, where temporary protection has a tendency to turn into permanent protection, the same could very easily be true of this suggested payment system. In the United States, for example, the temporary welfare measures that were passed during the 1930s depression are mostly still in force. In some cases, families receiving government payments are now into the third generation — the children and grandchildren of people who received welfare payments in the 1930s are also receiving welfare payments. Rather than working and leading productive lives, these people are a drain on society. They are being paid not to work, and the incentive to work has been taken away from them.[36] If they get a job, their welfare benefits will be taken away from them (as they should be, because they no longer need welfare).[37]

The conclusion, then, is that there is no easy solution. The best solution, from a rights perspective, is total and immediate free trade, regardless of the consequences. This solution is the only one that does not violate the right to contract and property. It is also the only policy that is in keeping with the "servant" theory of government, the view that government should be the servant of the people — the protector of life, liberty, and property — and not a redistributor of wealth.[38] Total and immediate free trade would also cause resources to be reallocated to more productive uses faster, whereas a gradualist approach would retard this shifting of resources. Thus, the standard of living would rise faster under the total and immediate free trade approach.

However, if policymakers deem that a policy of total and immediate free trade cannot be implemented, for whatever reason, what would be the second-best solution? Of the two gradualist approaches outlined above — infant industry protection and unemployment payments

— the unemployment payment approach is the less costly and less dangerous of the two. Implementing the unemployment payment approach is a much cheaper way to realize the goal of protecting workers from the ravages of unemployment, but there are problems with the unemployment payment approach, because the temporary payments might become permanent payments. If policymakers adopt an unemployment payments approach, they will have to make sure that the system of temporary payments does not evolve into a welfare bureaucracy that allows individuals to live at the expense of others for more than a few months. Some safeguards must be built into the system that would prevent a temporary system of unemployment insurance from turning into a permanent way of life, as has happened in the United States. The prospects for building in such safeguards are not good, given past history. Also, even if safeguards could be built into the system to prevent temporary welfare from becoming a permanent way of life, the policy still violates rights, because those who work are having a portion of their property (income) forcibly transferred to others who do not work. Thus, it is an improper policy.

The possibility of building in safeguards to prevent temporary help from becoming a permanent subsidy is remote, based on past experience. The tendency, both in the United States and in the welfare states of Western Europe, has been to expand welfare and decrease the incentive to work, which is exactly the opposite of what the policy should be. Perhaps this is because the people whose idleness is being subsidized are also voters, and politicians feel pressured to pander to the masses, so to speak. Certainly, a politician who promises to cut welfare payments is not as likely to get the vote of someone who is on welfare as someone who promises to increase welfare payments.

One way to prevent this pandering effect from getting out of hand would be to prohibit anyone on welfare from voting. Another possibility would be to adopt a voting system that is weighted, so that those who contribute the most to the system also have the most clout at the polling place. For example, rather than allowing each individual to cast one vote, computer technology now makes it possible to have a system in which each individual can cast one vote for each dollar of taxes paid since the last election. This system would be more fair, because the individuals who pay a lot in taxes should have more say about who gets elected than individuals who pay little or no taxes. Such an approach to voting is not new. Corporations have been using this method for decades. Each shareholder gets one vote for each share of stock owned, so those who have a larger investment in the company have more say in deciding who gets elected.

Applying this system of voting to political elections would also act as a brake on the tendency of the relatively poor majority to exploit the relatively richer minority, because the poor tend to vote for politicians who promise to redistribute wealth in their direction. Also, implementing such a system in emerging democracies might be easier than trying to implement it in a long-established democracy where one person–one vote has long been the rule. Anyone who becomes unemployed can be provided for by private charities, such as the various Catholic, Protestant, and Jewish charitable groups and the Salvation Army. People would be more willing to contribute to these charitable groups if they knew that the money would go to a good cause, and private charities are more likely and able to weed out the malingerers from the truly needy.[39]

However, discussion of the second-best approach causes us to misdirect our attention from the best solution. Although providing temporary cushions to the unemployed is better than subsidizing infant industries, neither approach is as good as establishing a policy of total and immediate free trade regardless of the short-term consequences. Total and immediate free trade is the only policy that does not violate rights. Paying people not to work forces the productive members of society to part with their property; thus, it violates property rights. Providing protection for an infant industry, even if protection could be kept temporary, violates the rights of consumers to enter into contracts with the producer of their choice and forces consumers to pay more for foreign products than would be the case in a free market. Government forcibly redistributes wealth from consumers to producers under any infant industry policy. Just as the total and immediate abolition of slavery regardless of the consequences was the only moral policy toward slavery in the nineteenth century, the only moral policy toward trade is the total and immediate abolition of all laws and regulations that prevent trade from being totally free.

Therefore, we must conclude that total, immediate, and unilateral free trade is the best solution. It is the most efficient, which satisfies utilitarians, and it is the only solution that does not violate rights, because individuals, under a totally free trade regime, will be able to buy what they want from whomever they want and will not have a portion of the fruits of their labor confiscated to subsidize those who do not work.

NOTES

1. "Officials Outline IRS Help in Setting up Polish Tax System," *Daily Tax Report (BNA)*, April 6, 1992, p. G-1.

2. For documentation of these abuses, see George Hansen, *To Harass Our People: The IRS and Government Abuse of Power* (Washington, D.C.: Positive Publications, 1984); David Burnham, *A Law unto Itself: Power, Politics and the IRS* (New York: Random House, 1989).

3. "Repeal the Protectionist's Charter," *The Economist*, June 15, 1991, p. 20.

4. Ibid.

5. Ibid. For more on the European Community's antidumping policy, see Seema P. Chandnani, "European Community Antidumping Regulation: Law and Practice,"

Boston College International & Comparative Law Review 13 (1990): 391–413; Eugeniusz Piontek, "Anti-Dumping in the EEC — Some Observations by an Outsider," *Journal of World Trade Law* 21 (1987): 67–93; Stuart A. Christie, "Anti-Dumping Policy of the European Community and the Growing Spectre of Protectionism in Technology-Related Goods," *Rutgers Computer & Technology Law Journal* 16 (1990): 475–507.

6. "Repeal the Protectionist's Charter."

7. "The Korean Semiconductor Boom Boomerangs," *Business Week*, October 5, 1992, p. 107.

8. Kim Nak-Hieon, "EC Slaps Tax on Korean DRAMS," *Electronics*, September 28, 1992, p. 3.

9. It is not the purpose of this chapter to compare and contrast the antidumping policies of the various Western countries. Besides, although the specifics in each country may be somewhat different, the underlying philosophy and the effect on competition and economic growth is the same. For those who would like to read a comparative study, see U.S. General Accounting Office, *Comparison of U.S. and Foreign Antidumping Practices*, September, 1990, GAO/NSIAD-91-59; Edwin A. Vermulst, "The Anti-Dumping Systems of Australia, Canada, the EEC and the United States of America: Have Anti-Dumping Laws Become a Problem in International Trade?" *Michigan Journal of International Law* 10 (1989): 765–806.

10. For a discussion of some issues involved with the possible admission of Hungary and Austria into the European Community, see Emese Péter Fàyné, *Enlargement of EC: Case of Austria and the Hungarian Attitude*, paper presented at the Second Integration Symposium, Confederation of European Economic Associations, September 13–15, 1990, in Lille, France.

11. For a discussion of some of these structural changes as they relate to Hungary, see Emese Péter Fàyné, "Structural Changes in Eastern European Countries — Case of Hungary," *Artha Vunana* 33 (December 1991): 345–51.

12. Of course, some of this price rise might be due to inflation, which has nothing to do with switching from a centrally planned economy to a market economy.

13. For more on this point, see Edward P. Lazear, *Prices and Wages in Transition Economies* (Stanford, Calif.: Hoover Institution, Stanford University, 1992).

14. Most texts on economic development devote some space to this theory, which has been called the "dependency theory" or the "theory of unequal exchange." This theory has most often been used to explain post–World War II underdevelopment in Latin America. However, recent studies have found that Latin American underdevelopment is the result of adopting mercantilist policies that restrict trade and disparage property rights. For documentation of this point, see Hernando DeSoto, *The Other Path: The Invisible Revolution in the Third World* (New York: Harper & Row, 1989).

15. A variation on this theme is the "terms of trade" literature that permeates the development economics literature. The Prebisch Report and the United Nations Conference on Trade and Development literature are often cited to support the position that government intervention, in the form of central planning, is needed by third world countries in order to achieve economic growth. These theories have been refuted for years, yet they continue to appear in the literature. For one critical analysis of this literature, see P. T. Bauer, *Dissent on Development* (Cambridge, Mass.: Harvard University Press, 1976), pp. 233–71.

16. For more on this point, see Deepak Lal, *The Poverty of Development Economics* (London: Institute of Economic Affairs, 1983), pp. 20–24.

17. Some emerging market economies recognize this point and have tried to adopt policies to attract foreign investment and expand foreign trade. For the Hungarian case, see "Hungary: Government Views the Attraction of Foreign Capital

and Trade as Critical Factors in Restructuring the Economy," *Business America*, November 6, 1989, pp. 18–20.

18.   For several treatises on this point, see Steve H. Hanke and Alan A. Walters, eds., *Capital Markets and Development* (San Francisco, Calif.: ICS Press, 1991).

19.   For a discussion of the relationship between economic growth and property rights, see Alan Rufus Waters, "Economic Growth and the Property Rights Regime," *Cato Journal* 7 (1987): 99–115.

20.   The Hungarian Act XCVIII of 1990 removed the requirement for government approval of foreign investment. The Polish Foreign Investment Law substantially reduced, but did not completely eliminate, the need for government approval in the investment process. Part of the problem with attracting foreign investors in Hungary, Poland, and elsewhere is the lack of clearly defined property rights. Recent legislation in some of these emerging market economies has sometimes been unclear, and the provisions of some laws are in conflict with the provisions of other laws. Thus, foreign investors have been hesitant to invest. For more on these points, see Steven A. Velkei, "An Emerging Framework for Greater Foreign Participation in the Economies of Hungary and Poland," *Hastings International and Comparative Law Review* 15 (1992): 695–723.

21.   Some material for this section was synthesized from James Bovard, *Washington's Iron Curtain against East European Exports*, Cato Institute Foreign Policy Briefing No. 15, January 7, 1992.

22.   Bruce Barnard, "Going to Market," *Europe*, March 1992, pp. 6–7. The European Community's abolition of scores of quotas on manufactured products in 1990 helped to trigger a 40%–50% jump in Hungarian and Polish exports to the European Community in 1991.

23.   For more on the application of U.S. countervailing duty laws to nonmarket economies, see Randall B. Marcus, "An Argument for Freer Trade: The Nonmarket Economy Problem under the U.S. Countervailing Duty Laws," *International Law and Politics* 17 (1985): 407–51.

24.   For a treatise on the relationship between protectionism and comparative advantage, especially as applied to lesser developed countries, see Melvyn B. Krauss, *Development without Aid: Growth, Poverty and Government* (Lanham, Md.: University Press of America, 1983), pp. 46–66.

25.   I am not saying that economists are correct to use the utilitarian approach, only that they tend to favor it over the rights approach.

26.   For a modern critique of the infant industry argument, see Robert E. Baldwin, *Trade Policy in a Changing World Economy* (Chicago, Ill.: University of Chicago Press, 1988), pp. 148–59.

27.   James Bovard, *The Fair Trade Fraud* (New York: St. Martin's Press, 1991), p. 71. The farm program Congress passed in 1985 guaranteed U.S. sugar beet and sugar cane farmers about 21.5 cents a pound for their product when the world market price was about 4 cents a pound. Janet Novack, "Three Yards and a Cloud of (Sugar) Dust," *Forbes*, September 4, 1989, p. 39.

28.   Steven Greenhouse, "Trade Curbs: Do They Do the Job?" *New York Times*, April 16, 1992, p. D10. The Big-3 automakers in Detroit suffered even greater losses in 1992.

29.   Anne O. Krueger and Baran Tuncer, "An Empirical Test of the Infant Industry Argument," *American Economic Review* 75 (1982): 1142; Lila J. Truett and Dale B. Truett, *Economics*, (St. Louis, Mo.: Times Mirror/Mosby College Publishing, 1987), p. 726.

30.   Charles P. Kindleberger, "International Trade and National Prosperity," *Cato Journal* 3 (1983/84): 630; Larry E. Westphal, *Empirical Justification for Infant*

Industry Protection (Washington, D.C.: World Bank, 1981); Edward Tower, "Some Empirical Results on Trade and National Prosperity," *Cato Journal* 3 (1983/84): 642.

31.   William R. Cline, *The Future of World Trade in Textiles and Apparel* (Washington, D.C.: Institute for International Economics, 1990), p. 193. Cline estimates the cost to be $20.3 billion, but this estimate is based on wholesale prices. At retail, the cost might be double, or $40 billion, because markups are about 100% in the textile and apparel industries.

32.   Cline, *The Future of World Trade in Textiles and Apparel*, p. 194. The $134,686 and $81,973 figures are based on wholesale prices. The actual costs might be double these amounts.

33.   U.S. Department of Labor, Bureau of Labor Statistics (1985), *Displaced Workers, 1979–83* (Washington, D.C.: Department of Labor, 1985), pp. 28–29, as cited by Cline *The Future of World Trade in Textiles and Apparel*, p. 195.

34.   Ibid. points out that displaced apparel workers earned about 2.5% less on their new jobs and displaced textile workers earned about 3.3% more on their new jobs. Of course, these figures would differ for different industries. In autos and steel, for example, displaced workers from Western countries would probably earn less on their new jobs, because autoworkers and steelworkers earn more, on average, than other industrial workers.

35.   The author knows of one instance in which an acquaintance in the state of Pennsylvania lost his job and received unemployment benefits equal to about 60% of previous pay for 52 weeks. During this time, he did not even try to find other employment. He treated his unemployment as a paid vacation. When the benefits ran out in week 53, he found another job. Therefore, even if unemployed workers are paid a percentage of their former wages, an unemployment compensation system may have a tendency to reduce the incentive to work.

36.   For some treatises on the failure of the U.S. welfare system, see Martin Anderson, *Welfare: The Political Economy of Welfare Reform in the United States* (Stanford, Calif.: Hoover Institution Press, 1978); Charles Murray, *Losing Ground* (New York: Basic Books, 1984); Charles Murray, *In Pursuit of Happiness and Good Government* (New York: Simon and Schuster, 1988); Clarence B. Carson, *The Welfare State 1929–1985, A Basic History of the United States* (Wadley, Ala.: American Textbook Committee, 1986); Clarence B. Carson, *The War on the Poor* (New Rochelle, N.Y.: Arlington House, 1969). For a recent suggestion for improvement, see Marvin Olasky, *The Tragedy of American Compassion* (Washington, D.C.: Regnery Gateway, 1992).

37.   Adoption of welfare state policies, with all their attendant bureaucracy and inefficiency, are especially harmful to lesser developed countries, which can least afford to have their economic growth retarded. For more on this point, see Melvyn B. Krauss, *Development without Aid: Growth, Poverty and Government* (Lanham, Md.: University Press of America, 1983), pp. 139–53.

38.   Even if one subscribes to the redistributionist approach, it is difficult to justify redistribution from consumers to producers, which is exactly the kind of redistribution that takes place under protectionism. Protectionism results in higher prices, which consumers must pay to producers.

39.   For a detailed discussion of what is wrong with the current welfare system in the United States and what can be done to improve (and privatize) it, see Olasky, *The Tragedy of American Compassion*.

Bibliography

Agreement on the Implementation of Article VI of the General Agreement on Tariffs and Trade. Art. 2, 19 U.S.T. 4348, 4348-49, T.I.A.S. No. 6431, pp. 3–4, 651 U.N.T.S. 320, 322, 324, June 30, 1967.

Ahlstrom, Bjorn. "Protecting Whom from What?" *The Freeman* 39 (1989): 153.

Alexander, Mary. "Antidumping Amendment Dumps on Consumers." *Citizens for a Sound Economy*, November 5, 1987.

____. "No Dumping on Consumers." *Houston Post*, November 24, 1987

Algoma Steel Corp. v. *United States*. 865 F.2d 240, 241 (Fed. Cir), cert. denied, 492 U.S. 919, 1989.

American International Auto Dealers' Association. "Import Dealers See Continuing Fight Over MPV Tariffs; Demand End of 25% Duty." February 16, 1989.

____. "Auto Import Group Calls Reclassification of Multi-Purpose Vehicles a 'Consumer Rip-Off.'" January 17, 1989.

Anderson, Benjamin M. *Economics and the Public Welfare*. Indianapolis, Ind.: Liberty Press, 1979.

Anderson, James E. "The Relative Inefficiency of Quotas." *American Economic Review* 75 (1985): 178–90.

Anderson, Martin. *Welfare: The Political Economy of Welfare Reform in the United States*. Stanford, Calif.: Hoover Institution Press, 1978.

Antidumping Act of 1921. Pub. L. No. 67-10, 42 Stat. 11, codified as amended at 19 U.S.C. §§ 160-171.

Aristotle. *The Politics*. I: VII, chap. 4.

Armentano, Dominick T. *Antitrust and Monopoly: Anatomy of a Policy Failure*. 2nd ed. New York: Holmes & Meier, 1990.

____. *Antitrust Policy: The Case for Repeal*. Washington, D.C.: Cato Institute, 1986.

____. *The Myths of Antitrust*. New Rochelle, N.Y.: Arlington House, 1972.

Baker, William L. "Native Pottery Only." In *Free Trade: The Necessary Foundation for World Peace*, edited by Joan Kennedy Taylor, pp. 52–55. Irvington-on-Hudson, N.Y.: Foundation for Economic Education, 1986.

Baldwin, Robert E. *Trade Policy in a Changing World Economy*. Chicago, Ill.: University of Chicago Press, 1988.

Baldwin, Robert E., ed. *Trade Policy Issues and Empirical Analysis*. Chicago, Ill.: University of Chicago Press, 1988.

Baldwin, Robert E., and Richard K. Green. "The Effects of Protection on Domestic Output." In *Trade Policy Issues and Empirical Analysis*, edited by Robert E. Baldwin, pp. 205–26. Chicago, Ill.: University of Chicago Press, 1988.

Barnard, Bruce. "Going to Market." *Europe*, March 1992, pp. 6–7.

Barnes, Harry Elmer. *In Quest of Truth and Justice*. Colorado Springs, Colo.: Ralph Myles, Publisher, 1972.

——. "A.J.P. Taylor and the Causes of World War II." *New Individualist Review* 2 (1962): 3.

Barry, Brian. *The Liberal Theory of Justice*. Oxford: Oxford University Press, 1973.

Bastiat, Frédéric. *The Law*. Irvington-on-Hudson, N.Y.: Foundation for Economic Education, 1968.

——. *Economic Harmonies*. Irvington-on-Hudson, N.Y.: Foundation for Economic Education, 1964.

——. *Economic Sophisms*. Irvington-on-Hudson, N.Y.: Foundation for Economic Education, 1964.

——. *Selected Essays on Political Economy*. Irvington-on-Hudson, N.Y.: Foundation for Economic Education, 1964.

——. "What Is Seen and What Is Not Seen." In *Selected Essays on Political Economy*, Frédéric Bastiat, pp. 1–50. Irvington-on-Hudson, N.Y.: Foundation for Economic Education, 1964.

——. "La Loi." Reprinted in *Sophismes Économiques*, Vol. I, *Oeuvres Complètes de Frédéric Bastiat*, Frédéric Bastiat, pp. 343–94. 4th ed. Paris: Guillaumin et Cie, 1878.

——. *Sophismes Économiques*, Vol. I, *Oeuvres Complètes de Frédéric Bastiat*. 4th ed. Paris: Guillaumin et Cie, 1878.

Batemarco, Robert. "GNP, PPR, and the Standard of Living." *Review of Austrian Economics* 1 (1987): 181–86.

Bauer, P. T. *Dissent on Development*. 2nd ed. Cambridge, Mass.: Harvard University Press, 1976.

Baughman, Laura Megna. *Analysis of the Impact of the Textile and Apparel Trade Act of 1987*. International Business and Economics Research Corporation, 1987.

Baughman, Laura Megna, and Thomas Emrich. *Analysis of the Impact of the Textile and Apparel Trade Enforcement Act of 1985*. International Business and Economics Research Corporation, 1985.

Baumol, William J., and Janusz A. Ordover. "Use of Antitrust to Subvert Competition." *Journal of Law and Economics* 28 (1985): 247–65.

Baysinger, B., R. Ekelund, and R. Tollison. "Mercantilism as a Rent Seeking Society." In *Towards a Theory of the Rent Seeking Society*, edited by James M. Buchanan, Robert Tollison, and Gordon Tullock, pp. 235–68. College Station, Tex.: Texas A & M University Press, 1980.

Becker, J. *Das Deutsche Manchestertum*, 1907.

Bergsten, C. Fred, Kimberly Ann Elliott, Jeffrey J. Schott, and Wendy E. Takacs. *Auction Quotas and United States Trade Policy*. Washington, D.C.: Institute for International Economics, 1987.

Bhagwati, Jagdish N. *Protectionism*. Cambridge, Mass.: MIT Press, 1988.

"Big Three Auto Firms Move to Appeal Decision on Sales of Toyota Minivans." *Wall Street Journal*, August 7, 1992, p. B-3.

Block, Walter, and Michael Walker. *Lexicon of Economic Thought*. Vancouver: Fraser Institute, 1989.

Bluestone, Barry, and Bennett Harrison. *The Deindustrialization of America*. New York: Basic Books, 1982.

Blustein, Paul. "Unfair Traders: Does the U.S. Have Room to Talk?" *Washington Post*, May 24, 1989, p. F1.

Boorstein, Randi. "The Effect of Trade Restrictions on the Quality and Composition of Imported Products: An Empirical Analysis of the Steel Industry." Ph.D. dissertation, Columbia University, 1987.

Boorstein, Randi, and Robert C. Feenstra. "Quality Upgrading and Its Welfare Cost in U.S. Steel Imports, 1969–74." In *International Trade and Trade Policy*, edited by Elhanan Helpman and Assaf Razin, pp. 167–86. Cambridge, Mass.: MIT Press, 1991.

Bork, Robert H. *The Antitrust Paradox: A Policy at War with Itself.* New York: Basic Books, 1978.

Bovard, James. "U.S. Protectionists Claim a Russian Victim." *Wall Street Journal,* June 8, 1992, p. A-10.

____. "Washington's Iron Curtain against East European Exports." Cato Institute Foreign Policy Briefing No. 15, January 7, 1992.

____. *The Fair Trade Fraud.* New York: St. Martin's Press, 1991.

____. "High Cost of Textile Protection." *Journal of Commerce,* December 10, 1991, p. A-12.

____. "No Justice in Anti-Dumping." *New York Times,* January 28, 1990, p. F13.

____. *The Farm Fiasco.* San Francisco, Calif.: ICS Press, 1989.

____. Bradley, Robert L., Jr. *The Mirage of Oil Protection.* Lanham, Md.: University Press of America, 1989.

Branson, William H. "The Myth of Deindustrialization." In *Plant Closings: Public or Private Choices?* edited by Richard B. McKenzie. Washington, D.C.: Cato Institute, 1984.

Bryan, Michael F., and Owen F. Humpage. "Voluntary Export Restraints: The Cost of Building Walls." *Economic Review, Federal Reserve Bank of Cleveland* (Summer 1984): 17–37.

Buchanan, James M. "Free Trade and Producer-Interest Politics." In *Essays on the Political Economy*, James M. Buchanan, pp. 52–66. Honolulu, Hawaii: University of Hawaii Press, 1989.

____. *Liberty, Market and State.* New York: New York University Press, 1985.

____. *Freedom in Constitutional Contract: Perspectives of a Political Economist.* College Station, Tex.: Texas A&M University Press, 1977.

____. *The Limits of Liberty: Between Anarchy and Leviathan.* Chicago, Ill.: University of Chicago Press, 1975.

Buchanan, James M., Robert Tollison, and Gordon Tullock, editors. *Towards a Theory of the Rent Seeking Society.* College Station, Tex.: Texas A&M University Press, 1980.

Buchanan, James M., and Gordon Tullock. *The Calculus of Consent.* Ann Arbor, Mich.: University of Michigan Press, 1962.

Burnham, David. *A Law unto Itself: Power, Politics and the IRS.* New York: Random House, 1989.

Butler, Henry, and Larry Ribstein. "State Anti-Takeover Statutes and the Contract Clause." *Cincinnati Law Review* 57 (1988): 611.

Caine, Wesley K. "A Case for Repealing the Antidumping Provisions of the Tariff Act of 1930." *Law & Policy in International Business* 13 (1981): 681–726.

Cantillon, Richard. *Essai Sur la Nature Du Commerce en Général [Essays on the Nature of Commerce in General].* New York: Macmillan, 1755/1931.

Canto, Victor A. "U.S. Trade Policy: History and Evidence." *Cato Journal* 3 (Winter 1983/84): 679–96.

Canto, Victor A., R. Eastin, and A. Laffer. "Failure of Protectionism: A Study of the Steel Industry." *Columbia Journal of World Business* 17 (1982): 43.

Canto, Victor A., and Arthur Laffer. "The Effectiveness of Orderly Marketing Agreements: The Color TV Case." *Business Economics* 18 (January 1983): 38.

Canto, Victor A., Arthur Laffer, and J. Turney. "Trade Policy and the U.S. Economy." *Financial Analyst Journal* (September/October, 1982): 237.

Carson, Clarence B. *The Welfare State 1929–1985, A Basic History of the United States,* Vol. 5. Wadley Ala.: American Textbook Committee, 1986.

____. *The Rebirth of Liberty: The Founding of the American Republic, 1760–1800.* Greenville, Ala.: American Textbook Committee, 1973/1976.

____. *The War on the Poor.* New Rochelle, N.Y.: Arlington House, 1969.

____. "The Mercantile Impasse." In *The Rebirth of Liberty: The Founding of the American Republic, 1760–1800,* Clarence B. Carson. Reprinted in *Free Trade: The Necessary Foundation for World Peace,* edited by Joan Kennedy Taylor, pp. 41–51. Irvington-on-Hudson, N.Y.: Foundation for Economic Education, 1986.

Cass, Ronald A., and Stephen J. Narkin. *Antidumping and Countervailing Duty Law: The United States and the GATT.* Washington, D.C.: Brookings Institution, 1990.

Chaikin, S. "Trade, Investment, and Deindustrialization." *Foreign Affairs* 60 (1988): 836.

Chamberlin, William Henry. *America's Second Crusade.* Chicago, Ill.: Henry Regnery, 1950/1962.

Chandnani, Seema P. "European Community Antidumping Regulation: Law and Practice." *Boston College International & Comparative Law Review* 13 (1990): 391–413.

Chodorov, Frank. "The Humanity of Trade." In *Free Trade: The Necessary Foundation for World Peace,* edited by J. K. Taylor. Irvington-on-Hudson, N.Y.: Foundation for Economic Education, 1986.

Choo, Ai Leng. "New Zealand Braces for Loss in Kiwi Sales." *Wall Street Journal,* July 20, 1992, p. A10B.

Christie, Stuart A. "Anti-Dumping Policy of the European Community and the Growing Spectre of Protectionism in Technology-Related Goods." *Rutgers Computer & Technology Law Journal* 16 (1990): 475–507.,

Clifford Winston and Associates. *Blind Intersection? Policy and the Automobile Industry.* Washington, D.C.: Brookings Institution, 1987.

Cline, William R. *The Future of World Trade in Textiles and Apparel.* rev. ed. Washington, D.C.: Institute for International Economics, 1990.

____. *American Trade Adjustment: The Global Impact.* Washington, D.C.: Institute for International Economics, 1989.

____. *The Future of World Trade in Textiles and Apparel.* Washington, D.C.: Institute for International Economics, 1987.

____. "Reverse the Course on Textiles," *Washington Post,* August 7, 1987.

Cole, A. H., ed. *Industrial and Commercial Correspondence of Alexander Hamilton.* New York: Kelley, 1968.

Collyns, Charles, and Steven Dunaway. "The Cost of Trade Restraints: The Case of Japanese Automobile Exports to the United States." *International Monetary Fund Staff Papers,* March 1987, pp. 150–75.

Congressional Budget Office. *Has Trade Protection Revitalized Domestic Industries?* p. 96. Washington, D.C.: U.S. Government Printing Office, 1986. Quoted in *Protectionism's Adverse Economic Impact,* written testimony of Daniel Oliver (former chairman of the Federal Trade Commission) before the U.S. International Trade Commission, Investigation No. 332–325, October 14, 1992.

Consumers for World Trade. *How Much Do Consumers Pay for U.S. Trade Barriers?* Washington, D.C.: Consumers for World Trade, 1984.

Corden, W. M. *Trade Policy and Economic Welfare.* New York: Oxford University Press, 1974.

Cowen, Tyler, ed. *The Theory of Market Failure: A Critical Examination.* Fairfax, Va.: George Mason University Press, 1988.

Cox, J., and A. Wright. "A Tariff Policy for Independence from Oil Embargoes." *National Tax Journal* 28 (March 1975): 29.

Crandall, Robert. "The Effects of U.S. Trade Protection for Autos and Steel." *Brookings Papers on Economic Activity* 1 (July/August 1987): 271–88.

____. "Detroit Rode Quotas to Prosperity." *Wall Street Journal*, January 29, 1986, p. 30.

____. "Import Quotas and the Automobile Industry: The Costs of Protectionism." *Brookings Review* 2 (1984): 14.

____. "Federal Government Initiatives to Reduce the Price Level." *Brookings Papers on Economic Activity* (1978).

Curtiss, W. M. *The Tariff Idea*. Irvington-on-Hudson, N.Y.: Foundation for Economic Education, 1953.

Dale, Richard. *Anti-Dumping Law in a Liberal Trade Order*. New York: St. Martin's Press, 1980.

Dardis, Rachel, and Carol Young. "The Welfare Loss from the New Sugar Program." *Journal of Consumer Affairs* 19 (1985): 127.

deHamel, Beth, James R. Ferry, William W. Hogan, and Joseph S. Nie, Jr. *The Export of Alaskan Crude Oil: An Analysis of the Economic and National Security Benefits*. Cambridge, Mass.: Putnam, Hayes, and Bartlett, 1983.

Denzau, Arthur T. *The Unlevel Playing Field: How High Steel Prices and Trade Protection Help Deindustrialize America*. St. Louis, Mo.: Washington University, Center for the Study of American Business, 1989.

____. *How Import Restraints Reduce Employment*. St. Louis, Mo.: Washington University, Center for the Study of American Business, 1987.

____. *American Steel: Responding to Foreign Competition*. St. Louis, Mo.: Center for the Study of American Business, 1985.

DeSoto, Hernando. *The Other Path: The Invisible Revolution in the Third World*. New York: Harper & Row, 1989.

Destler, I. M. *American Trade Politics*, 2nd ed. Washington, D.C.: Institute for International Economics, 1992.

____. *American Trade Politics: System under Stress*. Washington, D.C.: Institute for International Economics, 1986.

Destler, I. M., and John S. Odell. *Anti-Protection: Changing Forces in United Sates Trade Politics*. Washington, D.C.: Institute for International Economics, 1987.

DiLorenzo, Thomas. *The Myth of America's Declining Manufacturing Sector*. Washington, D.C.: Heritage Foundation, 1984.

Dinopoulos, Elias, and Mordechai E. Kreinin. "Effects of the U.S.–Japan Auto VER on European Prices and on U.S. Welfare." *Review of Economics & Statistics* 70 (1988): 484–91.

Dorn, James. "Trade Adjustment Assistance: A Case of Government Failure." *Cato Journal* 2 (1982): 865.

Dowd, A. "What to Do about Trade Policy." *Fortune*, May 8, 1989, p. 106.

Dowdle, Barney, and Steve H. Hanke. "Public Timber Policy and the Wood-Products Industry." In *Forest Lands, Public and Private*, edited by M. Bruce Johnston and Robert Deacon. Cambridge, Mass.: Ballinger Publishing, 1984.

Doxey, M. *Economic Sanctions and International Enforcement*. Washington, D.C.: Institute for International Economics, 1980.

Duke, M. I. "David Hume and Monetary Adjustment." *History of Political Economy* 11 (1979): 572.

duPont, Pete. "Tigers by the Tail." *American Spectator*, September 1992, pp. 41–42.

Durant, Will. *The Story of Philosophy*. New York: Washington Square Press, 1952.

Ekelund, Robert B., Jr., and Robert D. Tollison. *Economics*, 2nd ed. Glenview, Ill.: Scott, Foresman, 1988.

Epstein, Richard A. "Toward a Revitalization of the Contract Clause." *Chicago Law Review* 51 (1984) 703.

Fausten, D. K. "The Humean Origin of the Contemporary Monetary Aproach to the Balance of Payments." *Quarterly Journal of Economics* 93 (1979): 655.

Fay, Sidney Bradshaw. *The Origins of the World War.* New York: Macmillan Company, 1939.

Fàyné, Emese Péter. "Structural Changes in Eastern European Countries — Case of Hungary." *Artha Vunana* 33 (December 1991): 345–51.

———. "Enlargement of EC: Case of Austria and the Hungarian Attitude." Paper presented at the Second Integration Symposium, Confederation of European Economic Associations, Lille, France, September 13–15, 1990.

Feenstra, Robert C. "How Costly Is Protectionism?" *Journal of Economic Perspectives* 6 (Summer 1992): 159–78.

———. "Quality Change under Trade Restraints in Japanese Autos." *Quarterly Journal of Economics* 103 (February 1988): 131–46.

Finger, J. Michael. "Trade Policies in the United States." In *National Trade Policies*, edited by Dominick Salvatore. Westport, Conn.: Greenwood Press, 1992.

———. "The Political Economy of Trade Policy." *Cato Journal* 3 (Winter 1983/84): 743–50.

———. "Incorporating the Gains from Trade into Policy." *World Economy* 5 (December 1982): 367.

Finger, J. Michael, H. Hall, and D. Nelson. "The Political Economy of Administered Protection." *American Economic Review* 72 (1982): 14.

Finger, J. Michael, and Patrick A. Messerlin. *The Effects of Industrial Countries' Policies on Developing Countries.* Washington, D.C.: The World Bank, 1989.

Finger, J. Michael, and J. Nogues. "International Control of Subsidies and Countervailing Duties." *World Bank Economic Review* (1987): 23.

Fisher, Franklin M. "On Predation and Victimless Crime." *Antitrust Bulletin* 32 (Spring 1987): 85–92.

Folsom, M., and S. Lubar, editors. *The Philosophy of Manufactures: Early Debates over Industrialization in the United States.* New York: Kelley, 1980.

Friedman, Milton. "The Social Responsibility of Business." *The New York Times Magazine* 33 (1970): 122–26. Reprinted in Kurt R. Leube, editor. *The Essence of Friedman.* Stanford, Calif.: Hoover Institution Press, 1987.

Friedman, Milton, and Rose Friedman. *Free to Choose.* New York: Harcourt Brace Jovanovich, 1979/1980.

Gable, Wayne. *Myths about International Trade.* Washington, D.C.: Citizens for a Sound Economy, n.d.

Gardner, Bruce L. "The United States." In *Agricultural Protectionism in the Industrialized World*, edited by Fred H. Sanderson. Washington, D.C.: Resources for the Future, 1990.

Gomez-Ibanez, Jose A., Robert A. Leone, and Stephen A. O'Connell. "Restraining Auto Imports: Does Anyone Win?" *Journal of Policy Analysis and Management* 2 (1983): 196–219.

Greenhouse, Steven. "Trade Curbs: Do They Do the Job?" *New York Times*, April 16, 1992, p. D10.

Grubel, H. G. "Ricardo and Thornton on the Transfer Mechanism." *Quarterly Journal of Economics* 75 (1961): 292.

Gutfeld, Rose, and Dana Milbank. "U.S. Steel Firms Get Early Boost in Import Fight." *Wall Street Journal*, August 11, 1992, p. A-2.

Gwo-Jiun, M. Leu, Andrew Schmitz, and Ronald D. Knutson. "Gains and Losses of Sugar Program Policy Options." *American Journal of Agricultural Economics* 69 (1987): 591–602.

Haberler, Gottfried. *Quantitative Trade Controls, Their Causes and Nature.* Cambridge, Mass.: Harvard University Press, 1943.

Hamilton, Carl. "An Assessment of Voluntary Restraints on Hong Kong Exports to Europe and the U.S.A." *Economica* 53 (1986): 339–50.

____. *An Assessment of Voluntary Restraints on Hong Kong Exports to Europe and the U.S.A.* Stockholm: Institute for International Economic Studies, University of Stockholm, 1985.

____. *Voluntary Export Restraints on Asia: Tariff Equivalents, Rents and Trade Barrier Formation.* Stockholm: Institute for International Economic Studies, University of Stockholm, 1984.

Haney, Lewis H. *History of Economic Thought.* New York: Macmillan, 1949.

Hanke, Steven H. "U.S.-Japanese Trade: Myths and Realities." *Cato Journal* 3 (1983/84): 757–69.

Hanke, Steve H., and Alan A. Walters, editors. *Capital Markets and Development.* San Francisco, Calif.: ICS Press, 1991.

Hansen, George. *To Harass Our People: The IRS and Government Abuse of Power.* Washington, D.C.: Positive Publications, 1984.

Hartigan, J., and E. Teller. "Trade Policy and the American Income Distribution." *Review of Economics & Statistics* 72 (1982): 261.

Hayek, F. A. *Prices and Production.* London: Routledge & Sons, 1931/32 and 1935/39.

Hazlitt, Henry. *The Failure of the "New Economics": An Analysis of the Keynesian Fallacies.* Princeton, N.J.: D. Van Nostrand, 1959.

____. *Economics in One Lesson.* New York: Harper & Brothers, 1946.

Hazlitt, Henry, editor. *The Critics of Keynesian Economics.* New York: D. Van Nostrand, 1960.

Helpman, Elhanan, and Assaf Razin, editors. *International Trade and Trade Policy.* Cambridge, Mass.: MIT Press, 1991.

Henderson, W. O. "Prince Smith and Free Trade in Germany." *Economic History Review* 2 (1950): 295.

Heyne, Paul. "Do Trade Deficits Matter?" *Cato Journal* 3 (1983/84): 705–16.

Hickok, Susan. "The Consumer Cost of U.S. Trade Restraints." *Federal Reserve Bank of New York Quarterly Review* (Summer 1985): 1–12.

Hirst, Francis W., editor. *Free Trade and Other Fundamental Doctrines of the Manchester School.* New York: Augustus M. Kelley, 1968.

Hopkins, Thomas D. *Cost of Regulation.* Rochester, N.Y.: Rochester Institute of Technology, 1991.

Hoppe, Hans-Hermann. *A Theory of Socialism and Capitalism: Economics, Politics, and Ethics.* Boston, Mass.: Kluwer Academic Publishers, 1989.

____. *Praxeology and Economic Science.* Auburn, Ala.: Ludwig von Mises Institute, 1988.

Horngren, Charles T., and Gary L. Sundem. *Introduction to Management Accounting,* 7th ed. Englewood Cliffs, N.J.: Prentice-Hall, 1987.

Horton, Tracey, and Hal Colebatch. *Who Pays for Protection.* Australian Institute for Public Policy, 1988.

Horwich, G., and E. Mitchell, editors. *Policies for Coping with Oil-Supply Disruptions.* New York: Praeger, 1982.

Hudgins, E. *Robust U.S. Textile Industry Needs No More Protection.* Washington, D.C.: Heritage Foundation, 1987.

Hufbauer, Gary Clyde, Diane T. Berliner, and Kimberly Ann Elliott. *Trade Protection in the United States: 31 Case Studies.* Washington, D.C.: Institute for International Economics, 1986.

Hume, David. *Of Money and of the Balance of Trade,* 1752.

"Hungary: Government Views the Attraction of Foreign Capital and Trade as Critical
    Factors in Restructuring the Economy. *Business America*, November 6, 1989,
    pp. 18–20.
Husbands, Samuel H. "Free Trade and Foreign Wars." In *Free Trade: The Necessary
    Foundation for World Peace*, edited by Joan Kennedy Taylor, pp. 97–105.
    Irvington-on-Hudson, N.Y.: Foundation for Economic Education, 1986.
Hutt, W. H. *The Keynesian Episode: A Reassessment*. Indianapolis, Ind.: Liberty
    Press, 1979.
____. *A Rehabilitation of Say's Law*. Athens, Ohio: Ohio University Press, 1975.
____. *Keynesianism — Retrospect and Prospect*. Chicago, Ill.: Henry Regnery, 1963.
"Is the Boss Getting Paid Too Much?" *Business Week*, May 1, 1989, pp. 46–93.
Ives, R., and J. Hurley. *United States Sugar Policy: An Analysis*. Washington, D.C.:
    Department of Commerce, 1988.
Johnson, Bryan T. *A Guide to Antidumping Laws: America's Unfair Trade Practice*.
    Washington, D.C.: Heritage Foundation, 1992.
Johnson, Harry G. "Forward." In *Trade Effects of Public Subsidies to Private
    Enterprise*, G. Denton, S. O'Cleireacian, and S. Ash, p. xxxiii. London: Trade
    Policy Research Centre, 1975.
Jouvenel, Bertrand de. *The Ethics of Redistribution*. Cambridge: Cambridge
    University Press, 1952.
Kaldor, Nicholas. *The Causes of the Slow Economic Growth of the United Kingdom*.
    Oxford: Oxford University Press, 1966.
Kalt, Joseph P. "The Political Economy of Protectionism: Tariffs and Retaliation in
    the Timber Industry." In *Trade Policy Issues and Empirical Analysis*, edited by
    Robert E. Baldwin, pp. 339–64. Chicago, Ill.: University of Chicago Press, 1988.
Kaplan, Gilbert B., Lynn G. Kamarck, and Marie Parker. "Cost Analysis under the
    Antidumping Law." *George Washington Journal of International Law and
    Economics* 21 (1988): 357–418.
Kennedy, Kevin C. "A Proposal to Abolish the U.S. Court of International Trade."
    Dickinson Journal of International Law 14 (1985): 13–37.
Keynes, John Maynard. *General Theory of Employment, Interest and Money*. New
    York: Harcourt Brace, 1936.
Kindleberger, Charles P. "International Trade and National Prosperity." *Cato
    Journal* 3 (1983/84): 623–37.
Knoll, Michael S. "United States Antidumping Law: The Case for Reconsideration."
    Texas International Law Journal 22 (1987): 265–90.
Knorr, K. *The Power of Nations*. New York: Macmillan, 1975.
Koller, R., Jr. "The Myth of Predatory Pricing: An Empirical Study." *Antitrust Law &
    Economics Review* 4 (1971): 105–23.
"The Korean Semiconductor Boom Boomerangs." *Business Week*, October 5, 1992, p.
    107.
Krauss, Melvyn B. *Development without Aid: Growth, Poverty and Government*.
    Lanham, Md.: University Press of America, 1983.
____. *The New Protectionism: The Welfare State and International Trade*. New York:
    New York University Press, 1978.
Kreinin, M. "Wage Competitiveness in the U.S. Auto and Steel Industries."
    Contemporary Policy Issues 4 (January 1984): 39.
Kronby, Matthew S. "Kicking the Tires: Assessing the Hyundai Antidumping
    Decision from a Consumer Welfare Perspective." *Canadian Business Law
    Journal* 18 (1991): 95–117.
Krueger, Anne O., and Baran Tuncer. "An Empirical Test of the Infant Industry
    Argument." *American Economic Review* 75 (1982): 1142.

Lal, Deepak. *The Poverty of Development Economics*. London: Institute of Economic Affairs, 1983.

Lazear, Edward P. *Prices and Wages in Transition Economies*. Stanford, Calif.: Hoover Institution, Stanford University, 1992.

Lerner, Abba. "The Symmetry between Import and Export Taxes." *Economica* 3 (1936): 306.

Leube, Kurt R., editor. *The Essence of Friedman*. Stanford, Calif.: Hoover Institution Press, 1987.

Locke, John. *The Second Treatise on Civil Government*. Buffalo, N.Y.: Prometheus Books, 1986.

Luciano Pisoni Fabrica Accesori v. *United States*, 640 F. Supp. 255, 260-61 (CIT 1986).

Luttrell, Clifton B. *The High Cost of Farm Welfare*. Washington, D.C.: Cato Institute, 1989.

Machlup, Fritz. "The Mysterious Numbers Game of Balance-of-Payments Statistics." In *International Payments, Debts, and Gold: Collected Essays*, Fritz Machlup, 2nd ed. New York: New York University Press, 1976.

Mack, Eric. "In Defense of 'Unbridled' Freedom of Contract." *American Journal of Economics and Sociology* 40 (1981): 1.

Madaj, Edwin J., and Charles H. Nalls. "Bifurcation without Direction: The United States International Trade Commission and the Question of Petitioner Standing in Antidumping and Countervailing Duty Cases." *Law & Policy in International Business* 22 (1991): 673–88.

Magnusson, Paul. "U.S. Shoots Itself in Foot in Tariff Skirmish." *Detroit Free Press*, May 24, 1987, p. F7.

Marcus, Randall B. "An Agrument for Freer Trade: the Nonmarket Economy Problem under the U.S. Countervailing Duty Laws." *International Law & Politics* 17 (1985): 407–51.

Martin, James J. "Pearl Harbor: Antecedents, Background and Consequences." In *The Saga of Hog Island*, James J. Martin, p. 114. Colorado Springs, Colo.: Ralph Myles, Publisher, 1977.

———. *The Saga of Hog Island*. Colorado Springs, Colo.: Ralph Myles, Publisher, 1977.

Matsushita Electric Industrial Co. Ltd. et al. v. *Zenith Radio Corp. et al.*, 475 U.S. 574 (1986).

McGee, John. "Predatory Price Cutting: The Standard Oil (N.J.) Case." *Journal Of Law & Economics* 1 (1958): 137–69.

McGee, Robert W. "Trade Deficits and Economic Policy: A Law and Economics Analysis." *Journal of Law and Commerce* 11 (1992): 159–74.

———. "The Economic Thought of David Hume." *Hume Studies* 15 (1989): 184–204.

———. "Mergers and Acquisitions: An Economic and Legal Analysis." *Creighton Law Review* 22 (1988/89): 665–93.

McKenzie, Richard B. *The American Job Machine*. New York: Universe Books, 1988.

———. *Competing Visions: The Political Conflict over America's Economic Future*. Washington, D.C.: Cato Institute, 1985.

———. *National Industrial Policy*. Dallas, Tex.: Fisher Institute, 1984.

McKenzie, Richard B., editor. *Plant Closings: Public or Private Choices?* Washington, D.C.: Cato Institute, 1984.

Melo, Jaime de, and David Tarr. "Welfare Costs of U.S. Quotas in Textiles, Steel and Autos." *Review of Economics and Statistics* 72 (1990): 489–97.

Mendez, Jose A. "The Short-Run Trade and Employment Effects of Steel Import Restraints." *Journal of World Trade Law* 20 (September/October 1986): 554–66.

Messerlin, P. *The Long Term Evolution of the EC Anti-Dumping Law: Some Lessons for the New AD Laws in LDCs.* Washington, D.C.: World Bank, 1987.

Mill, John Stuart. *Utilitarianism and Other Writings.* New York: New American Library, 1962.

Mises, Ludwig von. "The Economics of War." In *Free Trade: The Necessary Foundation for World Peace*, edited by Joan Kennedy Taylor, pp. 77–83. Irvington-on-Hudson, N.Y.: Foundation for Economic Education, 1986.

———. *Epistemological Problems of Economics.* New York: New York University Press, 1981.

———. *The Ultimate Foundation of Economic Science.* Kansas City: Sheed, Andrews and McMeel, 1978.

———. *Omnipotent Government.* New Rochelle, N.Y.: Arlington House, 1969.

———. *Human Action*, 3rd ed., rev. Chicago, Ill.: Henry Regnery, 1966.

———. "Lord Keynes and Say's Law." *Freeman* 1 (1950): 83. Reprinted in *The Critics of Keynesian Economics*, edited by Henry Hazlitt, pp. 315–21. New York: D. Van Nostrand, 1960.

Munger, Michael C. *The Costs of Protectionism: Estimates of the Hidden Tax of Trade Restraint.* St Louis, Mo.: Washington University, Center for the Study of American Business, 1983.

Murphy, Antoin E. "Richard Cantillon — Banker and Economist." *Journal of Libertarian Studies* 7 (1985): 185–215.

Murray, Alan. "As Free-Trade Bastion, U.S. Isn't Half as Pure as Many People Think." *Wall Street Journal*, November 1, 1985, p. 1.

Murray, Charles. *In Pursuit of Happiness and Good Government.* New York: Simon and Schuster, 1988.

———. *Losing Ground.* New York: Basic Books, 1984.

"The Myth of Managed Trade." *The Economist*, May 6, 1989, pp. 11–12.

Nak-Hieon, Kim. "EC Slaps Tax on Korean DRAMS." *Electronics*, September 28, 1992, p. 3.

NAR, S.p.A. v. *United States*, 707 F.Supp. 553 (CIT 1989).

Nettels, C. *The Roots of American Civilization. Chicago: University of Chicago Press, 1963.*

"New Competitive Realities Show Japanese Auto Quota Is Obsolete." *Worldwide Information Resources*, November 20, 1987, p. 4.

Niskanen, William A. "U.S. Trade Policy." *Regulation* 1 (1988): 34–42.

Note. "Managing Dumping in a Global Economy." *George Washington Journal of International Law & Economics* 21 (1988): 503.

Novack, Janet. "Does Big Steel Really Need Protection?" *Forbes*, March 16, 1992, p. 37.

———. "Three Yards and a Cloud of (Sugar) Dust." *Forbes*, September 4, 1989, p. 39.

Nozick, Robert. *Anarchy, State, and Utopia.* New York: Basic Books, 1974.

"Officials Outline IRS Help in Setting up Polish Tax System." *Daily Tax Report (BNA)*, April 6, 1992, p. G-1.

Olasky, Marvin. *The Tragedy of American Compassion.* Washington, D.C.: Regnery Gateway, 1992.

Oliver, Daniel. *Protectionism's Adverse Economic Impact*, written testimony before the U.S. International Trade Commission, Investigation No. 332–325, October 14, 1992.

Olson, Sherry H. *The Depletion Myth: A History of Railroad Use of Timber.* Cambridge, Mass.: Harvard University Press, 1971.

Olson, Walter. "Don't Slam the Door." *National Review* 35 (1983): 248.

Organization for Economic Cooperation and Development. *Costs and Benefits of Protection.* Paris: OECD, 1985.

Osterfeld, David. "The Nature of Modern Warfare." In *Free Trade: The Necessary Foundation for World Peace*, edited by Joan Kennedy Taylor, pp. 84–90. Irvington-on-Hudson, N.Y.: Foundation for Economic Education, 1986.

Outboard Marine Corp. v. *Pezetel*, 461 F. Supp. 384 (D. Del. 1978).

Palmeter, N. David. "Exchange Rates and Antidumping Determinations." *Journal of World Trade* 22 (1988): 73–80.

____. "Torquemada and the Tariff Act: The Inquisitor Rides Again." *International Lawyer* 20 (1986): 641.

Pareto, Vilfredo. *Manual of Political Economy*. Various publishers, 1927.

Passell, Peter. "The Victim Has a Blue Collar, but Free Trade Has an Alibi." *New York Times*, August 16, 1992, p. E4.

Paul, Jeffrey, editor. *Reading Nozick: Essays on Anarchy, State, and Utopia*. Totowa, N.J.: Rowman & Allanhead, 1981.

Petrella, Frank. "Adam Smith's Rejection of Hume's Price-Specie-Flow Mechanism: A Minor Mystery Resolved." *Southern Economic Journal* 34 (1968): 365.

Phillips, M. "The Life and Times of the Contract Clause." *American Business Law Journal* 20 (1982): 139.

Piontek, Eugeniusz. "Anti-Dumping in the EEC — Some Observations by an Outsider." *Journal of World Trade Law* 21 (1987): 67–93.

Plato. *Laws*, IV, 705a.

Plummer, J. "United States Oil Stockpiling Policy." *Journal of Contemporary Studies* 4 (1981): 5.

Pomfret, Richard. *International Trade: An Introduction to Theory and Policy*. Oxford: Basil Blackwell, 1991.

"Predatory Pricing, RIP." *Wall Street Journal*, April 1, 1986, p. 32.

Prusa, Thomas J. "Why Are So Many Antidumping Petitions Withdrawn?" *Journal of International Economics* 33 (1992): 1–20.

Raico, Ralph. "John Prince Smith and the German Free-Trade Movement." In *Man, Economy and Liberty: Essays in Honor of Murray N. Rothbard*, edited by Walter Block and Llewellyn Rockwell, Jr., pp. 341–51. Auburn, Ala.: Ludwig von Mises Institute, 1988.

Ravenal, Earl C. "The Economic Claims of National Security." *Cato Journal* 3 (1983/84): 729–41.

Rawls, John. *A Theory of Justice*. Cambridge, Mass.: Harvard University Press, 1971.

Read, Leonard. "I Pencil." *The Freeman*, December 1958. Reprinted in *Free Market Economics: A Basic Reader*, edited by Bettina Bien Greaves, pp. 40–42. Irvington-on-Hudson, N.Y.: Foundation for Economic Education, 1975.

Reed, Lawrence W. "Free Trade or Protectionism?" (cassette tape). Englewood, Colo.: Independence Press, 1985.

"Repeal the Protectionist's Charter." *The Economist*, June 15, 1991, p. 20.

Revenue Act of 1916, ch. 463, §§ 800-801, 39 Stat. 798, codified at 15 U.S.C. §72.

Ricardo, David. *Principles of Political Economy and Taxation*, 1817.

Rockwell, Llewellyn H., Jr., editor. *The Free Market Reader*. Burlingame, Calif.: Ludwig von Mises Institute, 1988.

Rodriguez, Carlos A. "The Quality of Imports and the Differential Welfare Effects of Tariffs, Quotas, and Quality Controls as Protective Devices." *Canadian Journal of Economics* 12 (1979): 439–49.

Rosenthal, N. "The Shrinking Middle Class: Myth or Reality?" *Monthly Labor Review*, March 1985.

Rothbard, Murray N. "Protectionism and the Destruction of Prosperity." In *The Free Market Reader*, edited by Llewellyn H. Rockwell, Jr. Burlingame, Calif.: Ludwig von Mises Institute, 1988.

____. *The Ethics of Liberty*. Atlantic Highlands, N.J.: Humanities Press, 1982.

____. *For a New Liberty*. New York: Libertarian Review Foundation, 1978.

____. *Man, Economy and State*. Los Angeles, Calif.: Nash Publishing, 1970.

____. *America's Great Depression*. Los Angeles, Calif.: Nash Publishing, 1963.

Rowley, Charles K., Robert D. Tollison, and Gordon Tullock, editors. *The Political Economy of Rent-Seeking*. Boston, Mass.: Kluwer Academic Publishers, 1988.

Rueff, Jacques. "An All-Time Fallacy: The Trade Balance Argument." In *Balance of Payments: Proposals for Resolving the Critical World Economic Problem of Our Time*, Jacques Rueff, pp. 116–29. New York: Macmillan, 1967.

Russell, Dean. *Government and Legal Plunder: Bastiat Brought Up to Date*. Irvington-on-Hudson, N.Y.: Foundation for Economic Education, 1985.

Saint-Etienne, Christian. *The Great Depression 1929–1938: Lessons for the 1980s*. Stanford, Calif.: Hoover Institution Press, 1984.

Salvatore, Dominick, editor. *National Trade Policies*. Westport, Conn.: Greenwood Press, 1992.

Sanderson, Fred H., editor. *Agricultural Protectionism in the Industrialized World*. Washington, D.C.: Resources for the Future, 1990.

Schmidtz, David. *The Limits of Government: An Essay on the Public Goods Argument*. Boulder, Colo.: Westview Press, 1991.

Schram, M. "'M. 'Big Fritz': Tough Talk and a Flag." *Washington Post*, October 7, 1982, p. 1.

Schultze, Charles L. "Industrial Policy: A Dissent." In *Plant Closings: Public or Private Choices?* edited by Richard B. McKenzie, pp. 155–75. Washington, D.C.: Cato Institute, 1984.

Schumacher, E. *Small Is Beautiful*. Englewood Cliffs, N.J.: Prentice-Hall, 1973.

Sennholz, Hans F. "Protectionism and Unemployment." In *Free Trade: The Necessary Foundation for World Peace*, edited by Joan Kennedy Taylor. Irvington-on-Hudson, N.Y.: Foundation for Economic Education, 1986.

____. "Welfare States at War." In *Free Trade: The Necessary Foundation for World Peace*, edited by Joan Kennedy Taylor, pp. 91–96. Irvington-on-Hudson, N.Y.: 1986.

____. *Age of Inflation*. Belmont, Mass.: Western Islands, 1979.

Shapiro, A. "Why the Trade Deficit Does Not Matter." *Journal of Applied Corporation Finance* 2 (1989): 87.

Shapiro, R. "A Hidden Tax on All Our Houses." *U.S. News and World Report*, March 21, 1988, p. 52.

Shughart, William F., II. *Antitrust Policy and Interest-Group Politics*. Westport, Conn.: Quorum Books, 1990.

Siegan, Bernard H. *Economic Liberties and the Constitution*. Chicago, Ill.: University of Chicago Press, 1980.

Smith, Adam. *An Inquiry into the Nature and Causes of the Wealth of Nations*. Various publishers, 1776/1937.

Smith, Alasdair, and Anthony J. Venables. "Counting the Cost of Voluntary Export Restraints in the European Car Market." In *International Trade and Trade Policy*, edited by Elhanan Helpman and Assaf Razin, pp. 187–220. Cambridge, Mass.: MIT Press, 1991.

Smoot-Hawley Tariff Act of 1930, Pub. L. No. 71-361, 46 Stat. 590, 19 U.S.C. §§ 1671–1677g, 19 U.S.C.A. §§ 1673–1673i (1980 & 1992 Supp.).

Sorokin, Pitirim A. *The Crisis of Our Age: The Social and Cultural Outlook*. New York: Dutton, 1941.

Sowell, Thomas. *Say's Law*. Princeton, N.J.: Princeton University Press, 1972.

Staley, C. E. "Hume and Viner on the International Adjustment Mechanism." *History of Political Economy* 8 (1976): 252.

"Talking Loudly and Carrying a Crowbar." *The Economist*, April 29, 1989, pp. 23–24.

Tarr, David. "Effects of Restraining Steel Exports from the Republic of Korea to the United States and the European Economic Community." *World Bank Economic Review* 1 (1987): 379–418.

Tarr, David, and Morris E. Morkre. "Aggregate Costs to the United States of Tariffs and Quotas on Imports." Bureau of Economics Staff Report to the Federal Trade Commission, December 1984.

Taylor, A. J. P. *The Origins of the Second World War*. New York: Athenium, 1983.

Taylor, Joan Kennedy, editor. *Free Trade: The Necessary Foundation for World Peace*. Irvington-on-Hudson, N.Y.: Foundation for Economic Education, 1986.

Tollison, Robert D. "Public Choice and Antitrust." *Cato Journal* 4 (1985): 905–16.

Tornell, Aaron. "On the Ineffectiveness of Made-to-Measure Protectionist Programs." In *International Trade and Trade Policy*, edited by Elhanan Helpman and Assaf Razin, pp. 66–79. Cambridge, Mass.: MIT Press, 1991.

Tower, Edward. "Some Empirical Results on Trade and National Prosperity." *Cato Journal* 3 (1983/84): 639–44.

Trade Act of 1974, 19 U.S.C. § 160 (1976).

Trade Agreements Act of 1979, Pub. L. No. 96-39, tit. I, § 106(a), 93 Stat. 193., codified at 19 U.S.C. §§ 1673–1673i, 19 U.S.C.A. §§ 1673–1673i (1980 & 1992 Supp.).

"Trade: Mote and Beam," *The Economist*, May 6, 1989, pp. 22–23.

Trela, Irene, and John Whalley. "Global Effects of Developed Country Trade Restrictions on Textiles and Apparel." *Economic Journal* 100 (1990): 1190–1205.

———. "Do Developing Countries Lose from the MFA?" National Bureau of Economic Research Working Paper No. 2618, June 1988.

Truett, Lila J. and Dale B. Truett. *Economics*. St. Louis, Mo.: Times Mirror/Mosby College Publishing, 1987.

Tullock, Gordon. *The Economics of Special Privilege and Rent Seeking*. Boston, Mass.: Kluwer Academic Publishers, 1989.

———. "The Welfare Costs of Tariffs, Monopolies, and Theft." *Western Journal of Economics* 5 (1967): 224–32.

Tullock, Gordon, editor. *Explorations in The Theory of Anarchy*. Blacksburg, Va.: Center for the Study of Public Choice, Virginia Polytechnic Institute and State University, 1972.

Turner, L. C. F. *Origins of the First World War*. New York: W. W. Norton, 1970.

U.S. Congress, Senate Committee on Finance. *Nonmarket Economy Imports Legislation*. Washington, D.C.: Government Printing Office, 1984.

U.S. Department of Agriculture. *Sugar: Background for 1985 Legislation*. Agriculture Information Bulletin 478. Washington, D.C.: U.S. Department of Agriculture, 1984.

U.S. Department of Commerce. *United States Sugar Policy — An Analysis*. Washington, D.C.: Government Printing Office, 1988.

U.S. Department of Commerce, Administrative Hearing. *Certain Red Raspberries from Canada*. Investigation No. A-122-401, March 22, 1985.

U.S. Department of Labor, Bureau of Labor Statistics. *Displaced Workers, 1979–83*. Bulletin 2240. Washington, D.C.: Department of Labor, 1985.

U.S. General Accounting Office. *Uranium Enrichment: Unresolved Trade Issues Leave Uncertain Future for U.S. Uranium Industry*. GAO/RCED-92-194. Gaithersburg, Md.: U.S. General Accounting Office, June 19, 1992.

———. *Comparison of U.S. and Foreign Antidumping Practices*. GAO/NSIAD-91-59. Gaithersburg, Md.: U.S. General Accounting Office, September 1990.

———. *Use of the GATT Antidumping Code*. July 1990.

190   Bibliography

____. *U.S. Administration of the Antidumping Act of 1921*. Gaithersburg, Md.: U.S. General Accounting Office, March 15, 1979.

____. *Minivans from Japan*. Publication No. 2529. July 1992.

U.S. International Trade Commission, *Fresh Kiwifruit from New Zealand*. Publication No. 2510. May 1992.

____. *Uranium from the U.S.S.R.* Publication No. 2471. December 1991.

____. *Certain High-Information Content Flat Panel Displays and Display Glass Thereof from Japan*. Publication No. 2413. August 1991.

____. *Minivans from Japan*. Publication No. 2402. July 1991.

____. *Fresh Kiwifruit from New Zealand*. Publication No. 2394. June 1991.

____. *U.S. Imports of Textiles and Apparel under the Multifiber Arrangement: Annual Report for 1990*. Publication No. 2382. May 1991.

____. *Certain Telephone Systems and Subassemblies Thereof from Korea*. Publication No. 2254. January 1990.

____. *Sweaters*. Publication No. 2312. 1990.

____. *Sweaters (Hong Kong, Republic of Korea, Taiwan)*. Publication No. 2311. 1990.

____. *Tapered Roller Bearings and Parts Thereof and Certain Housings Incorporating Tapered Rollers from Hungary*. Publication No. 2245. December 1989.

____. *The Effects of the Steel Voluntary Restraint Agreements on U.S. Steel-Consuming Industries*. Report to the Subcommittee on Trade of the House Committee on Ways and Means on Investigation No. 332-270 Under Section 332 of the Tariff Act of 1930. U.S. International Trade Commission Publication 2182. May 1989.

____. *Dry Aluminum Sulfate from Sweden*. Publication No. 2174. March 1989.

____. *Fresh Cut Flowers*. Publication No. 2119. 1988.

____. *Tapered Roller Bearings (Italy, Yugoslavia)*. Publication No. 1999. 1987.

____. *Stainless Steel Pipes and Tubes*. Publication No. 1919. 1986.

____. *Carbon Steel Products*. Publication No. 1642. 1985.

____. *Summary of Statutory Provisions Related to Import Relief*. Washington, D.C.: U.S. International Trade Commission, n.d.

Vaughn, Karen Iversen. *John Locke: Economist and Social Scientist*. Chicago, Ill.: University of Chicago Press, 1980.

Velkei, Steven A. "An Emerging Framework for Greater Foreign Participation in the Economies of Hungary and Poland." *Hastings International & Comparative Law Review* 15 (1992): 695–723.

Vermulst, Edwin A. "The Anti-Dumping Systems of Australia, Canada, the EEC and the United States of America: Have Anti-Dumping Laws Become a Problem in International Trade?" *Michigan Journal of International Law* 10 (1989): 765–806.

Victor, A. Paul. "Injury Determinations by the United States International Trade Commission in Antidumping and Countervailing Duty Proceedings." *New York University Journal of International Law and Politics* 16 (1984): 749–70.

____. "Antidumping and Antitrust: Can the Inconsistencies Be Resolved?" *N.Y.U. Journal of International Law and Politics* 15 (1983): 339–50.

Viner, Jacob. *Dumping: A Problem in International Trade*. Chicago, Ill.: University of Chicago Press, 1923; New York: Augustus Kelley, 1966.

Ward, Colin. *Anarchy in Action*. London: Freedom Press, 1988.

Waters, Alan Rufus. "Economic Growth and the Property Rights Regime." *Cato Journal* 7 (1987): 99–115.

Weidenbaum, Murray. "The High Cost of Protectionism." *Cato Journal* 3 (1983/84): 777–91.

____. *Business, Government, and the Public.* Englewood Cliffs, N.J.: Prentice-Hall, 1981.

Wells, Sam. "The Myth of the Trade Deficit." In *The Free Market Reader,* edited by Llewellyn H. Rockwell, Jr. Burlingame, Calif.: Ludwig von Mises Institute, 1988.

Westphal, Larry E. *Empirical Justification for Infant Industry Protection.* Washington, D.C.: World Bank, 1981.

White, T. "The Danger from Japan." *New York Times Magazine,* July 28, 1985, p. 23.

Willett, Thomas D., and Mehrdad Jalalighajar. "U.S. Trade Policy and National Security." *Cato Journal* 3 (1983/84): 717–27.

Williams, Walter. *All It Takes Is Guts: A Minority View.* Washington, D.C.: Regnery Gateway, 1987.

Worldwide Information Resources. "New Competitive Realities Show Japanese Auto Quota Is Obsolete." November 20, 1987, p. 4.

Wu, Y. *Economic Warfare.* New York: Macmillan, 1952.

Yeager, Leland B., and David G. Tuerck. "Realism and Free-Trade Policy." *Cato Journal* 3 (1983/84): 645–66.

Zenith Radio Corp. v. *Matsushita Elec. Indus. Co.,* 513 F. Supp. 1100, 1120 (E.D. Pa. 1981), 723 F.2d 238 (3d Cir., 1983), 475 U.S. 574 (1986).

Index

ABOUT THE AUTHOR

Robert W. McGee is a Professor in the W. Paul Stillman School of Business at Seton Hall University in South Orange, New Jersey. He is the author/editor of more than 30 books and monographs and has written many articles and reviews for a variety of professional and scholarly journals. Among his recent books is *Business Ethics & Common Sense* (Quorum, 1992).